Mind R Your World

How to think yourself into better health, greater happiness, and more success!

This as proved by 36 Leading Exponents of New Thought
throughout the United States and Canada

Edited by
Ernest Holmes
and
Maude Allison Lathem

COMMEMORATIVE EDITION 2015

International New Thought Alliance

Mind Remakes Your World
International New Thought Alliance
www.newthoughtalliance.org

Printed in the USA

First Printing – 1941
First Commemorative Printing – 2015

Printing – Panoramic Press
www.panoramicpress.com

ISBN # 978-1-4951-2953-7

This book is authorized by a publication committee of the International New Thought Alliance, chosen for this purpose, and is dedicated to the Christ who lives in all people. The oneness of all life is its keynote. "That ye all may be One," is the prayer breathed from cover to cover. May every reader become more consciously aware of the omnipresence of God and the eternal principle of life, love, truth, and beauty. May it go forth into the world to bless every hand that touches it, every mind that receives it, and every heart that welcomes it.

CONTENTS

CONTENTS

CONTENTS

CONTENTS

Preface

Rev. Dr. Blaine C. Mays is past President of The International New Thought Alliance, a position he held since 1974. He is senior minister for Community Church of New Thought in Mesa, Arizona.

Mind Remakes Your World: The spiritual energy shared by the inspired New Thought writers in this book is powerful; capturing the dedication, integrity, and the convictions of those blessed ones who have preceded us on our spiritual journey and leadership. As with each one who reads this powerful book, the writers probably did not realize the impact their teachings had on the many lives they touched. In honoring a part of the dynamic history of The International New Thought Alliance, we are proud to have this great book republished and available for the Alliances' Centennial Congress as well as thereafter.

Foreword

Rev. Larry Swartz is President of The International New Thought Alliance. He is Co-Minister, along with his wife Rev. Mary Ellen, of Unity of Tucson in Tucson, Arizona.

What a personal honor it is for me to write the foreword for the reprinting of *Mind Remakes Your World*. When it was originally printed in 1941, I was a mere 3 years old. Today as I read the various chapters, my mind and heart key into the Truths that were shared then, and again now for us today. I am humbled to be part of the organization that has as its antecedents writers whose names I recognize, yet people I didn't have the pleasure of knowing, along with others I have had the privilege of at least meeting, if not personally enjoying a relationship.

Many of our organizations stand and exist today upon the shoulders of pioneers who boldly spoke the Truth of how the very process of our lives work, and how in the words of William Henley we can truly be, "The master of our fate and the captain of our soul."

If I were to synthesize the messages found within these chapters, it would be to realize that life isn't a spectator sport. It is the realization that we are always in the loop of choices made that form consciousness that then become our world.

The writers spoke to levels of understanding that once implemented within Mind are life changing. It is the beginning of a fantastic ride.

INTRODUCTION

The New Thought Movement is essentially spiritual. Dealing with the laws of Mind, it is also scientific. It assumes that God is not only the final Reality, He is the only present Reality. Everything that is real is of Him. Our own being is God manifest as personality.

The New Thought Movement has been likened to applied Christianity. It is both unique and practical, since it seeks to make definite use of spiritual power in everyday living. This attempt to re-evaluate the philosophy of Christianity in terms of practical application definitely originated in the New Thought Movement, and became its chief impulsion, its outstanding characteristic. *It is this practical application of spiritual causation to human needs which has drawn the attention of millions of people in America and other millions throughout the world to a new outlook on life, and to new hope.*

Whatever the New Thought Movement may owe to other systems, and it owes much, it is unique in this, it has placed a new and dynamic meaning to the relationship between God and man, between the invisible and the visible. With Jesus, it has insisted that faith shall be made manifest in works; that the Creative Power of God is individualized in every soul. Spiritual faith, belief and conviction, are not merely terms used to designate the devotional life, they are dynamic and creative instruments to be used in everyday living.

While there is a wide range of opinion among the New Thought leaders, teachers, practitioners and laymen, this one underlying purpose runs through the entire Movement: the immediate availability of Good; conscious and practical application of spiritual thought force to the solution of human problems; the inevitable necessity that good shall come to every soul; the belief in immortality and the continuity of the individual stream of consciousness, and eternal expansion of the individual life; the awakening, not to an absorption of man's identity in Deity, but to his complete unity with the Whole. Thus every man becomes an individualized center of God Consciousness, eternally expanding.

The International New Thought Alliance Congress, held at the Palace Hotel in San Francisco, California, July 1940, by a unanimous vote of its members, instructed Erma W. Wells, president of the organization, to appoint a Publication Committee with full authority to act in the publishing of a book representing, as nearly as possible, a true cross-section of the spiritual philosophy and methods for practice which are today being taught by leading teachers, authors, and lecturers in the New Thought field. The Committee subsequently appointed consisted of Ernest Holmes, Chairman, Maude Allison Lathem, Vice-Chairman, Reverend Elizabeth Towne, Reverend James E. Dodds, Reverend Nona L. Brooks, Dr. Emmet Fox, Wallace Kibbee, Ervin E. Seale, Carrick-Cook, Reverend Murrell Powell-Douglas and Reverend Mary L. Butterworth.

Executive members of this committee, after having carefully considered all the material sent in, because of its fine quality have seen fit to incorporate in this book practically all view-points submitted, since each throws a unique light on the subject. The committee feels deeply indebted to all those who have made contributions to this book, for the beautiful spirit of cooperation which has been made manifest.

The following articles may be considered a true, if not entirely complete, presentation of the teachings and practice of the New Thought Movement in America today. Those represented in this book are not, necessarily, better than other teachers in this field, but they are representative.

It did not seem at all necessary to write an exhaustive history of the New Thought Movement. This has already been adequately done.* It is well

---

* History of The New Thought Movement, by Horatio W. Dresser. Published by Thomas Y. Crowell Company, New York, 1919.

however to explain just what is meant by New Thought, and what the leaders of this Movement in America today, teach and practice.

The New Thought Movement is metaphysical, but not in a strict philosophical sense. Metaphysics in terms of New Thought means a practical idealism, which emphasizes spiritual causation and the accessibility of spiritual mind power, acting in accord with law and available to all people. From this standpoint, "Christian Metaphysics" means the philosophy of the New Testament, practiced as a science.

It is the purpose of the New Thought Movement to prove the teachings of Jesus relative to the spiritual universe and man's relationship to it. The New Thought Movement in many ways is unlike most of the Oriental teachings, for in following the philosophy of Jesus more closely than that of other teachers of antiquity, it emphasizes the importance of individualism. In this it is quite American, which is natural, since the Movement started here. Yet it would be a mistake to deny the heritage which this Movement has received from many sources. It is an outgrowth of all that has gone before. It has borrowed much from the idealistic philosophies of the ages, particularly Plato, Socrates and the Neoplatonists. It has been profoundly influenced by the teachings of the Old Testament, the precepts of Buddha and the Sacred Writings of the East. It owes an enormous debt of gratitude to many of the spiritual philosophies of the Middle Ages, and in our own country is particularly indebted to Emerson and many others with whose writings we are all familiar.

But as much as it owes to other systems of thought, it is still a unique American Institution, in that it started in this country, and, although it has spread over the world, it has flourished and grown here more than elsewhere. It probably would be safe to estimate that from fifteen to twenty million people in America today are influenced by its teachings.

The Movement itself is the outcome of a number of contemporaneous systems of thought which have emphasized the inner life. As Dresser stated in his History of New Thought Movement, "The last century witnessed the rediscovery of the inner life.... The new age bids us go to the sources for ourselves."

Probably more than on the work of any other one person, the New Thought Movement of America has been built upon the teachings of Phineas Quimby, who was born in New Hampshire in 1802 and who passed from this plane in the state of Maine in 1866. This man was one of the few original thinkers of the ages. He had a deep intuition as well as an unusually pronounced psychic development. He believed that we are living in a spiritual universe now, but that the freedom of our choice, backed by the law of Mind, makes possible the experience of discord and limitation. He said: "Can a theory be found capable of practice which can separate Truth from error? I undertake to say there is a method of reasoning which, being understood, can separate one from the other. . . . Man is made up of truth and belief; and, if he is deceived into a belief that he has, or is liable to have, a disease, the belief is catching, and the effect follows it."

Quimby laid his chief emphasis on spiritual mind healing, rather than on the control of conditions through the creative power of thought. He claimed that disease is but a dream from which one may be awakened. His method, according to his son, George Quimby, was to "change the mind of a patient, and disabuse it of its error and establish the truth in its place, which, if done, was the cure."

He was completely convinced that the Creative Spirit within us is God, and that we have an immediate relationship to the Divine. This relationship is creative. Quimby never sought to control others; he made no suggestions to them. That is, he did not practice suggestive therapeutics. His whole method of procedure was spiritual explanation. His idea was that symptoms would disappear with the changed viewpoint. In this he anticipated the discoveries of modern psychology, except that his was a more spiritual method.

He spoke of mind as *spiritual substance*, and often referred to what he called the real or the spiritual man who needed to be summoned to the aid of the man who is mentally and physically sick.

Quimby believed in a spiritual body. He taught that there is no disease independent of mind. Thus he said, "Disease being in its root a wrong belief, change the belief and it will cure the disease. By faith we are thus made whole."

The New Thought Movement in America today, owes much to this man's life, teaching and practice. Most of its early teachers were instructed by him. Thus we find most of them emphasizing the Divine Spark in man, which, despite all appearances to the contrary, is always there.

Shortly after Quimby passed in 1866, several of his devout students, most of whom he had healed, began to teach and write. Each branched out freely and naturally, each added his own ideas to what he had received from Quimby. Among those early teachers were people who had already been theologically trained, several of them in the Swedenborgian Church, and it was not difficult for them to follow Quimby since they had already been taught to believe in a law of spiritual correspondences. Whatever the difference of opinion among these earlier teachers may have been, they all seem unanimous in emphasizing mental and spiritual causation and the thought that the material universe possesses no independent life and intelligence. Of course, this was before the day of the new physics. They all taught that spiritual mind healing of the physical body is a result of touching the springs of life in the soul of the patient. Naturally the different teachers chose different names, such as Divine Science, Metaphysical Clubs, Applied Christianity, Practical Christianity and innumerable other names, and in England the term Higher Thought was used, all of which have a common meaning. The New Thought Movement has always been very individualistic and in many respects has stood for a protest against ecclesiastical or spiritual authority. Finally, an attempt was made to weld the whole movement into a national alliance for the purpose of clarity of thought and the dissemination of its teaching.

The following declaration of purpose is taken from one of its earliest records: "Organized to promote an active interest in a more spiritual philosophy and its practical application to human life. Its spirit is broad, tolerant and constructive, and its object an impartial search for truth. All who sympathize with these purposes, without regard to past or present affiliations of sect, party or system, are cordially invited to cooperate."

In another statement drawn at an early date we read: ". . . It seeks the spark of infinitude in the seemingly finite, and seeks to fan it into a blaze that shall be the light of the world. It is therefore striving to bring into hearty cooperation all the individual potencies that have tended toward the high end which it has in view, believing that thus a resistless impulse might be given to the development of life on the highest attainable plane."

It was the purpose of the New Thought Movement not only to stand for a method of spiritual healing, but for a positive and affirmative philosophic idealism of religion, of applied Christianity, and to emphasize the rediscovery of the Gospel teachings relative to healing and everyday life.

In 1900 The International Metaphysical League held its second convention in New York City. In its revised Constitution, the following "purposes" were adopted: "The Purpose of the League is: To establish unity and cooperation of thought and action among individuals and organizations throughout the world devoted to the Science of Mind and of Being, and to bring them, so far as possible, under one name and organization; to promote interest in, and the practice of a true spiritual philosophy of life; to develop the highest self-culture through right thinking, as a means of bringing one's loftiest ideals into present realization; to stimulate faith in, and the study of, the highest nature of man, in its relation to health, happiness, and progress; to teach the universal Fatherhood and Motherhood of God and the all-inclusive Brotherhood of Man; that One Life is immanent in the universe, and is both Center and Circumference of all things visible and invisible, and that this Intelligence is above all and in all; and that from this Infinite Life and Intelligence proceed all Light, Love and Truth."

The following statement of purpose is taken from the Alliance meeting in 1916: "To teach the infinitude of the Supreme One; the Divinity of Man and his infinite possibilities through the creative power of constructive thinking and obedience to the voice of the Indwelling Presence, which is our source of Inspiration, Power, Health and Prosperity." And in St. Louis in 1917 the following declaration of principles of the International New Thought Alliance was adopted, and is now in use:

DECLARATION OF PRINCIPLES
INTERNATIONAL NEW THOUGHT ALLIANCE

We affirm the freedom of each soul as to choice and as to belief, and would not, by the adoption of any declaration of principles, limit such freedom. The essence of the New Thought is Truth, and each individual must be loyal to the Truth he sees. The windows of his soul must be kept open at each moment for the higher light, and his mind must be always hospitable to each new inspiration.

We affirm the Good. This is supreme, universal and everlasting. Man is made in the image of the Good, and evil and pain are but the tests and correctives that appear when his thought does not reflect the full glory of this image.

We affirm health, which is man's divine inheritance. Man's body is his holy temple. Every function of it, every cell of it, is intelligent, and is shaped, ruled, repaired, and controlled by mind. He whose body is full of light is full of health. Spiritual healing has existed among all races in all times. It has now become a part of the higher science and art of living the life more abundant.

We affirm the divine supply. He who serves God and man in the full understanding of the law of compensation shall not lack. Within us are unused resources of energy and power. He who lives with his whole being, and thus expresses fullness, shall reap fullness in return. He who gives himself, he who knows and acts in his highest knowledge, he who trusts in the divine return, has learned the law of success.

We affirm the teaching of Christ that the Kingdom of Heaven is within us, that we are one with the Father, that we should not judge, *that we should love one another, that we should heal the sick, that we should return good for evil*, that we should minister to others, and that we should be perfect even as our Father in Heaven is perfect. These are not only ideals, but practical, everyday working principles.

We affirm the new thought of God as Universal Love, Life, Truth and Joy, in whom we live, move, and have our being, and by whom we are held together; that His mind is our mind now, that realizing our oneness with Him means love, truth, peace, health and plenty, not only in our own lives but in the giving out of these fruits of the Spirit to others.

We affirm these things, not as a profession, but practice, not on one day of the week, but in every hour and minute of every day, sleeping and waking, not in the ministry of a few, but in a service that includes the democracy of all, not in words alone, but in the innermost thoughts of the heart expressed in living the life. "By their fruits ye shall know them."

We affirm Heaven here and now, the life everlasting that becomes conscious immortality, the communion of mind with mind throughout the universe of thoughts, the nothingness of all error and negation, including death, the variety in unity that produces the individual expressions of the One-Life, and the quickened realization of the indwelling God in each soul that is making a new heaven and a new earth.

We affirm that the universe is spiritual and we are spiritual beings. This is the Christ message to the twentieth century, and it is a message not so much of words as of works. To attain this, however, we must be clean, honest and trustworthy and uphold the Jesus Christ standards as taught in the Four Gospels. We now have the golden opportunity to form a real Christ movement. Let us build our house upon this rock, and nothing can prevail against it. This is the vision and mission of the ALLIANCE.

* ERMA WELLS, *President, I.N.T.A.*

ERNEST HOLMES, Chairman,
Publication Committee

** MAUDE ALLISON LATHEM, Vice-Chairman,
Publication Committee.

* Erma Wiley Wells. Born and educated in Iowa. Received her Bachelor of Science Degree from Iowa State College in 1905. Teacher of High School Mathematics in Couer d'Alene, Idaho, and Spokane, Washington for three years. For several years served as Associate Pastor of the Church of the Truth in Spokane. Organized and was pastor of the Church of the Truth in Couer d'Alene. When Dr. A. C. Grier, founder of the Spokane church, resigned in 1924, she was named pastor and has held that position ever since. Founder and director of L.T.L., international young people's organization. Editor for several years of the *Truth Magazine* and now edits *The Fountain.* Author of several small books. Active in Spokane Sorosis (Literary Club), P.E.O. Sisterhood, Pi Beta Phi, Altrusa (Service Club for Women). Has served as president of the International New Thought Alliance since 1938.

** Maude Allison Lathem, editor of Science of Mind Magazine. Formerly Western Editor of Photoplay Magazine. Later free-lance writer, contributing regularly to ten or twelve leading Motion Picture Magazines. Twelve month's series of articles for Progress Magazine. Twenty-five years study of Metaphysics. Teacher and practitioner at Institute of Religious Science, Los Angeles, California.

MIND REMAKES YOUR WORLD

THAT FOR WHICH WE STAND
BY V. MANLEY AYERS

V. Manley Ayers, who founded the Sacramento Branch of the Church of Truth in 1938 and continues as its minister, was trained for the Christian Ministry in the Church of Truth at Spokane, Washington, and for several years following this he was a faculty member of their University of Metaphysics. Prior to his ordination by the Spokane Church in 1937, he served as student minister of the Church of Truth, Couer d'Alene, Idaho.

ALL of the great allegories of the world tell the same epic story of man's journey from the realm of "the way things SEEM" to the realm of "the way things ARE," from "seeming" to "being," from "apparent fact" to "eternal Truth."

As a teacher of The Church of The Truth, I interpret human experience as man's journey from "sense" to "Soul." Evolution, as life's predominating theme, is not the evolution of things, but the evolution of man's sense of things. This is therefore primarily a mental journey, not a progression from place to place, but from consciousness to consciousness—"from glory to glory."

The Creation story itself, the Deluge, the emancipation of the Jews under the leadership of Moses, the wanderings of the Children of Israel in the wilderness, and above all that incomparable New Testament parable of the Prodigal Son, illustrate graphically, in great detail and a rich variety of terms, the return of the sense man to a consciousness of his true spirituality. Some call the process "progressive evolution." Some call it the "path of regeneration." Some call it "soul enfoldment."

To some it is the eternal quest for the "fleeing perfect." It is really man's unquenchable thirst for the knowledge of Truth. True, we often reach forth blindly for it, and do not always recognize it when it is at hand; but none the less the individual's quest for divine satisfaction is the quivering of the compass needle, which is never still until it finds its North. This knowledge of Truth is man's divine birthright. It belongs to him and he shall have it. This consciousness of complete satisfaction is the most personal necessity of the individual,—it is the Father's plan for him, it is his ultimate destiny!

As the spiritual offspring of God, Spirit, man is unlimited in possibilities, abilities and capabilities, containing within himself absolute knowledge, peace, faith and love. Man is not merely body—man is individualized Spirit: Soul, Self. Being a child of the unconditioned God, he is a creature of free choice, not bound by any external fate, determinism, mechanism. Affirming that man is primarily a "spiritual being, living in a spiritual world, governed by spiritual law," the futility of attempting to explain the universe in terms of its material manifestation is perceived. Since the fundamental nature of the universe is Mind, the permanent nature of the Cosmos has no earmarks of matter, such as extension, weight or inertia. However, as the mode is indispensable to the Whole, relative forms of being are not denied. It is denied that the universe of modes and effects has existence apart from the reality which supports it. God alone is acknowledged as Cause. The supreme purpose of the Whole is the discovery by each individual that the macrocosm and the microcosm (the universe in its vastness and its minuteness) are one, and that the individual is a reproduction of the Whole, from which he can in no wise be separated. God is life and life is consciousness. There is no cessation of consciousness, therefore there is no cessation of life. The most ancient sacred writings say, "Nothing takes place without an Onlooker." Truly, were there no omnipresent Intelligence there would be no existence. Ignorance is oblivion. Knowledge is life. There can be no end of knowledge where awareness is; therefore there can be no end to life. That which appears to be death is a change of form, a change of "broadcasting station," for a new and higher expression of the Self.

There is no final judgment. All judgment is continuous self-judgment. ("Multitudes, multitudes in the valley of decision.") Human experience is largely a matter of choice between the Truth and the appearance. Judgments based upon sense perceptions will not be found to be accurate. Judgments according to the Christ standard of perfection within man shall be found to be sound. There is no "final" condition to life. The very genius of life is growth and expansion.

There is an objective in life and it is this: In "the beginning" all was pronounced "good"—perfect; and in "the end" the same perfectness appears, fully recognized. Each soul shall be fully aware of that perfectness which was his from the beginning. Shall we remember that the evolutionary process is not evolution of matter as biologists often indicate, but an evolution of man's consciousness of the good?

Any form of ceremony, we consider, is legitimate to the degree that it truly raises the consciousness; but all forms of ceremony need to be looked upon with suspicion if they become substitutes for consciousness. Likewise, with creeds and formulations. Statements are not to be employed as final, unalterable standpoints. Creeds which are more than a formulation of one's present understanding can be of infinitely more harm than good to the beginner. Open-mindedness is essential to vital religion, whose only credo is, "I believe in my Indwelling Christ." Religious terminology is not essential to the presentation of scientific Truth, but this writer finds it the most adequate means of communicating himself. To ignore this personal factor would in a sense be a denial of his belief in the personalness of God.

METHOD OF PRACTICE

The only test of a theory being the pragmatic one, "Does it hold water?" "Does it cut ice?" "DOES IT WORK?" our teaching is largely determined by the practical results attained from the standpoint of practitionership. These have been abundant, every step of the way, paralleling in some degree the works of the Master, and testifying to the effectuality of scientific prayer. While essentially prophylactic, preventative, in effect, the therapeutic aspect of the Jesus Christ teaching is an important phase of the "Religion of healthy-mindedness." None the less, we consider the greatest demonstration of Truth to be to "so live that you have nothing to overcome." In my experience the sick have been healed, lepers have been cleansed, the dead have been raised, "devils" have been cast out through the ministry of the Word. While direct silent realization has been the ideal, the following suggestions for individual prayer-practice have been found to be particularly effectual.

First, *stop thinking of the problem; think of God.* This clears the consciousness and establishes poise. This can also be done (silently or verbally) by the reading of some good text, the denial of the false belief and affirmation of the Truth of spiritual man. Direct realization is not as difficult as many seem to think, for it is largely a matter of personal training.

Second, *lift up your thought to your highest conception of God, Man, Heaven.* Do not remain on the level of your problem. Do not treat conditions. You must not have one eye on the material world or the problem; do not heed "improvement" or "relapse"; keep the eyes on the Truth. Realize that nothing can in any way interfere with the direct, instantaneous action of God.

Third, *continue treating until you touch the point of releasement.* You alone will know when the work is done "in earth as it is in heaven," A flood of warmth and joy, accompanied by a great sense of security, will tell you that the work is completed and that no more treatment is needed in that specific direction. Faithfulness is required. Many short periods of treatment are suggested for beginners, rather than long hours, until the prayer-without-ceasing attitude is attained.

Mr. E. W., in desperation from lack of work, demanded another practitioner be called for cooperation as a bolster to his faith. No sense of emergency touched the practitioner, but he assented, with the realization that "God's man is always employed in the right place at the right time." No sooner was the call placed in the hands of Western Union than a perception of the needlessness of other support told the practitioner that the work was done. In less than an hour Mr. E. W. called back, overwhelmed with joy that he had found work in his own line.

Personal treatment, directing attention to a personal man and his problem, has been found to be the least satisfactory method, involving as it does all of the pitfalls of personal sense. All too often it attaches the problem to the "patient" and aggravates the evil. Often it qualifies the healing, limiting it to the specific sphere of the practitioner's knowledge.

An emergency call came from C, who was apparently choking with asthma. This is the realization we held: "Nothing can interfere with the free, orderly, sequential flowing of God's ideas. Man receives and passes on God's ideas with perfect facility and ease." It was later learned that asthma was not the only problem: the mind had become hazy and the blood had almost ceased to circulate. All three of these conditions were met by this one impersonal realization.

Absent treatment has been found to be particularly successful where there is any tendency to be "caught in the picture" or carried away by the suggestion of evil.

Self-treatment denies the necessity of a professional practitioner's services, and reveals that all can be instruments of healing. F. M., student with marvelously clear consciousness in certain directions, found himself in the middle of the office floor coughing up quantities of blood. The office force was frightened, witless, and wordless. With a detachment from the problem unequaled in my experience, F. M. saw the whole scene as an impersonal picture. Touched by the ridiculousness of it, that he, a son of God, a spiritual being, could bleed to death, he laughed aloud, even while he lay in the pool of blood. That laugh was the denial that "saved his life." This man, almost perversely doing the things which it was thought would kill him in the succeeding days, gained better health than he had known for years.

From a signed statement in our files we bring another testimonial: Shirley Lucille Grant, three and a half years old, caught the index finger of her left hand in a car door. Only the cord and about an eighth of an inch of flesh held the finger to the hand. After the first shock, one cry (as though she had hit her hand with a hammer) there was no crying and no pain. The doctor, the father (who is a Truth student) and the head nurse at the hospital testify to these facts. Three weeks later it was revealed that only one small spot about the size of a pin-head had not knitted in the bone. Feeling at the tip of the finger is normal. She is able to use the finger perfectly now. This was the father's instantaneous treatment, directed as much, possibly, to the fearful mother as to the child: "This is God's child more than yours. He is the force that cares for her. He is the power in every cell of her body. He can take care of her better than you can." Yes, "ye shall know the Truth and the Truth shall make you free."

Mr. W., a man with the greatest capacity for suffering that I have ever seen, revealed by the same token that his capacity of appreciation and enjoyment were tremendous. Purely a "mental type," his emotional energies and magnificent intellect had run him ragged through lack of direction. It was difficult to distinguish his exhausted nervous condition from insanity-- in fact, the police were holding him for psychopathic scrutiny. After convincing officials that he was perfectly sane, we secured his release from the hospital. On our knees before the altar in the darkened church (an emotional outlet was a necessity) he poured out his soul in the Lord's prayer. There on my knees I followed him by phrase in realization; "Our Father which art in heaven," Infinite Parent-Spirit of us all, enthroned in the divinity of man's soul: all Presence, all Knowledge, all Power, "Hallowed be Thy Name." Thy nature is Wholeness, Harmony, Peace. "Thy kingdom come." Establish the kingdom of Peace in man's conscious awareness; "Thy will be done in earth, as it is in heaven." As Thou art willing Peace to man, so man is willing peace to his fellowman. Let Thy Peace come forth in manifestation as it is in Divine Mind! "Give us this day our daily bread." Satisfy our hungers and thirst and desires daily, according to our constantly expanding capacity to receive. Feed us with the very substance of Thy Peace! "And forgive us our debts as we forgive our debtors." Fulfill our obligations to our fellowman with a fullness of Thy Peace, even as he in a fullness of Peace, fulfills his obligations to us and to the whole! "And lead us not into temptation." Let not our freedom of will, great gift from Thee, lead us into a sense of turmoil or warfare. "But deliver us from evil,"—deliver us from the miasma of confusion. And, then, in grateful acknowledgment of the completed demonstration we affirmed, "For Thine is the Kingdom and the Power and the Glory forever." For Thou art the only Power and the only Intelligence, supreme in authority, might and majesty. The government is upon Thy shoulder. Of the increase of Thy government and Peace there shall be no end. Amen. And Peace descended upon that mind and spirit and those raw nerves, and the storm of the emotions subsided, and instability fled before the Presence of God.

THE CREATIVE PRINCIPLE AT WORK
BY FREDERICK W. BAILES

Dr. Frederick William Bailes, head of the Institute of Religious Science at Long Beach, California, was born in New Zealand. Educated as a medical missionary at University of New Zealand, Beloit College, Wisconsin, and London Homeopathic Hospital, England. Became interested in metaphysics following a personal healing of diabetes. Lectured and taught classes in the subject on three world tours. For years specialized in application of mental law to sales and business life. Taught its relationship to classes made up of Realty Boards, Executives' Clubs, and similar groups. Also personally trained large sales organizations for industrial concerns such as Aluminum Corporation of America subsidiaries. Author of : *Getting What You Go After and Your Mind Can Heal You.*

As MIGHT be expected, the presentation of this truth is colored by the training and background of the one presenting it, as is always the case where different speakers present the same type of message. In this instance, the writer's original training in medicine has given him a scientific point of view in approaching man's problems, in addition to the philosophical view which characterizes this teaching.

We consider that man's chief problem is to find his place in the universe. He comes into a world to which he is a stranger, and from the cradle to the grave he is endeavoring to find out "what it is all about." In other words, his supreme effort is to make a true and proper adjustment of himself to the universe, to his fellowman and to God.

One of the first things of which he becomes conscious is that he lives in a physical universe. His mind naturally asks the question, "What is matter?" He can determine that it is a dead, obstructing substance, from which he must separate himself as completely as possible. But if he does this he finds himself with a dual universe, in which spirit and body are mutually antagonistic, and where God and Creation are inherently hostile the one to the other.

We teach and believe that God and the universe are mutually complementary to one another. That Spirit needs a universe of form as its vehicle of expression, and that these forms need the indwelling Spirit to make manifest the divine perfection. We believe that God and the universe are essentially One; that matter is actually a lowered vibration of God, to use a somewhat overworked term.

We feel it is scientific to believe that Spirit, Mind and Substance all coexisted from the beginning, the three making up the constituents of the Godhead. That all are noble, and the flesh not something to be despised. That Spirit, desiring form through which It could express, spoke the Word that sent Mind into action along this specific line, to bring the universe into being, following a definite, ordered, graded plan, which science now calls the process of evolution.

Spirit is always the deciding, determining phase of the Godhead, forever impressing Its will upon Mind, which is the working phase of the Godhead, formulating and fabricating the desire of Spirit into form. Matter is always the more condensed phase of the Godhead, whether simple electric particles or vibrations, or gaseous, liquid or solid form.

To reverse these three, matter possesses no power of voluntary activity. It must always be operated upon by a force outside itself. We believe this force to be Mind Power. This Universal. Mind Power we believe to be subjective, forever subject to the word and will of Spirit. We see no differences in "Godness" here; each phase of the Trinity operates according to its own inherent nature, Spirit determining, Mind obeying Spirit, and

Body obedient to Mind.

These facts are not dependent upon any sacred writing—they are evident to any careful observer. Thus our belief in the healing power of Mind is based upon logical premises. Just as the three levels of Divine activity are seen in the universe, so are they seen in the life of man, for man as spirit reasons and chooses, determining that which he intends shall be manifest; man's subjective mind obeys his objective mind, swinging into action to follow its dictates, and it in turn influences and molds man as body or material possessions.

From the above we gather that when the body is sick, it could not have produced that sickness of itself, for it can only move in any direction as it is moved by mind. Therefore the sickness is really a distortion of the mental processes, which have become evident only because we are able to observe bodily changes from the outside. Therefore it follows that the physical disorder is an effect, and that the mental malformation is the real disorder. In other words, all manifestations which are called disease begin in the mind, and consequently must end there, if healing is to be.

We teach that material, bodily, physical conditions are reflections of mental states. But we go farther—we teach that *they are* the identical mental states themselves condensed into form. Since we live in a universe which is One, and since that universe is, in the last analysis, nothing but energy in varying degrees of condensation, we can see that Dr. Bucke was stating a profound truth when he declared that "the Universe is a Living Presence."

We know that in the material universe all vibrations are one vibration of varying lengths, thus they are received through various kinds of apparatus. Those of a certain length are caught by the retina and carried along the optic nerve to the brain, where they are "seen" as light. Those of a different length are caught by the organ of Corti and transmitted through the auditory nerve into the brain, where they are "heard" as sound.

In reality, light and sound are one, except that they are received differently. The radio wave, the X-ray, cosmic rays are all one, differing only in their wave length. Electricity, the basis for all formed substances, is merely another form of energy, a vibration of a different length.

Since the chirp of a chicken and the roar of a lion are one and the same thing, except for their wave length, and the toot of a piccolo and the rumble of a steamer horn are the same, we feel that it is not unreasonable to believe that Spirit, Mind and Body are one and the same thing, at different wave lengths, if we might be permitted to use this term here. Whether we apply the thought to man as an individual, or to God as a Trinity, we feel that we are well within the bounds of reason, and in this we are supported by the discoveries which pour daily out of the scientific laboratories all over the world.

We believe that there is a fundamental harmony in and throughout the entire universe, up to and including the Godhead. Therefore, wherever we see that which is inharmonious we know that it is a false inharmony—that fundamentally it is an error of finite vision, fostered and given apparent reality by the race-consciousness, encouraged by the belief of our neighbors as well as our own past belief.

To dissolve this distorted view, we believe that man, having the power of choice, is privileged to turn his back upon that which "appears to be," and face toward that which really is —the Divine Perfection in man, and the Divine Harmony of the universe and its Living Presence. His healing comes from an inner, conscious awareness of his inseparability from his Divine Source, and of the active, momentary receptivity of all that Spirit is. In other words, he gives the lie to every inharmonious manifestation, and affirms the truth of his being, that God is in his holy temple, the body, the business, the property, the paycheck. Faith is the giving of substance to things hoped for, the giving of evidence to things not seen.

We teach that there is only One Mind throughout the universe. That man in thinking thinks with that Mind, or with as much of It as he is able to draw within his thinking space. Man's subjective mind, which controls his bodily conditions, is merely that much of Universal Subjective Mind as he allows to flow through him. Therefore we do not speak much of "concentration," valuable though we know it to be. We feel that, compared to the vast surrounding ocean of Mind, man's mind is finite in its scope. But we believe that man's thought becomes part of the universal thought, and that as he unifies his thought with that harmonious thought of Spirit, that awareness of perfection which he has embodied is carried out into the ceaseless, creative Mind, and becomes form. This is done "not by might, nor by power, but by my Spirit, saith the Lord." In other words, man's will power, mental labor and striving do not accomplish the result, but a release of his inner awareness to Universal Creative Mind places his treatment where permanent healing can take place.

More than this, we endeavor to rise to the highest realization of spiritual power when treating, for the higher the concept of the power that is working, the higher the result. When the problem is of such a nature that analysis and explanation are required, we use them, but we never lose sight of the fact that these belong in the preliminary stages of the work, and are useful ONLY as a means of clearing the ground preparatory to the erection of the temple, which is the reproduction in the seeker of what Spirit is in Itself. Anything less than this is incomplete work, and cannot be permanent.

We find, then, that this Intelligent Mind works always by Law. The Law of Mind is as inflexible as the law of electricity, *and differs from Mind itself as Me law of electricity differs from electricity.* It works only where directed. In many people there is a continuous direction toward the negative, morbid, limited, poverty, sickness state. It is not that they consciously desire these things; but this is where their contemplation most easily turns; they live in fear, or they carry the negative thought patterns of hatred, jealousy, grudges, selfishness. These destructive hidden mental states are the only direction which the Law of Mind receives, or they are the principal pattern upon which this Law has to build. The result is—themselves perpetuated in form, until the trouble-ridden individual cries out, "0 wretched man, who shall deliver me from this body of death?"

Since this Law is impersonal, and swings its activity only in the way to which it is directed, it becomes a blessing where before it had seemed to be a curse. Man can consciously, deliberately and scientifically choose to eradicate this former destructive thought pattern, and substitute one more to his liking. Then, and only then will his circumstances commence to change for the better. For the same Law which impersonally brought the negative into form will now bring the positive—he can be sure of this. Therefore he works with a certainty before him, not merely a hope. This is why Truth is in reality a "Science of Mind."

Before leaving the subject of matter and the body, we might add that we see this Law of Life daily working in our bodies, following quite evidently a pattern laid down ages ago by the Spirit. We see it in the ceaseless flow of intelligence to every part of the body, growing hair and finger nails, maintaining digestion, assimilation and elimination, maintaining the body always at a temperature of ninety-eight and a half degrees, setting off an impulse of the heart seventy-two times every minute, repairing cuts, bruises and breaks without man's conscious assistance—in short, maintaining the body economy at normal. The only time it deviates from this norm is when man, by his negative mental states, interposes a false pattern, or as in the case of infants, the parents interpose a fear pattern.

This Intelligent Law seems to have a passion for saving the body. We do not have to plead for healing—we have merely to comply with this Cosmic Law, and healing will be resumed at the point where it was interrupted by our mental obstructions.

We teach that, while the Science of Mind is not a get-rich-quick scheme, man has a right to expect that he shall have abundant supply when he complies with the Law of abundance. We believe that much harm has accrued to the metaphysical cause by the teaching that man can go into the Silence and through affirmations alone materialize automobiles, houses and millions. We believe in affirmations, but those affirmations must come out of an integrated personality. As long as one's inner unity is disintegrated his earning power is lost, and a disturbed, anxious, fearful soul sitting in a closet affirming millions is incongruous. Jesus put the horse before the cart when he said to seek first the Kingdom, then these other things will come.

Until the inner life is unified, and one is "in tune with the Infinite," he will continue to be disappointed, if financial troubles are his chief concern. For his outer world is merely his inner world condensed into form. The financial distress is merely the echo of the mental distress. As long as a person is whipped within, he cannot be victorious without. There must be a sense of his complete adequacy in the universe; he must know that his services are useful; that he is fully aware of his usefulness; that all men are aware of his worth; that he has the full assurance of supply; that he is not merely uttering words given him by a practitioner or found on a printed page.

There must be a recognition that money, like health, is first spiritual; it is spiritually conceived. The deep consciousness of this must become a living awareness within one. He must form what we call his *Mental Equivalent,* because only that will manifest in the outer of which he himself has formed a mental equivalent in the inner. In other words, *his inner consciousness of money means much more than the actual words of an affirmation.*

As a rule, improvement in finances comes gradually, not in a big jump. This is because inner acceptance comes gradually, light dawns slowly in most people; the scattered inner life, as a rule, is put together by picking up the scattered pieces and setting them in place, a piece at a time, until finally the inner personality is unified and integrated. While this is going on there is usually a gradual improvement in one's earning power, or his ability to attract money.

We do not wish to appear to be saying something here which contradicts our thesis—that perfection is ever within. It is true—and we teach it—that in some people this integration of the true Self sometimes comes in a moment. But we are speaking of things as we observe them in the majority of cases, and our observation is that the process is usually a gradual one. As a general rule, one's consciousness does not change from defeat and despair to inward victory in a moment, although we rejoice when we see this occur, just as we do when we see an instantaneous healing of cancer or some other so-called *incurable disease.*

We teach that demonstrations come best when one lives in a continuous state of supply. Too many metaphysicians seek to demonstrate money only when they get into a pinch. The rent is due, or a payment has to be made, and the person becomes panicky. In this condition one treats frantically, *but his affirmative words are belied by his inner anxiety.* The Law is perfect—it *could* cause thousands of dollars to flow into form for him. But his consciousness is imperfect—there is discord within him instead of peaceful harmony. God can only do for us what He does THROUGH us. Everything that we get comes through one channel alone—the channel of our own mind. If our consciousness is pinched, then our supply cannot be anything but pinched.

Therefore we seek to encourage our students to a mode of life which promotes prosperity. This is the way that nature manifests supply. The trees in the forest keep drawing upon the moisture, and expecting it. The birds of the air live in the expectancy of daily supply. Man alone in all creation worries about his supply. His worry and fear tend to shut it off— his faith and expectancy of the good reopen it. When his inner peace is destroyed his ability to earn begins to suffer. This is seen in the lives of business men and salesmen every day.

The prime factor in drawing supply is an unshakeable, inward, unforced peace of mind. This comes from knowing that one lives in a universe which is harmoniously inclined toward him, and with which he himself is entirely at peace. If he is poorly adjusted to life, or to his surroundings, he finds supply shutting off. One must be true to his deep inner self, must feel that inner harmony which sometimes comes through following his inner light, even though it leads him to a decision or decisions which are violently opposed by others. If his mode of life is one which is pointed toward an enlarged vision, then he may have to cut away or drop some attitudes or connections which have been the cause of deep-seated inner turmoil. But if this is the way to the reestablishment of his integrated self, the way to substantial peace and power, then he is true to society as well as to himself, and most important of all, he is true to the universe which has never agreed with his hidden inharmony. We teach this as a prerequisite to power in the life.

THE NEW TEACHING FOR THE NEW AGE
BY RAYMOND CHARLES BARKER

Raymond Charles Barker, an ordained minister of the Unity School of Christianity, is minister of the Unity Church of Truth, Rochester, New York, and the Syracuse Unity Center, Syracuse, New York. He has been vitally active in the I. N. T. A. for eight years and has been a member of the Executive Board of the Alliance for the past five years. He is a well known Field lecturer in the New Thought Movement having spoken in most of the New Thought ministries in the United States.

"THERE is nothing so powerful as an idea whose time has come." New Thought is an idea of the nature and processes of a God whose time has come. Ideas of religion are eternally in a state of flux and New Thought is a fresh interpretation of the reality of the spiritual universe designed to fit the needs of the Twentieth Century. It is practical Christianity in its most comprehensive sense.

An essential belief of New Thought is that the universe is an intelligent creation of an intelligent Mind. This Mind is God. The older theologists have proclaimed God as the Creator, but have not always given a logical or intelligent outline of the method by which the Creator becomes the created. The New Thought Movement, with its understanding of God as Mind, explains creation as a logical result of the Divine Mind giving birth to ideas, which ideas take form. This process is an eternal one, for creation is never complete; it is forever going on.

This Spiritual Process by which the cosmic system has come into being is based upon divine law, a law of mind action. This law operates not only in the Universal Mind of God, but also in the individual world by means of thought. The conditions, limitations and possibilities of each man are dependent upon the ideas his consciousness projects into form. Man was created in the "image and likeness" of the Universal Mind, and, as Jesus said, has been given all power and all authority to be the Light of his own world.

This indwelling power and authority consists in man's ability to grasp the spiritual ideas of the God-mind and to think those ideas into form. Man is a spiritual being living in a spiritual universe governed by spiritual law. If the outer body and affairs of man do not seem to bear witness to this fact, it is due to his own misuse of ideas.

Jesus Christ redefined man's oneness with Spirit. God is Spirit and man is made in the image and likeness of that Spirit. Jesus came to inject into the consciousness of man the idea of man's own divinity. He assured the individual that *every thing that the Christ in Jesus of Nazareth accomplished could be accomplished by the Christ of each individual.* The indwelling Father to which Jesus referred, is the universal Christ Principle in every Son of God. As students of this Truth we apply our knowledge of the perfection of man and his relationship to God to human needs and thereby heal the sick, prosper the poor, and bring peace to confused minds.

The healing of body and affairs is the natural result of spiritual Causation operating through the mind of man. Health, happiness and prosperity are the inevitable result of man's thinking the thoughts of God after Him. A perfect Cause does not produce an imperfect result. As man's thought turns to Spirit as the "cause, medium and effect" in his life; as he recognizes his oneness with God and therefore with all of the attributes of God, realizing that nothing unlike Perfection can belong to the Christ man, he brings forth into his life "the fruits of the Spirit," some of which are happiness, health and prosperity.

These great benefits, resulting from the immutable Law of God (which is always the Law of Good), are impersonal and omnipresent. They work for one and all. Creed, race, and personality have nothing to do with this immutable law of mind in action.

Heaven and hell are the results of man's use of ideas. If man turns to the indwelling Christ Mind and draws his ideas from that Source, he lives in Heaven here and now. If he turns to the external world and the opinions of others, he builds for himself a hell here and now. New Thought affirms that man is in Heaven here and now and is as spiritual as he ever will become. As man turns from the race beliefs in sin, sickness, lack and death, to the living ideas of Jesus Christ (which are life eternal, opulence, radiant health, and permanent harmony) he will create for himself a wonderful world in which he will live as an intelligent spiritual being.

New Thought is not so much a religion as it is an approach to spiritual Truths. It does not tell man what to do; it tells him what he is, and man, by perceiving his own spiritual nature, automatically begins to change his attitude of mind and with the adjustment of his thought, outer conditions in his life are changed accordingly.

We stand on the platform of works accomplished and we are willing to be tested by the standard of Jesus Christ which was, "By their works ye shall know them." The New Thought Movement is proving, in the lives of every sincere student who applies it, the practical results of thinking with the Christ Mind and loving with the Christ Heart.

DIVINE SCIENCE
BY NONA L. BROOKS

Nona L. Brooks, president and cofounder of the Divine Science College, Denver, Colorado (parent organization of the Divine Science Colleges over the country) was born in Louisville, Kentucky. She received her B.A. degree at Charleston College, Charleston, S.C., taught five years in the public schools in Colorado, and later attended Wellesley for special work in English and Latin. On January 1, 1899, Miss Brooks and her sisters organized the first Divine Science Church in Denver and she was chosen minister and continued in that capacity until 1929. In 1916, she went to the Boston University to take work in Journalism and Theism. Miss Brooks was secretary of the Colorado Prison Association seven years; president of the Denver Philosophical Society for a term; president of the Divine Science College for sixteen years. Then she resigned from both the College and the Church to work in other parts of the world. She went to Europe in 1926 and taught classes in London and in other cities, continuing her trip around the world. The year 1929 she spent in Australia and New Zealand. 1938 the demand was so insistent that she again took up her work as president of the College in Denver, and continues in that capacity. Author of *Short Lessons in Divine Science, Mysteries, What is Real and What Illusion, The Prayer that Never Fails, Studies in Health.*

THE dictionary defines "divine" as that which pertains to God; and "science" as knowledge coordinated, arranged and systematized. Then let us think of Divine Science as the knowledge of God systematized with reference to the fundamental principles of life and the method of highest individual attainment.

Divine Science is a philosophy, a science and a religion; it covers the entire field of life, universal and individual. It deals with fundamental principles and the laws by which they can be demonstrated in your and my life. In the life of every human being when be applies them faithfully. Through the study and application of Divine Science we can attain an ever higher and higher realization of Life eternal, the gift of God to us, His children.

As a philosophy, Divine Science satisfies my intellect. It is reasonable. It satisfies my needs as an individual by giving me a working basis for daily living through which I may realize the truths that its philosophy teaches.

As a science, Divine Science shows us the value of systematizing our knowledge of God. System is necessary in all attainment, why not in our study of the One Universal Presence? Knowledge is of much more value to us if it is in usable form.

As a religion, Divine Science satisfies my heart; it brings me into touch with life in an understanding way. It regards and interprets man and the facts and forms of life in a logical way from the standpoint of the universal. Omnipresence is its basic principle, the basis of all its teachings. It is important in the life of every one that he accept the omnipresence of God definitely, not merely intellectually, but as a foundation principle by which to live. If this were done by all human beings there would develop in us the *consciousness of unity (love)* which would transform the world. There could be no more quarrels; gossip would cease; criticism, which stirs up so much inharmony, would fall away; wars would be no more, life on this beloved planet would be what it should be, harmonious throughout, abounding in good at every point. We should then realize the abundant life which Jesus said he wished to reveal to the world. We should be living in a very haven of beauty and wonder and joy. For through Divine Science one gains a new realization of the universe and of all life.

The moment one postulates the Omnipresence of God as a principle to live by, to be demonstrated, life comes to have a new meaning to him, a rich and blessed meaning. Divine Science gives the fullest and most consistent interpretation of Omnipresence. It points its students to this truth as the basis of their thinking and living. They are not trammeled by personal leadership. Never have I known a religion or a philosophy that dealt with omnipresence so earnestly and so deeply as a working hypothesis, a sure basis for right thinking and true living.

Divine Science teaches us to think in accord with this fundamental Principle and to live in accord with it. With the thought of God everywhere present as our guide at all times we are not in need of personal leaders or outside helps. The practice of this foundation truth in thinking and in living brings its own individual revelation of truth. This proves to us that God is open to every earnest seeker. While leaders and others may be helpful, we should not say that anything is true because some one says it is the truth. Divine Science believes in the Voice of God, in the soul of man, as the only certain guide.

Divine Science is progressive. Its teachings never point to finality in outer expression. It never says to us, "Here is the end." As a religion it teaches and expects continuous revelation. Jesus did not tell us that we could never know aught except what he had given us. Jesus told his disciples that the Spirit would lead them into all truth and that men would do greater works in the future than he had done, if they would be true spiritually. Jesus and Paul both taught that we work out our own salvation through seeking and living the highest spiritual truth. By bringing the truth we know into our daily living, we come to perceive and understand still greater truth.

The whole of truth is always *here*, open to us; however, it is necessary that we find it for ourselves. Each of us, in order to come into an understanding knowledge, must have his own revelation of truth, of God. This throws the responsibility of the spiritual unfoldment of the individual upon the individual himself. It shows us that no one can take another and put him into the Kingdom of God, but the realization of the glories of this kingdom depends upon each one of us. The Spirit of Truth leads us into all truth, for the Spirit is open and ready to lead.

Divine Science is inclusive. It endeavors to understand and interpret, not to deny. The only things that this teaching denies are those that are unlike God—self-centeredness, impurity, separation and lack with their dire results, sin, sickness, death. It accepts God in fullness and sees His universe as a living organism to be understood and trusted by the one who is open to truth and free to understand.

Divine Science teaches that man is in God, of God and like God. Omnipresence, its supreme affirmation, shows that God includes man; "In him we live, move and have our being," says Paul. God not only includes man but, "He hath given us of His Spirit," God is within man. Paul speaks of this divinity within man as the Christ of us; "Christ in you your hope of glory," "Ye have the mind of Christ." We believe that God includes the body of man also. Therefore, we do not deny the body or the visible universe, instead we glorify them; therefore, we believe in healing which means that man may come into the realization of his rightful body, his Divine Body, his God-given Form. Those who understand the Presence and who feel that they are the children of this One, the living Reality, know what healing means.

We realize that God is not a respecter of persons; God does not select certain ones for His special blessings. God is universal life, health, harmony, and these belong to each of us. We are given the right of choice, to accept or reject these gifts. Each of us may choose health and be healed, if he does his part.

Divine Science does not deny process: God is continually expressing Himself; His creative power is forever active and man is always coming to know more and more of truth. We believe in evolution—God expressing Himself in the consciousness of man, and man becoming more and more aware of what God is and of what God does. Evolution is merely God's method of creating. The rose does not come into being full blown but unfolds through a wonderful and beautiful process until it presents to our appreciative eyes the Divine Idea worked out by a Divine Plan. Man does not spring into being full grown— what we should miss if he did, if there were no babies, no children. God's way is always the best. When we really know Life, we shall see that there is only God and God in action, and that all process is good.

Divine Science affirms that we have a right to the perfect body. We cannot study biology and not believe that the body is the living presence of God and as such we glorify it by knowing it to be God's spoken word in form.

One of the joys in Divine Science is that it includes in its outlook every process of life, from the tiniest to the sublimest, and declares that God is in action in each one, unfolding His plan, impelling the different forms of nature to move forward.

We feel assured that the inner process that is going on in man has no end. We cannot fully conceive infinity, but we know that love is an infinite and universal quality and that all process is in the care of this love. Therefore, we look forward to an eternity of joy for we believe that there is continuous and limitless revelation ahead. Life is the immediate as well as the infinite Presence of God.

I believe that Omnipresence leads us to the sanest and truest interpretation of life. It brings to one who fully understands it a feeling of unity with his fellow man. I never really loved Jesus and found him companionable until I studied his life in the light of omnipresence. I think of him now as an elder brother who came to show us the Father, for his emphasis is never upon himself but always upon God.

Divine Science gives us the highest ideals and it also gives us the assurance that we can live up to them. It has the optimism of true knowledge for it says, "Truth can be known and demonstrated. Here and now it can be done. Millions are proving this."

When I was a child, I was told occasionally of a God of Love and Power, but oftener there was impressed upon me that God was angry with the wicked every day; and with that I was told that I was a sinner and could not please God. Total depravity was a doctrine put to the front of nearly every sermon. I came to believe that I was weak and sinful. I became hopeless so far as God and myself were concerned. What terrible psychology to bring a child up on. I was much concerned that we must go on sinning. It was useless then to try to do anything else. You can imagine what a comfort it was to me when I learned of Omnipresence; it taught me that I am one with the God of Love and Power and within me is the ability to live up to the divine ideal.

Through this teaching I have learned that health is a spiritual reality and that it includes environment as well as body; that God's will for us is freedom and happiness. There are millions today who believe this and who are proving the truth of God's presence and power in their daily lives by their release from sin and sickness. Think of it! The knowledge of God's universal presence and the application of that truth to our daily experience brings to the student the realization of the abundant life, the life of health, harmony, power; the life that abounds in good and that frees us from every limitation.

The teaching of Divine Science is, I believe, the nearest to Jesus' message of any I have found, after years of study of many other religions. It is Jesus' idea of salvation as I interpret it. Divine Science calls us to truer living; it places upon each one of us the responsibility of using the principle he accepts steadfastly until he realizes its deepest and fullest meaning.

Divine Science rejoices in the truth wherever it is found; in those who sometimes claim that they are not religious, in other churches by whatever name they are called. It says to the individual, "Come to this church if it gives you what you need. If not, go where you find the most satisfaction, and God bless you." I have been asked, "Miss Brooks, is it fair for others to come to this church to get what you are giving, then take it to another church?"

I answer, "One of the best things about this teaching is its interpretation of Truth. We are not working to build organization or sect. There is something much bigger than any organization and we must work for the larger thing. It is of course necessary to have a name. I wish it were not. We should all be workers in the body of Christ."

We rejoice in the truth wherever given. We believe we have something worthwhile to give here and now. We invite others to share it with us. We are happy when they are benefited by their work for the Church Invisible—the Church Universal.

Our method of work is similar to all other metaphysical groups. In a nutshell, it is this: Keep your thoughts and feelings true to the foundation principle of the universe, God's universal presence. This will bring the realization of God's immediacy. Here are some affirmations we like to make. They are very simple but they give briefly the truth of every moment; the truth which, when realized through our practice of true thinking, brings us to the realization of health, peace and power.

Affirmations

God is everywhere, therefore God is here.

What God is, is everywhere; therefore what God is, is here. Whatever God is is here; therefore, health, joy, love, wisdom, supply and power are here. This knowledge is my certainty of good.

THE UNASSAILABLE POWER
BY EDGAR WHITE BURRILL

Edgar White Burrill, B.A., M.A., Amherst College; D.S.B., Denver; Ps. D., D.D., Indiana; Ph.D., California. Taught at Northwestern and Columbia Universities in English Literature, etc., for sixteen years. Created and directed New York City's famous "Literary Vespers," in Town Hall for fourteen years. Conducted lecture tours throughout the United States and on the Continent. Dr. Burrill, who is now Leader of the Buffalo Unity Center, has served as Associate Pastor of Divine Science Church, Denver, Colorado, and as Summer Leader of Victoria (Canada) Truth Center. Contributor of many articles to Science of Mind, Divine Science Magazine, Think What You Want, etc. Author of *Literary Vespers, Master Skylark, Modern Dream, The Fortunes of Thought, etc.*

As THE air in this room and all about us is filled with countless unseen vibrations, so also is it filled with Good, God's presence. Scientific prayer is the practice of that presence. It is the affirmation of that which is true. This also constitutes a "treatment." A person is "healed" by a treatment when the spiritual Truth destroys the "error," by correcting it. Where does the error, or mistaken belief go? Well, where does darkness go when light dissolves it? It ceases to be. It doesn't go anywhere. It is swallowed up in victory, as death is when consciousness of everlasting life is awakened.

The understanding of our oneness with the ever-presence of Good bestows eternal life upon us. This power of Goodness is all about us, and it is sufficient for all our needs. It is supreme, omnipresent, unassailable, conquering all. Give yourself to it, let it have its way with you. It is indestructible and inexhaustible. The more you use it, the more you can have, and the stronger you will be. It is the greatest force in the universe, and it is yours to use, always, as much as you need. Nothing can stand against it. Nothing can hurt you when armed with it. When you use this unassailable Power, all evils must flee, as darkness is swallowed up in light. It is impenetrable by anything unlike itself, impervious to all attacks from those who would misuse it or destroy it.

Most of us do not turn to this power until in extremity. But when we do, we are saved and protected, like Daniel in the lion's den. True humility of self is the door. Self-effacement of the personal ego, self-abandonment to the divine, is the key. The use of this Almighty Power is yours by right of your divine heritage. "It is your Father's good pleasure to give you this Kingdom." Claim it. It is already yours. It is the same Power that holds the stars in their courses, that keeps all the heavenly planets in their orbits about their central suns.

This Power is God, it is the Principle of Goodness in action. It is not a person nor a thing, but a Power that is loving, intelligent and just, ever present everywhere and at all times, and all-powerful. It is the one and only operative power. Evil, if potent at all, would have to exist where God is, and that is impossible. So fear it not. If the One is Allness, then everything else is no thing, nothing. The instantaneous effect of such a realization is marvelous. It heals all our diseases, destroys all our fears, curing at once mentally, physically, financially, domestically, emotionally, socially.

This Mind-Power is supreme over its own conditions and creations. Hence, "None of these things move me;" no plague nor poverty nor pain, any more. But conquest of fear is possible only when our understanding is clear, our understanding of the unassailable power of Good. Wild beasts attack us only when we fear them, because we fear them. The psychological reaction to fear is a responsive fear. Fear forces animals to attack the thing that is afraid because it smells bad. It is a fact that fear causes an offensive emanation from the body that infuriates animals. Fear breeds fear in the beholder always. Even the tiny wild beasts called germs and bacteria become virulent and destructive when we are afraid of them. Otherwise they have no power to harm us. Sir Charles Napier found that he could force tigers to flee from him in the jungle when he looked fearlessly upon them, but only after he had overcome the tiger in himself. First say to the storm within yourself, "Peace, be still," and outwardly all will be well. Jesus never needed to conquer the stormy waves; when he had calmed his disciples' panic, they were expert enough to handle their threatened ship properly.

The first commandment decreed that we should have no other gods before Good; should recognize no other power than our own God-like I AM, the principle of our eternal being, spirit of His spirit. This is the one and only Source of all that is; it is the unassailable and all-inclusive power; it is the only Power. There is but one God, Good. It follows therefore that there is no evil. Hence, "I will fear no evil." Why should I? There is but the One Presence, in Whom all other presences are included. There is one Life, and it is everlasting; one Love, and it is all-inclusive; one Truth, which is universal. Everlasting Life, all-inclusive Love, universal Truth; this is the real Trinity. Father, Son, and Holy Spirit means one infinite Mind, its perfect Ideas, and their expression, manifestation, representation, in an infinite diversity of patterns, yet all of the same substance.

No power can rob me, therefore, of vitality. God won't; any lesser power can't. Therefore I possess eternal vitality; I have everlasting life. By realizing this perpetual, continuous, inextinguishable life, I can raise the dead to newness of life. "Though a man were dead, yet shall he live." I can bring the dying back to newness of life by bringing back to them the understanding of their unending vitality because one with this unassailable Power. Many have raised the dead: Elijah, Elisha, Jesus, Peter, Paul, and many another. Haven't you been raised from the dead many times, from despair and disaster and disbelief and discontent and the dark depths of doubt again and yet again?

We must not judge by appearances. They are usually false. There is 1, ONE, just 1 force in all this world; not two. When we see good *and* evil, we have a duality of power, and that is fatal. That is why those who eat of the Tree of the Knowledge of good and evil "shall surely die;" for they have forfeited their eternal life and given power to false gods. When we reverse this belief in evil as another power, it is as if we spelt EVIL backwards, and lo, we LIVE again. For to destroy belief in evil is to have everlasting life. When ignorance, error, or mistaken judgment creeps in, we must simply correct the mistake and go on as if it had not been. When you strike a wrong musical note, you correct it and proceed.

No one can rob you of your peace of mind, for your mind is a piece of the One Mind. Therefore when you cling fast to it, you will not make mistakes. But until you have learned how, it is not going to condemn nor punish you because you cannot yet achieve the perfect harmony. Try, try again, until you do. The powers that be are ordained of God, and so they are always good, part of the one Power that is Good. That is our perfect security. One Cause, One Creator, one series of Effects, all manifesting this One Omnipresence, Omnipotence, Omniscience.

If the Unassailable Power can hold the stars in heaven, as it does, can it not also hold you in all your activity serene and unafraid, 0 ye of little faith? Let it regulate all you do as it regulates all things great and small, whether "in the heavens above or in the earth beneath, or in the waters under the earth." In the most tremendous blazing sun or in the tiniest cell, the same unassailable Power is at work. Let it have its way with you, and work through you, as you. "When I think of the heavens, the moon and the stars which thou hast ordained . . . why should I fear what men may do unto me?" Why indeed? Whether we look through microscope or telescope, we shall marvel at the perfect order and harmony and incredible beauty of design that pervades every part of the Whole. From infinitesimal electron to vast starry galaxy there is glory and power and wonder unspeakable, indescribable.

And all this energy of the universe is yours to use. You can draw upon it whenever you want, as much as you need. Do you realize what that means? Think what it implies before you claim it as yours, as you may. Never blaspheme this heavenly Power by affirming evil of it. Never say I am ill, I am poor, I am unhappy, I am in pain; for that can never be true of holy you. Say, rather, I am God's beloved child, I am infinitely rich, I am well with the Wholeness of health, I am happy because I cannot but praise Good, I am at peace because God made me so, in His own image and likeness, I am one with the infinite energy of the Creator's Universe.

All the energy of all the coal mines, the water-power of all the streams, rivers, waterfalls, tides, the power of oil wells, gas deposits, the muscles of animals, the machines of men, the force of gravitation, the expansion of growing roots and fibers (a tiny tree root can split a whole cliff of granite by just growing!), the sum of all electricity, cosmic rays, winds, atoms, suns, fires, heat, cold, the pull of the planets, centrifugal and centripetal force, the reserves of power locked in every electron,—all this is but a drop in the infinite ocean of universal activity. And any part of this illimitable activity is yours to use at any moment, according to your developed capacity to use it. Divine Mind is the source of all this activity, and this mind is ever active. God rests in action. We rest in God. And His action is always harmonious and effective.

All this power is yours, said Jesus. It moves mountains, heals disease, raises the dead, produces plenty. It is unlikely that you will ever need more than a tiny fraction of this unlimited, undiminishing power. Yet all you need is yours now, freely. No taxes to pay on it, no meters, no sales slips, no checks to draw, no books to keep, no leases to sign: freely ye have received of it. Freely you may use it. Know that you already possess it. No one can claim your share. No one can take another's share from him. There is enough for all. You are the beloved child of this Power Almighty. You are one with it. You are part of it, and it is part of you. You are therefore not only powerful, but you are the Power itself made manifest as You.

You are a vehicle of its expression, and as such let it have its way with you, to express the wholeness of its quality in your oneness with it. It is made radiant through you. It is God made visible as you, in your own activity. Omnipotence is using you as its means of expression always. Let it. Give it a chance to function. Let it possess your consciousness. Let it work freely through you without hindrance or frictions. Let it be you as Itself individualized. For that is what you are: omnipotence particularized as you. God the Father, You the Son, your activity part of His total activity. How can you go wrong, be ill, or feel impoverished or unhappy when you know this? You have the power at all times and in all places to do anything that it is right for you to do. Claim your omnipotence now. Use it, for it is yours, from the Most High One.

But if an athlete does not use his muscles, he ceases to be strong. If a singer does not train his voice and keep in practice, he will not be a good singer. If a thinker of beautiful thoughts does not continue so to think, he finally loses the ability to think beautifully or perhaps to think for himself at all. If an executive does not assume responsibilities and control his business, *he* will not long have one nor be an executive. We grow by doing. We succeed by success. We love by loving.

Prayer implies no cessation of activity; it should be thus increased. The best part of Truth is understanding it and practicing it. There is no end to the activity of the Universal Mind; it is constantly arranging new powers and new patterns. There is no limit to the colossal forms it may build in beauty and order, no limitation to the scope of its infinite design, perhaps with stars for electrons and galaxies for organs, in the body of some cosmic being functioning beyond our human grasp.

The power of right ideas is always creative; it is the greatest power in the world, and it can become so for you. Every great and good thing was first an idea. The Infinite Mind conceives these perfect ideas, and man assists in their manifestation. This Mind power is the only real power there is, and it must function creatively. What are you thinking? So you will become. No rigor of land or climate or temperature can hold you back, once you have made up your mind to win. These things were no bar to those who desired greatly. America was first a dream. Columbus started its realization. The liberty-loving Pilgrims peopled it. Washington and Jefferson established it. Lincoln preserved its unity.

But the end is not yet. A new birth of freedom is demanded, and must come. As men are equal before God, and by the laws of men, so must they become in fact. Democracy and Christianity have this in common: They seek to make it evident that all men are equally important, each in his own way according to his diversity of gifts, to the same Creator of all. Without You, the infinite Design is incomplete and would be forever unfulfilled. God needs you as you need Him. But your country needs you, too, for its fulfillment politically, as much as Christianity needs you to battle for the Lord religiously. Democracy is the political front of Christianity, as Christianity is the background of true democracy.

And as the Puritans began to grow beyond the boundaries of their New England, seeking ever westward new frontiers and expanding horizons, so we should never be satisfied with present attainments. We are constantly to enlarge our powers, to make ourselves more and more receptive, day by day. Westward, ever westward, the course of empire made its way, towards the setting sun. The covered wagons of the pioneers never turned back, always moved forward. The American Expeditionary Force had been trained likewise always to advance, never to retreat; and so they also won. Wagon wheels making the trail, wagon wheels turning towards vaster horizons of plains and mountains and at last the sea. The Mormons in their two-thousand mile trek, many on foot, pushing their belongings on wheelbarrows, through storm and desert and cold, among Indians, over swamps and across great rivers, in spite of epidemics and doubt and despair. But they won their way and helped to build a great new world. Like the Pilgrim fathers, they could also thank God for victory, even when their first terrible winter had decimated their number by half.

Heed your own vision, make it come true. Be a divine instrument, an open channel of power, a flame, a pipe, a conduit, a wire through which energy is conducted to make your dream come true. Remember Thomas Edison, Henry Ford, Amelia Earhart. Edison believed he could bring light to a darkened world, but it cost him ten thousand experiments before he found the incandescent filament that would stand the test. Ford worked for ten years, amid the ridicule of his neighbors, before he constructed his horseless carriage and helped a world to ride. Amelia Earhart, alone but intrepid, did what no man had yet done, and at length met death still brave and unafraid over the uncharted seas, as she had hoped to do.

What these have done, we can do also, if we desire as greatly. Find your particular aptitude. Practice makes perfect; so try, try again. God will help you if you first help yourself. God is the only Cause and Creator. You are His beloved child. As His child, His creative powers find individualized and unique expression through you. As a child of the living God, you are a divine channel for the manifestation of all God's creative powers. But you must choose what you will do and be. For this cause came you into the world. It is your job to claim your own particular omnipotence, to do what you've set your heart on doing. No one can stop you, and God will bless you once you let Him guide and direct you. Give Him a chance. Rejoice, and be exceeding glad, for yours also is the kingdom and the power and the glory, now and always.

THE AWAKENING POWER OF CHRIST
BY MARY L. S. BUTTERWORTH

Rev. Mary L. S. Butterworth, Leader of the Chapel of Truth, 117 South Broad Street, Philadelphia, Pa., has been an active New Thought lecturer, metaphysician, radio speaker, teacher and writer for twenty-eight years. Has lectured and taught in most large cities of the United States and England. She is editor of "Truth Messenger," a monthly magazine now in its eighteenth year. Among her booklets are: *What Is Truth? Jesus Christ Is Passing By, Christ In Me, Truth Marches On, Thoughts That Heal, Demonstrating Supply, Where Dwellest Thou, Spiritual Interpretation of the Twenty-Third Psalm, Shifting into High.*

"ONE man was true to what is in you and me." Thus Emerson wrote about Jesus. The inspired message of Truth in the Twentieth Century which is called "New Thought" we believe to be the foundation upon which the true New World Order is being built. The foundation upon which this new edifice should be constructed is the teaching of him who spoke as never human being spoke before.

Jesus gained his victory over the flesh 'by applying one eternal God Power or universal spiritual Principle to the adjustment of human needs. Jesus called this Eternal Being, Principle or Power, "Our Father." Is it not reasonable to believe that, at least in some degree, we can do likewise. This most happy admission in our consciousness is the basis upon which we build the order of the new and higher thought, and let us not forget that this so called New Thought is merely reapproaching the teachings of Jesus as though we actually believed them and as though we really believed that the Power which he used is delivered into our keeping for our conscious use.

This New World Order governed by spiritual Truth is now in the making. Paul clearly stated: "I commend you to God (Spirit) and to the word of His grace, which is able to build you up." (Acts 20:32) We all know the world has been exposed to Christianity for 2000 years; but how much of the true spirit of Jesus Christ has acted through it as a divine contagion drawing fire from heaven within and reflecting the power of Spirit into life?

A consciousness of God was enthroned in the mind of Jesus as a great and ever present Reality. Peter announced that God is no respecter of persons and Jesus himself said, in substance, "Greater works than I have done will ye do." Certainly then, we have a right to believe in the divinity that is within. And surely we should expect to be able to use it even as he, the divine exemplar did, which was the purpose of his mission.

We cannot believe that there is any barrier between man and his spiritual perfection other than a false belief which inhibits the action of man's divinity through his humanity. How are we going to arrive at a realization of the presence of God other than by a constant shift of consciousness from the mortal to an immortal perception; from a finite and human sense to a more nearly Infinite Divine sense?

It is written that even Jesus continuously expanded his consciousness, grew in grace, and more and more manifested the glory of God. The harder the mortal struck at him the more completely he drew upon Reality, perfecting his consciousness more and more as the God Principle and the God Power flowed through him. Thus did he make a more complete and effective use of the Law of Mind. "God's Power is ever present," and "Christ is All in All." Isaiah said—there is a "Rock out of which all are hewn." In other words, back of, around, and within each one exists the God Power with all of its fullness, inexhaustible and ever present. Each has an equal opportunity to apply this Power. While in the flesh the Master proved this to a materially minded world; thus he attained the full stature of Christ, the Divine Principle of all being, which he called the "I Am" or "The Way, the Truth and the Life."

We should become aware of the Omnipresence, the Rock, the Christ Principle upon which Jesus built the universal but invisible Church of God. This is the New Thought Church, the constant awareness of Divine Reality giving fresh inspiration, calming our fear, inspiring new courage and guiding us to that Truth which makes prayer or metaphysical treatment effective. Returning in Spirit to the Almighty we are rebuilt in the manner we desire.

The Great Teacher emphasized the need of knowing the Truth in order to become free. What was it that Jesus inferred we should be freed from, or know the truth about, other than the belief that there are two creative principles, two ultimate powers and two natures of man. If we are to "stand fast therefore in the liberty wherewith Christ hath made us free" (Gal. 5:1); if we are to become conscious of the heavenly kingdom which is at hand, we must know that there is but One Perfect Power, One Divine Presence and One Eternal Law of wholeness. We must be willing to become God governed, for anything else than this would be license.

In New Thought we strive not only to honor the most excellent Teacher, but we seek to imbibe the spirit of that Mind which was also in Him. Our goal is to become God conscious even as he was God conscious. If Jesus, the great way-shower, constantly labored toward his victorious Christhood, should we not do likewise?

We need not beg God to send us blessings, since He has already endowed us with His own Spirit, this Spirit of Christ or God Idea ever present with us and ever available in meeting human needs. If we would walk the perfect way and not perish in our mistakes; if we would be blessed with Spiritual Power; then we must live in accord with the God Principle, with our true sonship; for we are forever linked with the perfect law of Cause and Effect, and as a man sows so must he reap.

We must practice expanding our consciousness that it may take in more and more of God, and join in the triumphant song of Jesus, believing that "all that the Father hath is mine." In this practice we shall find periods of ebb and flow in the tides of our life and its daily affairs, but let us perceive that the Divine dominates.

Jesus on the cross, symbolizing the unity of God with man, lifts us to our own divinity, for this was the symbolic meaning of the Crucifixion. Through his vision on the Cross which rent the veil of the temple, Jesus beheld the victory and the power, and the majesty and the might of his own Divine origin. Thus he said that if he were lifted up from the earth he would draw all men unto him, not meaning his personality but to the Reality of all.

The emphasis of New Thought is placed upon this uplifting, this transcendent and dominating spiritual principle, which we call the Law of Mind in action. This is the great offering which New Thought makes to a waiting world. Jesus advanced a workable science for daily living and taught men the definite use of a spiritual Law or Principle in nature, which is available to every one. It is upon the realization of this Divine Presence as an inspiring guide, and a recognition of a universal Law of Mind as a usable principle, that the New Thought bases its faith and its action for the abundant measure of life now.

New Thought believes in the healing of mind, body and affairs; that God is Life and ever present with us. It accepts the riches of His creation and beholds God's masterpiece on this planet as Man. We believe that God is Love as well as Righteousness and that He has nothing but good to give us. Placing our entire confidence in Divine Goodness, we feel that there is nothing in the universe to be afraid of.

New Thought gives a transcendent meaning to life, for if we are sustained by the Divine Presence, upheld by the Infinite Love and guided by the Eternal Mind, then we should no longer claim that we are poor, weak, sick or unhappy, but rather that we are healthful, happy, harmonious sons of God. Let the one, then, who believes in various forms of human negation make this divine claim upon the "All Sustaining Beauty" and the Perfect Law. Let him honor the Truth and not the lie, and let him continue until his legitimate desire is made manifest.

Nothing is too good for the Son of God, and it is written that "Beloved, now are we the sons of God." Let us see each other in the light of this divine sonship and transcending our former beliefs, pass from the agony of the cross to the glory of the crown. We have before us the magnificent example of Jesus, who, annihilating the negation, crossing out as it were, that which denied his sonship, ascended into the richness of Divine Bliss.

For the purpose of practical application, we must realize that a change of thought or consciousness alters conditions. The key to abundant life is through a true state of consciousness. For instance: when students come to me for help I try to explain to them that they are spiritual beings, and endeavor to get them to cooperate with me through a method similar to the following:

First, I ask the student to lift his thought toward the Infinite Good, thus helping him to take his mind from his problem. This proves to be very helpful. Next, I ask him to become conscious of peace, of freedom, of Divine Order, and Harmony. As he continues in this uplifted consciousness, I state, sometimes audibly and sometimes to myself, "There is but One Presence, Power and Perfect Life. This person is included in this Divine Wholeness. Anything and everything which does not belong to his complete and divine Perfection has no existence in God's Will or in God's Creation, hence no real existence in this man's experience or in his physical being. Love and Life and Wholeness and Perfect Freedom are his now." In this silent contemplation of the Divine Perfection within the patient, and the God Presence in, around and through him, I seek to realize his complete freedom from every negative condition.

Frequently following such a treatment, I seek to build up a realization of spiritual truth in the patient by discussing certain fundamental propositions with him. For instance, I ask him if he believes that there is more than one creator. Generally he answers no, upon which I ask him if he thinks that this One Creator *could* be imperfect. Almost invariably he says no. Next I ask him if a perfect Creator could project an imperfect creation, and more often than not he replies by saying he does not believe that a perfect Creator could project an imperfect creation. The next question is very vital: "Are you one of His perfect creations?" Usually he hesitates, but generally answers yes. Now comes the crux of the whole matter. "If you are one of his Perfect creations, or manifestations, and if God is all there is, and if there is but One Life, is that Life in you?" Naturally he answers that it must be.

What I am trying to convey to him is the recognition that the Spiritual Principle is perfect and that any and all imperfect appearances and experiences are but the result of a wrong belief in and application of the Law of Life. I point out to him that the mind is the silent builder of the body, the silent creator and projector of circumstances, and that when the mind is dominated by the harmonious spirit of the Christ Principle it creates only that which belongs to the Kingdom of Good. I ask him how he is going to get anything imperfect out of a Perfect Principle, a Perfect God and a Perfect Law, and I explain to him that all negation is a denial of the great affirmation of Life, "I am that I am beside which there is no other." It is here that the awakening generally comes.

With Jesus, the great Teacher, we must admonish our students to judge not according to appearances but to judge from the standpoint of a conscious union with the Law of Love and the Presence of Perfect Life.

It has been my privilege to work with thousands of cases over a period of more than a quarter of a century. I have used many methods to produce the spiritual awakening, and *I find that each one is effective in such a degree as it awakens a corresponding reflection of freedom within the mind of the student.*

One outstanding case which I think should give encouragement to many, is that of a man who was impelled to walk with crutches. He naturally had a great longing for freedom. Looking at him with a deep intensity of purpose, I asked him if he believed that this crippled body represented his true being. For some moments he did not answer but looked at me seriously, thinking. I questioned him further, "What has become of your spiritual Self?" Finally a light seemed to dawn upon his countenance as though something within were gradually awakening to a tremendous truth. "No," he said, "this is not me; I am of the Spirit, I am what God intended me to be." Instantly to my mind flashed the old command of Jesus, "Arise and walk!" Falteringly he did this, leaning on the furniture. He exclaimed, "I — think — I — can — walk!" All glory to the power that was within him; to Christ resurrected within his own consciousness, *he did walk!* When his wife returned to my study, he arose and greeted her.

It is indeed wonderful, this miracle-working Power which the Almighty has implanted in man, and what blessing can come to us greater than that of making use of It for our fellowmen.

I told this man that Spirit was the real crutch, and that he must exercise with the consciousness that the Spirit within him rises above pain, confusion and the limitation of physical bondage. This indeed is resurrection from sense to Soul.

In Luke 17:36 it says: "Two men shall be in the field; and one shall be taken and the other left." Suppose we interpret this to mean that the two men signify a belief in two natures, a belief that man is both human and divine. "One shall be taken and the other left." The truth about the real man cancels or robs us of the belief about the unreal man. The true Self remains intact. The true Self could always walk.

Metaphysically, or from the standpoint of New Thought, we must climb by the ladder of the Spirit to a new mental viewpoint. This flight of the mind to the divine Reality may be likened to the flight of a bird to a higher vantage point where the mountains and the valleys are united in one landscape. So our vision must rise Spiritward until the valley of our desolation is exalted to the mountain top of our understanding or faith where God walks with us. We are all climbers on the pathway of life, and though the trail is often winding, God has given us complete dominion for he has bequeathed to us the supreme gift, which is Himself. Christ, the Divine Sonship, is our true divinity, and it is only when the Divinity is seen permeating our humanity that we are conscious of Wholeness. This is true spiritual power endowing the mind with a transcendent creativeness. This is the Rock of our salvation, out of which our fuller, richer life is hewn day by day.

It is the business of the spiritual practitioner to so recognize the Christ Presence and Consciousness, that he is enabled to awaken a corresponding recognition within his patient. Jesus must have looked beyond the veil of fleshy form, away from the idea of bondage, and we, too, must cast our net (spiritual thinking) on the right, or true side, if we wish a full demonstration of the power of the Christ Consciousness. This we shall never do while we are caught in the belief in things as they *appear* to be.

The Real Man is identified with the Only God. When Jesus said, "I am the way, the truth and the life," he was referring to this divine and ineffable union of the soul with its center and source, which is the Living Spirit Almighty.

Those interested in New Thought know that the Power which heals is the same Power which Jesus used. In the New Thought Movement we recognize that physical healing, or what we call the demonstration of spiritual thought in human affairs, is a result (an effect) which follows the consecration of thought as it arises from the contemplation of fear, uncertainty, pain, limitation and want, to an inward perception of the Divine Creative Principle operating upon the word of the indwelling Christ, triumphant over the Cross and now resurrected into conscious union with God. Jesus on the Cross lifts all humanity to its Divinity. What else was it for?

MASTERY OF LIFE THROUGH DIVINE POWER
BY MYRTLE E. CATE

Mrs. Myrtle E. Cate, Director of the Center of Religious Education, Phoenix, Arizona. The Center is non-sectarian, non-denominational and devoted wholly to teaching and applying spiritual law as revealed and exemplified by Jesus Christ. Practically all of Mrs. Cate's adult life has been given to teaching, lecturing and healing. She calls this work Scientific Christianity.

TRUE spiritual education must be based upon a balanced perspective of spiritual knowledge gained through the teachings of Jesus Christ, together with other great spiritual leaders of the ages, which knowledge was so beautifully dramatized by Jesus in his unique healing ministry.

The message of spiritual Truth should be happy, enthusiastic and vital. Its scientific application should be taught in understandable terms. These teachings are based upon the understanding of spiritual laws and their application to our daily lives.

Scientific religion and the Science of Being, as we understand it today, is an accumulation of knowledge gained through experience, intuition, study and application. Because good does not come to every one in the same form, we endeavor to give the student such a clear background and establish him in such a firm foundation of spiritual Truth that he may recognize Reality regardless of what name or label any particular teaching may bear.

Naturally in all great systems of thought, God is the starting point: a God both true and changeless, universal as light, available as air, impersonal as law. The nature of this God is Love. The character of this God is omniactive, positive and constructive. The power of this God is law in operation. The Eternal Being is Infinite Spirit everywhere present, Whose life is forever birthless, deathless, indestructible and perfect; Whose substance composes everything seen and unseen, formed and unformed.

Those wishing to gain a clearer insight into the nature of God, must free themselves from the prejudices of the race mind which have been held for centuries. Who would fathom the mystery of Christ must become single minded before the throne of that Inner Light which illumined the thought of Jesus. The true interpretation of God is in the heart, not in some theological dogma.

Man being the offspring of the Divine Parenthood, because of his birthright is permitted to govern himself. He is free to work out his unfoldment by any method which best serves him on the road to the discovery that Divine Law and Power belong to him and are "closer than breathing, nearer than hands and feet." Man is destined to unfold a cosmic order that has been infolded in his being; to express the kingdom of God which rises from within him and which is at the center of all nature.

Spiritual science teaches that mankind, regardless of race or color or creed, is an expression of God and that each individual is a rightful heir to health, peace and abundance. We believe that these desirable conditions are attained and maintained in every day life by proclaiming the teaching of Jesus Christ, who, because of the vision within him, automatically became the Way-Shower. Jesus struck the cord of unity and universal brotherhood, free from prejudice, crystallized creeds or dogmatic doctrines. We do not need to go through all of the experience which he went through; it is not necessary that we become betrayed or crucified, but it is necessary that we embody the Christ Spirit proclaimed by these words, "By this shall all men know that ye are my disciples, that ye have love one to another."

We believe that every individual is a child or manifestation of God; that the One Universal Spirit and Life Principle is in all men, irrespective of racial heritage or sectarian attachment. We also believe that perfection is at the basis of everything that is real. Back of every form or manifestation is a perfect pattern or ideal. The Creative Process of the universe is available to and operative through the individual, because each individual is forever in union with the universal and cosmic scheme of things.

Man is today what he is and where he is, as a natural result of his thoughts, desires, aims and acts. He is not where he is because of a punishment or reward of an unyielding, unjust or afflicting God. There is an impartial Law which automatically produces outward conditions which correspond to the inner imagings of the heart, for the Law of God operates on those thoughts of man which are the ideals, goals and patterns most dominant in his heart and feelings.

We affirm that the truth of man's inseparable unity with this Life Principle and the immediate operation of the Divine Law on his thought and action, is a glorious revelation of the thought that "Before they call, I will answer, and while they are yet speaking, I will hear." Spiritual Truth can be demonstrated with mathematical certainty. Thus spiritual Realities may become scientific facts in the life of the one who recognizes and accepts them, and who is willing to allow himself to be transformed by the spiritual facts he recognizes and accepts. Consciously he must realize his innate God-likeness, his oneness with the Divine Father, and, as repeatedly announced and demonstrated by Jesus, he must recognize his own inner Christ Self.

The Spirit of Freedom is always striving for expression through the individual. As the earnest seeker becomes possessed of a higher consciousness, he gains freedom from the law of chance, discord, want and kindred negations in a degree which, to the average person, seems quite impossible.

When we get to the core of every problem we find that its solution lies in the spiritual understanding of God's Law and our cooperation with It. Results from spiritual help are obtained by allowing the action of God's

Mind to become operative in us as our individual mind. True Spiritual Science is not merely the acceptance of a creed, but deals with the purposes of life—with Life Itself liberated and freed into constructive self-expression. This Jesus declared in these words, "I am come that they might have life, and that they might have it more abundantly." (John 10 : 10).

The gift which God has made we must accept and use. One of America's greatest engineers recently said, "It is man's turn now. The Future belongs to himself from now on." We feel that there is a new consciousness in the world today, aflame with the Universal Fatherhood of God and Brotherhood of man. All men, black, red, brown, yellow, and white, must feel this unifying Presence, this Holy Spirit. They must awake to know directly, and immediately, how to contact God's Infinite Love, Wisdom and Power.

Many beliefs must become changed—beliefs that have been the cause of trouble; fear of disease; sense of loss in failure, all must be transferred to faith in God; faith in our oneness with good; faith in the ever available law which helps, maintains, heals, and sustains the children of the universe.

The power of spiritual treatment is in the recognition of the Spiritual Reality underlying all objective facts. The treatment proclaims something that is revealed as a present spiritual Reality. We do not try merely to make something become true, merely to manipulate some external condition or situation, rather we endeavor to open the doorway of recognition and acceptance. The treatment is a proclamation of a spiritual fact believed in as an ever present reality. Prayer without ceasing is the habitual activity of Truth in the mind of the individual; it is seeing perfection back of any appearance that denies God's Allness.

It is natural for God, or Perfection, instantly to come into manifestation. The element of time which enters into our healing work is a result of not instantly giving complete consent to the Divine Response, for God can respond to us only in such degree as we accept this response into our consciousness.

TREATMENT

Become still within. Let go of all hurry. Withdraw your attention from all outer things and from every disturbing thought. Open yourself in child-like trust and place yourself and your affairs completely in the hands of your all-loving and present Heavenly Father. Let go of every bit of uncertainty and doubt. KNOW you are encircled in Divine Love and Wisdom this moment—just where you are. There is nothing in the future for you to fear if you will realize God's grace and power are sufficient for your every need.

Prayerfully affirm in your heart that man is a divine idea sent forth in spiritual freedom, majesty and glory, into a world of law and order where Cosmic Spirit is ever responsive.

Recognize and accept that the presence of the thing you desire in your unlimited divine inheritance is already provided.

Know that the truth about this condition or circumstance comes to you direct from Infinite Intelligence and proclaim its perfection and presence in whole-hearted conviction and clarity. "Before they call, I will answer." "Father, I thank Thee." Treatment should begin and end with thanksgiving to God.

WHAT IS IT THAT WE HAVE?
BY RUTH E. CHEW

Ruth E. Chew, leader Unity Metaphysical Center, Helena, Montana, since 1930. Education: graduate Adelphi Academy, Brooklyn, N.Y. Alumna, B.L. Degree, Smith College, Northampton, Mass. Business experience: Teacher, Editor, Woman's Department on Daily News, Bridgeton, New Jersey. Department Editor, Butterick Publishing Company, Service Writer, Geo. Batten (Advertising) Company, New York. Author: Magazine and Newspaper Articles, Children's Stories and Plays. Publisher: *Dynamic Affirmations for Every Month, Joy Drill*. Truth student since 1909. Associate teacher, Rawson Center, San Diego, California, National Lecturer, I. N. T. A. District President for Montana. Member Official board I. N. T. A. Member, Helena Ministerial Alliance.

WHAT we have, we, the various clans of metaphysical workers who come together under the name, International New Thought Alliance, want all the world to have. What we have the world needs, needs desperately. And more and more, it is realizing the fact.

Take as an individual instance the good soul who for nearly fifty years had always given her church first place in her life. She never hesitated to tell people she had no use for "these newfangled religions," yet when the doctors told her that the operation she was facing in a few hours might prove fatal, she sent for a Truth friend. "Tell me," she demanded, "what is it that you have that will let me go through with this unafraid, whatever happens? I know you have it." With the telling came not only peace but life.

When a long series of terrific earthquakes rocked this part of Montana, girls in a home for the wayward, confided in one of their matrons: "We girls pray that when a big earthquake comes, we will be either with you or Mrs. T. (naming the one other Truth believer in the institution). You have something which makes you smile instead of scream and we feel safe." A member of the same faculty gave further corroboration: "You know," she confessed, "I am a deep, dyed-in-the-wool orthodox, but I must admit you have something I haven't."

Again and again physicians say of cases, metaphysically treated, "What have you, anyway, a rabbit's foot? You are a record case!" Husbands start attending the Center saying shyly, "You see, the wife has something she never used to have before she came here. She surely went through this ordeal of ours in great shape. Everything's working out fine, too."

Yes, we assuredly have something—to begin with, the noblest conception of God that the mind of man has yet been able to conceive of. A strong man's religion it is, for we accept the Bible teachings that literally God is "ALL And IN ALL," and, "BESIDE HIM THERE IS NONE ELSE." Thus we are in sound accord with the greatest intellects of our times who with each new discovery are constantly reaffirming the same truth, namely, that all phenomena originate from one and the same substance, which is invisible, intelligent, alive at every point. The great English scientist, Sir James Jeans, says, "We may as well call it God." This gives us a religion which, as our Dr. Grier points out, "Satisfies the soul of the saint, while it does no violence to the mind of the scholar."

Thus accepting God as SUM-TOTALITY provides a firm foundation, broad enough to include all mankind. The mere fact that we exist at all, is proof that we needs must be "part and parcel of the One Great Scheme," that right now we are actually living, moving and having our very being in a sea of Infinite Life, Love, Wisdom, Power. Paul sensed the great corollary which follows: "Sons of God! If sons, then heirs! If heirs, then JOINT-

HEIRS WITH JESUS CHRIST!" The Master himself by stating in such a matter-of-fact way, "The works that I do shall ye do also, and greater works than these shall ye do," gave authority to our divinity.

What a tremendous truth this is! What marvelous deductions logically may be made from it! At all times, under all conditions, whether we know it or are conscious of it, we are, every last one of us, "Endued with power from on High." But to benefit by this spiritual heritage, we must awaken to a realization of our real nature and learn how to deport ourselves as Royal Sons and Daughters of the Most High.

To have life unfold perfectly, divinely, we need to recognize our divinity and think and feel and act accordingly. To the degree that we succeed in so doing, do we automatically escape the realm of trouble and enter into the Kingdom of Good and good alone.

This knowing and this doing, however, is no child's play. Like the progeny of human royalty, we, the children of the King of Kings and Lord of Lords, need careful, definite training and discipline to fit us for our purpose here.

A good starting point is to realize that the power of God exists primarily, not for worship or adoration, but for USE. "The work of my hands, command ye them, saith Jehovah." Harry Emerson Fosdick points this moral in his story of the missionary who took with him to Africa a sun-dial that the natives might be able to tell the time of day. What did these ignorant folk do with such a practical object? No, they did not reject it, ridicule it nor yet despise it but they did do exactly what Christianity, too largely, has done with Jesus and His teachings—accepted it as something sacred, miraculous, but too precious for daily usefulness. So over the sun-dial they built a structure to keep off the sun!

Too many beginners in metaphysics assume the attitude that what we have is mostly a little different approach to prayer, one a little more likely, perhaps, to catch the ear of the Almighty, instead of realizing that all prayer, meditation, treatment and affirmation is for one purpose alone, of helping us to lose our human sense of bondage by becoming more and more conscious of Reality.

The Kingdom is ready prepared, filled to overflowing with every good and perfect gift. Waiting for us, the Bible promises, are Health, Strength, Length of days, Glory, Honor, Riches, Heaven on earth, Life Eternal. Not a single thing that the heart of man can crave is missing. We can have "All things whatsoever." To cap the climax we are told that even so, "Eye hath not seen nor ear heard, neither hath it entered into the heart of man to conceive" of the blessings beyond these.

What must we do to take possession?

From the nature of our high estate, we are strongly individualized, no two alike nor at the same point of unfoldment, so we of the I.N.T.A. do not try to insist at all on conformity of methods but only on the purity of the teachings concerning the laws of the Kingdom, then using them to the hilt.

One of these fundamental laws is, and I quote: "Not only is there an Intelligence which responds to us, but by reason of our own nature, *it can respond only by corresponding*" to that which we hold in consciousness.

Whether we receive or not, becomes then, not at all, a matter of God's willingness to bestow upon us the desired good. This at once does away forever with the old uncertainty, so destructive of faith, as to God's will in the matter. Our God is Love itself. We do Him the courtesy of taking it divinely for granted that His will is always, in all ways, good. We conform to His good and then naught but good manifests for us, through us, or as us.

This leaves the matter of receiving utterly and entirely up to us. It means that before we can receive our desire we must have a "change of heart." The original meaning of the word, Repent, we are told means just this.

Shaw illustrates this law in the beginning of his play, "Anthony and Cleopatra" where the young Egyptian queen, frantic with fear at the sudden approach of her country's enemy, the Roman General, Anthony, slips out on the desert to beseech help from her gods. There she stumbles upon Anthony himself. Not knowing him by sight, she confides in him her mortal dread and is advised at all costs, not to betray the slightest fear when she meets her adversary in royal conclave or all will be lost. Acting perfectly upon this counsel she saves her throne. Truly, "It is done unto us as we believe."

Cause and effect instead of reward and punishment, stand out strongly in our teachings because we find that such is universal law as well as Biblical statement. Until we ourselves change, our conditions remain in status quo. Far more difficult is this changing of our thoughts, this control of our emotions, than it is to go on believing that God will take over our affairs if we only beseech Him enough.

Our most arduous task, undoubtedly, is the dissolving of undesirable thought-patterns which we have unconsciously accepted from childhood as a part of our human heritage. The most profitable way of accomplishing this is daily meditation upon the truth that we are not merely humans with a divine spark within but that we are even now Spiritual Beings. It is our business to at least try our God-best to think and act as if we were! And how can we act divine and still carry around with us the poison of fears, worries, hates, prejudices, grief, discouragement or belief that accidents, illness, disgrace can get us or our dear ones? The answer is, "We can not." Let those who speak of metaphysical teachings as "easy religion" please take notice and try it.

But as Rawson has said, "Our progress heavenward is conditioned by the number of seconds a day we spend in reversing our negatives." Accepting life as a game, we enjoy this reversing business as a part of the fun of living. For instance, if self-pity attacks us, we replace it with joyous thoughts that after all, our right thinking can actually change the pathetic situation so there is really nothing to be sorry about. We make ourselves stop thinking hard-time, poverty thoughts by meditating on the Father's infinite abundance waiting our appropriation. When ignorantly, or weak of will, we have succumbed to fear and confusion until they have registered in the body (as flu) we deliberately fill our heart and mind with peace, faith, joy.

The greater the student's understanding of himself and his world as spiritual, rather than material, naturally the easier it is for him to make the desert bloom like the rose in his own individual affairs.

An all-important thing for him to discover early in his search for dominion is that words are alive with an invisible energy which has power to change conditions. To accomplish one must definitely and positively speak the word and so set this invisible energy in to motion. As Emilie Cady adds, "If we are quiescent, it, too, is quiescent," and no change occurs. A victory, impossible to human efforts alone, is often accomplished through this setting of Infinite Power into motion through our words, that is, by our thoughts, feelings, mental attitude, inner convictions. Languidly desiring is not enough. We must as Dr. Cady insists, "Maintain a definite, positive, will-not-be-put-off attitude."

"Whatsoever is not of faith is sin," says the Bible. "What then, do you make of faith?" you may ask. The Bible, we believe, is the outgrowth of religion rather than vice versa. Statements are not necessarily true because they are in the Bible, but because they are true, they are included in the inspired parts of the Scriptures. Now since modern scholarship realizes that the word, sin, means merely missing the mark, we can readily see how significant the above verse is. It states a reality: If we lack faith in what we do, we fail.

Practically every one needs to learn that faith does not descend like a dove from Heaven lighting only on a chosen few. Neither does it grow overnight anymore than does a rich, velvety lawn. Not a bit of it. But if you are willing to throw yourself enthusiastically, into cultivating faith, you can raise a bumper crop. Like a lawn, though, it takes active desire, knowledge, time, perseverance. Know, too, that the moment we look at appearances, that moment we have let go of whatever faith we had, that hoping to have our good at some future time, is only vain hope, not scientific faith. We must make ourselves think and feel, speak and act as if something delightful has already taken place and in a wonderful way.

This, I think, is what Jesus, the Master, meant when he said "When ye pray believe that ye have received and it shall be given you." Joyous persistency in holding a vision is true faith and brings results.

The pinnacle of all our principles in the International New Thought Alliance, however, is LOVE for we are discovering at last that all that the Bible says about love is true. It is, indeed, our very nature. Whatever, then, violates love, tears at our vitals. But, "Working with LOVE," all things are instantly possible, even to sustained world peace!

Rightly understood, religion is the most practical thing in the world. The International New Thought Alliance is consecrated to proving that following the teachings of Jesus, the Wayshower, leads from strife into Life, that it not only "Removes all tears," but also the cause of those tears. In this way we see a Great Light shining, when the Kingdom of Good will reign on earth, and men of good-will will live in heavenly peace.

THE OMNIPRESENCE OF GOOD
BY FLORRIE BEAL CLARK

Florrie Beal Clark, President of the Divine Science College of Oklahoma, Minister of First Divine Science Church of Oklahoma City, received her degree of D.S.B. and ordination in the Denver Divine Science College in May 1926. In the same year she began her work in Oklahoma. In 1934 she was delegated to represent the International New Thought Alliance in the British Alliance Congress which convened in London, England. In July, she taught classes in London and Glasgow, Scotland. Has filled summer engagements for the Divine Science Church, Washington, D.C., and the Church of Truth, New York City. She is also Field Secretary for the New Thought Alliance.

IT Is said to be sacrilegious to attempt any definition of the Unnamable One, but the Master, Jesus, told us that "to know God is Life Eternal." Hence, we do make the attempt to know God.

There are a number of synonyms used for the One-All. These four seem to express the meaning without limiting The Presence —Spirit—Reality— Principle—Truth. We are not arbitrary in the use of any of these terms, they are suggestions, and true to the Basis. Seven primary principles could come under these heads: Life, Substance, Intelligence, Love, Harmony, Power, Will. To realize all these in any degree is to bring into manifestation peace and joy, the fruits of the Spirit. That which is Unseen but is presupposed, bears witness in its objectivity as Life, love, protection, sustenance, happiness, peace. In these is sensed The Unmanifest One; to see the objective is to perceive Principle in Action.

The manifestation of The One is according to the scientific nature of all law, which is to step power down. With the Creator, the essence of which is never changed but tempered, it is Out into the visible—hence, in action we behold the One--Absolute---- Universal "That Which Is" taking form, becoming individualized, announcing Its manifest name to be forever "I Am that I Am." Accepting the One whose nature is Good, any description, amplification or analysis must hold true to this Premise of Oneness. This new age demands a new presentation of religious principles; it asks for clearer statements of ancient claims concerning God and man's relation to God. When man is taught that the Kingdom of God is within his soul and that this kingdom operates according to constructive laws for his own happiness, and that through the ages man has experimented and found that disobedience to these laws brings unhappy results, then he is ready to say "I see my God, I am willing to abide in the truth revealed by Principle."

There are many souls well advanced along certain lines of spiritual development who need to know the Principle for fuller expression of the Kingdom. The mind of man, ever expanding, demands larger concepts of life and asks "If God is *changeless*, why this change—If God is good, why confusion and despair?" The new religion must meet this demand, furnishing new approach, and greater proofs; in short, a practical and scientific presentation substantiated by personal experience in the believer's life. Fortunate is the religion of today that can present such premise and method, holding its high ideals and bringing these ideals into everyday experiences, helping man in his mind, soul, body and affairs—helping him attain a balanced and harmonious mode of life. This ideal and practical application of the Principle is given to the religious field by Divine Science.

Divine Science does not accept duality as real in the sense of two original powers. In manifestation, the positive and negative motion of the Principle constitute Its action, otherwise the visible would be static. These two activities are not antagonistic; they work together for the joy and pleasure of man's conscious accomplishment. Darkness is not opposed to light—it is simply its absence. If one desire light, the challenge is, learn the governing laws of light. Sickness is not opposed to health, it is the absence of consciousness of health and is a good friend, for without this warning man would remain in ignorance having no monitor telling him he has missed the way. When this purpose is fulfilled it is time to dissolve the wrong belief. Through all these opposites and seeming inconsistencies we realize there is a mental playground for man's growth and development. Despite all contrary appearance and experiences, Divine Science holds to the One Reality, the unchanging, undeviating principle of Good.

Proof of the Creator is in creation; man cannot deny his own existence. He may not correctly express perfection because of free will but the mere fact of his living, breathing self is evidence of an Unseen Actor. The object of our work is spiritual education, the steady unfoldment of every faculty of the true self, releasement of inner forces, the establishment of health through knowledge of governing laws, control of emotional nature, subduing selfishness and increasing mental power. We have a full program, through regenerated thought to attain the Christ consciousness, not by fantastic methods, but by natural unfoldment and application of Principle, moving onward to God's ideal for man—the realm of Power and Freedom.

The question is often asked "How do you deal with evil, if there is but One and that One is Good?" There is a rational answer for this seeming contradiction. Is the little green apple bad? No, it needs time for development. Is the energetic youth inherently bad? No, his energy needs direction.

The qualities used to deal intelligently with these problems are vision, wisdom, love, tolerance and patience. No problem is too complex to solve if all these factors are called into activity. If the individual has attained soul maturity he will use Truth methods; if not, the Impersonal Loving Law will provide the discipline. The only way to arrive beyond the realm of opposites is to transcend in mind into the higher plane, seeing The One before any manifestation. The Self-knowing Principle will, by its vital force, work out harmonizing results. This power is not to be induced by personal will, but by a faith that is alive. The comforting proof that God provides for His own manifestation is in the action of the great servant, the Law governing all outpicturing. There is no effect without cause—no cause without effect. This Law of justice gives encouragement and reward to motive and work. We do not deny planetary influence on nature and the natural man, but affirm when man knows the truth of himself, he can transcend the influence of the stars, for God has given him dominion. Also, we do not encourage psychic experiences, but when they come as a result of uplifted mind, heart and thought, they are apparently the reward of spiritual insight.

PHILOSOPHY

Divine Science participates in the philosophical realm of thought and reason as it recognizes Supreme Intelligence working out all things for good according to a plan of Wisdom in and for the universe and man; counseling the individual mind to hold its peace and poise during all process, advising one to look upon objective changes with impersonal and detached vision, doing his work, expanding his perception, holding to true values, keeping mental balance, living life with Divine indifference. As the artist needs perspective to find light, color and line all harmoniously in balance, so the philosophic observer must see the universe governed by law, and in its activity working out the great Artist's Plan. With unselfish motive in his heart, the observer sees all individual parts unified as instruments of a huge orchestra, giving expression to their own appointed part, thus harmonizing into a grand symphony—"All things working together for good."

PSYCHOLOGY

As speculation is the soul of philosophy, so analysis is the soul of Psychology. Divine Science deals in this phase of study with the One, All Inclusive Mind as Source, and with the individual mind that feels separateness as the actor. In Psychology is found the possibility of rightly placing every factor, rectifying all human inharmony, adjusting and readjusting until all entangled parts—whether this need for adjustment be in individual mind, in physical beliefs, or outer conditions—are harmonized into place or dissolved because out of place. "The Law of Love separates as well as unifies." The concerned mind may take one of two positions in solving its problems: Knowing God and the truth of God-Man and nothing beside; trusting and letting God Law make the adjustment without personal interference.

The second way is, the individual mind which is concerned in its disturbance and is not apt to see the Truth as a whole, separate the parts, and find the irritating factor. Testing the law of action and reaction by analysis and synthesis, all difficulties may be understood and solved. This is the hard way, but suited to some temperaments. This work takes love and understanding, but as God is All-Inclusive, it is a legitimate part of Mind Science. We believe that future psychology must be the Spiritual, that is based on the One Mind. As each individual has his problems which cannot be dealt with under general rules, this type of adjustment is the next step in the important work of restoring harmony in the individual mind as it harmonizes with the Universal Father Mind. The endeavor is vastly worth while to help the patient or client understand himself, that he may change his negative beliefs to positive by the process of thinking through, according to the Principle of Good.

RELIGION

The Religion of Divine Science is the Ideal and application of Divine Love, the love of the Creator for His creation, the act of poring Himself out, giving Himself—all that He is to His Sons— clothing them with His own substance, endowing them with His qualities of life, love, intelligence and power, inviting man to partake of and use, for "All things are for your sake." The practice of Divine Love and the giving of what "It Is" by man to man is termed religion, that which binds to our Father-God. The foundation for all true religion is the unity of the Creator and Creation, one in substance and action, the Beginning sanctifying the end of the Creative process. All is holy, "One Lord, one faith, one baptism;" man's part is in reenacting the pattern of Divine Love, giving of God's gifts to others, practicing the Law of Love. This is the soul's greatest test, involving deep purpose, consecration and unselfishness.

The Master did not at all times use the nonresistant attitude, as he cleared the temple of the money changers, using physical force, the only method they could understand, but he used it for constructive purpose, its inception being Love. The motive is always the index of love or hate. He also opposed by strong word the religious system that countenanced the "holier than thou" attitude, for this system was contrary to his teaching of the impersonal and loving Father and the belief that heaven may be attained by works, thus making God's free gift (grace) of none effect. Each soul has been given the power of decision "Yea, yea —Nay, nay." If this power is not used, man finds himself supporting destructive actions and systems, which involve him in sad experiences, but, used for constructive purposes, this decision endows man with dynamic power. The indecisive mind, so definitely associated with religion, is of no value to humanity. The true Christian Mystic is militant, decidedly on the side of the positive and true, thus he is held on the right track; he develops soul qualities, keeps the channel open to Divine Love flowing freely between his soul and the Oversoul. Through devotion to the One and practice of Divine Love, in all realms of thought, the At-one-ment is consummated between man and his God, man and his fellow man. "All is love, yet all is law."

PRAYER

In prayer for illumination, healing and adjustment, there can be but one perfect method, recognition, affirmation to the mental point of conviction by the use of the one ingredient necessary— Faith. Different techniques are allowable if the patient needs to support his faith by outer help. Intelligence is given man to use, and unfoldment is a legitimate mental law. To illustrate, if a man suffers a broken leg and is urged to walk by will power, the result will not turn out for the best. The progressive method is wiser; to bless the bandage or the crutch, hold to the ideal, keeps consciousness of the healing Power flowing, and the work is beautifully completed.

If the patient is also the practitioner and chooses the Absolute method of his own free will, depending on his God, nothing wavering, bolding to the idea of instantaneous healing and adjustment, he will experience wonderful and lasting results. We do not resist any sensible, helpful means of attaining results, but much that is called healing is simply a higher method of curing. Healing, to be perfect and complete, must be a conscious process in each individual soul, and results will correspond to the particular thought of the thinker. Perfect healing comes from changed thought in the patient and practitioner's mind. Jesus raised the dead, but the true resurrection must finally be the resurging of conscious Divine Life in the individual soul. Jesus healed many, but he warned them. to cease the negative thought which caused the illness lest they fall again. All sickness is the effect of deficiency; all inharmony has its inception in mental deficiency such as lack, selfishness, sensuality, and can only be overcome by filling the dark mental spot with God Presence. In Divine Science, healing is never relegated to theory; it must represent the Living, Ever-Healing stream of life. Belief of mortality must be replaced by belief in immortality, body as well as soul. This is the Master's teaching and demonstration.

There is a catalytic power which moves upon the substance of chemistry until the whole is reunited with the One Source— Spirit. This is not a fantastic dream, it is the ideal based on Jesus' experiences and is a matter of vibratory action. Any less ideal, transfers our teaching to the realm of theory. We do not deny the body nor visible creation, but seek understanding from the basis of Reality and the adjustment by knowing whether facts are true by the measure of Reality or untrue by the measure of unlikeness to God. The True spiritual body is the third part of the Trinity. This body is never lost, never sick, for the living temple cannot be something God is not. Therefore, we do not ask nor plead for health; the Healing Prayer is a Prayer of praise, thanksgiving. Man changes his beliefs from sickness to a realization of wholeness. "Behold what God hath wrought," and leave with Him the process of working it out.

RESUME

We go forward, with the Divine Science premise of Omnipresence, into the unexplored, uncharted spiritual and mental realm in confidence, knowing that if our Basis is true, as all prophets, seers, philosophers have affirmed, personal application has demonstrated and physical scientists are now proving in the laboratory, it will meet the challenge of any and all new findings of saint or scientist.

In the Principle of Good, nothing can be lacking. Knowing and using its laws, it will meet the full demand of mind, soul and body in the growing needs of man as he searches into the heights and depths to attain knowledge of other planes of Life. All doctrine of Truth teaching has not been formulated, nor all descriptive terms been perfected, but the Principle of All-Sustaining Love and Mind will provide for every step. Divine Science does not fear new findings of relative truths. There may be much adjustment but no reversal of Fundamentals. Direct discernment of Truth through the intuitive faculty is taught; the mind must be regenerated from fear, greed, hate, and learn to practice the Omnipresence of God, realizing any lack or limitation can be faced and overcome by knowledge of God and the true self.

God is the beginning and the end. If the individual mind cannot attain the exalted vision and experience at once, then it is right to consciously affirm new ideas mechanically; yes, even laboriously; in order to raise the thought to God; speaking words of Truth, going forth into action with Faith, not giving way to discouragement, persistently obedient to these necessary requirements; to think and know "All is Good," giving no power to another presence, certain the next step, however it may look from appearance, is part of God's process for the disciple, giving thanks for the already accomplished Good. Principle cannot fail, each soul is destined from the beginning to be well, happy and free.

After the student is reasonably grounded in metaphysical knowledge and has experienced some proof of his Basis, he is encouraged to go on into the delight of the true Mystic, developing his intuitive faculties, appreciating and enjoying the inner, deeper and higher phases of Truth, for Divine Science is truly a Mystical teaching, the whole object being conscious at-one-ment with God. In mystical meditation, Unity is attained and the individual will is one with God-Will, beyond the realm. of philosophical reasoning and mental analysis, in direct knowing with God. Mysticism calls for the disciplined mind, leaving methods and technique, transcending all ways and means, entering into eternal life and joy here and now. Ascension is the Ideal. Mental Ascension is the first step.

WHAT IS ABSOLUTE SCIENCE?
BY CARRICK-COOK

Carrick-Cook. Leader, Absolute Science Center, San Francisco. Resident Teacher, Metaphysical Library, San Francisco. Member Executive Board, International New Thought Alliance. District President Northern California, I.N.T.A. Chairman 1940 I.N.T.A. Congress, Palace Hotel, San Francisco. Ministerial Degree from Divine Science; Honorary Degree from Weltmer School of Missouri; Ministerial Degree, Christian Philosophical Institute, California. Writings of Mrs. Cook: *"Individual Completeness," "Science of Prosperity," "The Impossible and the Unexpected," "Metaphysical Terms Clarified."*

PROBABLY no metaphysical teaching has been so little understood by the field at large as that which is called "The Absolute Teaching." This is not because it is complicated or mysterious, but rather because it has seldom been made clear enough for the layman to understand. It is, therefore, a privilege and a joy to have the opportunity of stating what we believe, why we believe it, and how we apply our understanding to human needs.

We distinguish between a concept and an idea. A concept is an interpretation, or a belief about an idea; but an idea is an eternal verity. We affirm that health, completeness, harmony, love and joy are eternal verities in the Mind that we call God. It makes no difference how many false beliefs may be entertained about them; they remain perfect. No one can receive permanent healing or perfect adjustment from mental work who does not base his method of approach upon eternal verities.

Largely speaking, there are two great branches of New Thought, or two major approaches to the same goal. One is called the Relative and the other the Absolute. The Relative teachers have explained their attitude toward the appearance of sin, sickness and death. The Absolute student does not deny these conditions as appearances, but he *does* deny that they are realities. Herbert Spencer said: "That which is real is permanent; that which is not permanent is not real." The whole attempt of spiritual treatment is to cause the consciousness to have a *feeling* of this reality. A positive conviction always demonstrates. It is, therefore, highly advisable that the worker accept from the outset that that which gives joy and happiness is the real and—all appearances to the contrary—good is eternal.

"But how shall I know good from evil?" asks the seeker. "How shall I know true thought from false?" We reply: "That which gives you true peace of mind and happiness is good." All things return to harmony, for harmony is the natural state of being; upon it rests the principle of mathematics, the principle of music, the principle of all intelligent understanding. It is cosmos, as opposed to the chaos of human opinions.

It is very necessary for us to distinguish what is commonly accepted as logic, from *true* logic. Frederick L. Rawson, founder of the absolute message in England and America, was an excellent student and teacher of true logic. He was correct when he said that there cannot be two infinite powers. We claim that God is infinite, that He is good. There cannot be a power of infinite good with an opposing evil power. Either God is infinite, or He is not. Either He is all-Good, or He is not. We cannot have two infinite forces opposing each other throughout infinite time. Pure logic proves this.

Now, we will assume as our hypothesis that there is one power, infinite good, everywhere present, which we call Mind, or God. Assuming that Mind, Infinite Good, is everywhere evenly present, we then ask: "What does a mind do?" The reply is, of course: "Mind thinks." What it thinks are *Ideas*. We claim that the infinite ideas of Infinite Mind are the realities of every person, place, or thing in the universe.

It is frequently misclaimed about the Absolute teaching that it denies objects, the body, et cetera. This is not true. *It denies false concepts about them.* It affirms the perfect idea that underlies their appearance. For example: We do not deny the body, but we do deny that sickness is a real, or true part of Universal Mind. We claim it is only a false belief about *reality*. Reality is perfect health. We deny that age is truth about man; man is the perfect expression or reflection (thinking) of the One Mind. Therefore, age is only a false belief about him, for man is coexistent with that Mind, being ageless, birthless, deathless, and eternal.

We deny lack as a false belief about the omnipresence of Mind, since Mind, or God, is everywhere evenly present, so are Its ideas. There is, therefore, really no lack, although we admit that the appearance of it can be very unpleasant indeed. This same analysis we apply to companionship, freedom, success, or any desirable asset.

The Christian trinity is called Father, Son, and Holy Ghost. The metaphysical trinity may be stated as Mind, Idea, and Manifestation. Mind is the Father, Idea the activity of Mind, and Manifestation the offspring, the form which the Idea takes. For example, Mind—or Intelligence—desires to express repose and It creates, through man, a chair. The chair, or manifestation, is a form which the understanding of repose takes. Mind produces a companion for man to express the faithfulness of love, and we have a dog, symbolizing fidelity. Mind, expressing the continual vivifying action of life, produces rain, which symbolizes the multifarious ideas of God replenishing the earth. "He causeth the rain to fall upon the just and the unjust." Here we have a perfect example of Mind's impersonal attitude toward man. Mind judges no one. It gives of Its all to each one. What each receives is a question of how much he as an individual can avail himself.

Even the organs of the body are wonderful forms of divine understanding. They are qualities and characteristics of the Perfect Mind. Looking upon body in this way, we soon learn how to give an effective spiritual treatment. Let us examine the nature of some of the symbolic organs of the human body. Obviously, the breath reveals life and so the lungs symbolize God as Life. Now, the lungs themselves are not Life. If they were, a Apse could breathe. The lungs bear evidence to the presence of Life, but we have to know that Life is Mind. The heart symbolizes love, which causes the blood (joy) to circulate throughout the body (consciousness). The stomach symbolizes intelligence in the act of assimilation, digestion. It is really intelligence which digests and distributes our food.

In a way, we are indebted to the most advanced modern psychology for bringing to public notice the fact that so many physical diseases have their root in the mental life. It is logical, therefore, to suppose that the primary adjustment must be mental. This, the metaphysician claims, and he does his work at that level. It will help the seeker after Truth to know that to dwell in thought upon God as Love and to think of all the ramifications of Love in the universe, will improve the action of the heart. Interestingly enough, one does not even have to think of the heart as such. *The symbol automatically responds to its reality.* The same applies to the lungs. To think of God as Life, with all its loving, vital, dynamic action, is to improve and heal the action of the lungs. To make statement after statement to oneself about the perfect, orderly working of intelligence will permit the organs of digestion to assume normal functions.

Here we shall take up the much discussed subject of the reality or unreality of matter. Again we must express a debt of gratitude to our modern workers, the natural scientists. Through their steadily unfolding views of the universe, they have been proclaiming the new viewpoint about substance, which was formerly considered solid and indestructible. We have reduced matter from molecule to electron; from electron to menthoid; from menthoid to energy; and the Absolute Scientist claims that energy is the activity of Divine Mind. Therefore, we declare that strictly speaking there is no such thing as matter. It is but a form of interpreting Spirit or Mind, the only substance. Some metaphysical teachers call matter a form of Spirit. This is not quite correct, we think, for the forms of Spirit are ideas. Matter is an interpretation in time and is finally transcended in thought, when we get the new vision. For example, matter is a limitation. It is three-dimensional in belief. If matter were a reality, I would have to travel over miles of land to heal someone at a distance. Because I know that it is only a belief, and Mind is all, then to think the truth is to instantly help the person and to obliterate the false claims of time, space, matter and dimension.

Such absurd views were once held about the absolute teaching that objectors would ask: "Do you mean to say that this table isn't here? Do you mean to say I have no body? Do you mean to say that this chair upon which I am sitting is not of solid wood?" Of course the table is there! Of course your body is real enough! Of course you are sitting upon a chair! There is nothing in the teaching of Absolute Science that denies the world of experience.

Let us take for a moment the illustration of a dream. When we dream our bodies lie inert, yet in the dream experiences we have bodies. These bodies sometimes fall, cut themselves, and bleed. What produces that action? In dreams we sit upon chairs that do not let us down, we put objects upon tables that hold these objects up. What is the substance of all these phenomena? The reply, of course, is "Mind."

I once wanted to make this test literally, in order that I could honestly say to my students that I knew it to be a fact. Of course, I knew it theoretically. Whenever we have an honest desire, we know that it will sooner or later fulfill itself. The result was that I had a dream one night and in my dream I laughed and said to myself: "Now I am going to make a test; I am going to prove to myself that the phenomena of this dream are just as real as the phenomena of my waking experience. Then I can go back and tell my students that it is so." I arose from the chair upon which I was sitting, tapped the wall of the room, found it solid against the rap of my knuckles, and laughed again to see the simplicity of our theory so perfectly proven. When I awoke, I was filled with delight, and never since has it been difficult for me to understand the teaching of the unreality of matter as a thing in itself; nor has it been difficult for me to impart it to others.

"But what is the good of knowing all this?" you ask. Let us take the example of a spiritual treatment given to heal a growth, a tumor perhaps, or a cancer. If you believe that matter is substance, then the so-called laws of matter will have to be invoked in some way for that growth to be healed or destroyed, but we know that the only substance there is, is Mind. There is no truth, substantiality, or reality in matter. If this knowledge is stated sufficiently and clearly enough, the condition will be healed. It is only a matter of time and persistence. Sometimes the treatment is so clear the healing is instantaneous. At other times, it requires considerable repetition of the treatment before the belief yields, but in any event the allness of Spirit is the basis of our treatment.

Now let us take the problem of lack. If Mind, or Spirit, is the only substance, then the apparent lack of money is a false interpretation of the omnipresence of that substance. Intelligence is everywhere evenly present. We are told in the Scripture: "The Father knows what things you have need of before you ask Him," and again we read—"Before they call I will answer," showing that Mind has already provided the answer before we misinterpreted it as lack. To return in thought, therefore, to Mind or Spirit and declare that fact until we are convinced of the completeness of the situation, is the proper way to treat. Since matter does not exist as such, there is no material law of time or space that can defeat us. These so-called laws of phenomena, of a dimensional world, or of personal opinion, are immediately set aside by the invocation of a higher law of Absolute Truth. One of the beauties of this kind of treatment is that it requires no picturing or outlining on the part of the student. "The Father giveth the answer."

Automatically, the form of understanding comes into manifestation. We do not always know just what form will be made manifest and indeed we do not need to know. It is sufficient for us to declare the eternal verity in each case and so Absolute Science might be called a science of quality rather than quantity. For example, if I am treating anyone against a common cold, I do not have to know anything about the respiratory system; all I need to be clear about is the *opposite* of cold, i.e., the warmth of Divine Love, the absolute peace and harmony of the One Mind, which is controlling or functioning at the instant. If I become sufficiently clear about this in my consciousness, the body of the patient will automatically respond. Students who have worked with the "form" will find this a much simpler and more effective method. In fact, we teach that all permanent success depends upon the ability of the worker to get away in thought from the appearance and from the personality of the one for whom he is working.

Now, all treatment begins and ends in the consciousness of the person who is giving the treatment. It is stated thus by the Master Teacher, Jesus Christ—"I, if I be lifted up, will draw all men unto me." In other words, if the individual clears his consciousness sufficiently, all manifestation will be drawn unto him or will take on the quality of his true thinking. Strictly speaking, our world is our consciousness and the people, conditions, and things that we see in it can only be interpreted through the light of our own thinking, be it good or bad. As soon as the student sufficiently understands Absolute Science, he stops blaming other people, conditions, and objects for his difficulties.

He realizes that since this is a mental world, to change his perspective is to change his world. Everything, to us, is exactly as we believe it to be. Everyone, to us, is exactly as we think he is; nothing can change this unless we first change our thought; this is called treatment.

As a matter of fact, there is only one Creator, Infinite Mind, which works through man, or perhaps we can say which works as man, for man is the thinking, living, and loving of God. The Master said: "I of myself can do nothing." It was His supreme realization of the One Creator that released power and success through Him. Every genius, I suppose, consciously or unconsciously has realized this. Surely the boy Mozart did not know what was playing through him. Surely the poetry of Keats sang itself through him from some unknown source.

There is an argument, not so popular as it used to be, to the effect that God made man capable of choosing either good or evil in order that he might be free. This is one of the places where pure logic must be induced into the teachings. If God were capable of making such a man, He himself would have to be conscious of good and evil and therefore would not be Perfect Mind. The prophet, Habakkuk, has said it best: "Thou art of too pure eyes to behold iniquity." Also, we understand very clearly, in the light of modern metaphysics, the story in Genesis of the Garden of Eden. For the tree, which bore the forbidden fruit, was called the "tree of the knowledge of good and evil." And ever since, the sons of Adam—who have been eating of that double knowledge—have been dying or have seen the death of all they loved. It is only when we eat of the fruit of that other tree, spoken of in the allegory as "the tree of life," that we can have life; i.e., that we can have the consciousness of the permanence of all that we love.

This brings us to a helpful habit of working with opposites. Sickness, for instance, is only a lie about a truth called health and if health didn't exist, we couldn't even appear to see sickness, just as in the case of counterfeit money. If wealth didn't exist, or completeness, we could not experience poverty or lack. If love didn't exist, we could never be lonely. If harmony were not an eternal verity, we could never have the appearance of warfare and discord.

Our method of treatment consists of three simple steps:

First—turn your thought to God and Heaven. We define heaven as a perfect state of consciousness, or the "world of reality," as Huxley called it. Or, this world seen perfectly.

Second—deny that in that perfect Mind the evil thing seen, felt, or heard of can exist.

Third—affirm its direct opposite as being true. For example, if we were going to reverse or treat against the belief of anger, we would do it somewhat after this fashion:

I. "God is Love and the world of reality is a universe of absolute harmony where all men are loving to one another."

2. "In love, there is no anger."

3. "All is infinite peace, rest, harmony, and divine understanding."

The words do not matter; what counts is getting away in thought as far as possible from the so-called material world and thinking as clearly as one can of the nature of God, His kingdom, and His image and likeness, i.e., spiritual man.

Our spiritual striving should be to arrive at a joyous realization of what is really true. The denial should be short, terse, forceful, just as we would immediately deny a lie that was told to us about some dear friend. We elaborate the affirmation and dwell upon it that we may familiarize ourselves with the qualities of God and His kingdom. We have found that audible treatment is a great help. Of course, one should practice until he is able to work either audibly or silently, as there are times when it is not advisable to give audible treatment, but the beginners always find that they are able to arrange their thoughts more systematically and to watch the errant wrong thoughts that sometimes creep in, when they are making their statements audibly. We base our instruction upon the Bible statement: "The fervent prayer of a righteous man availeth much." Note the word "fervent." Prayer must be dynamic to be effectual. A "righteous man" is, of course, a right-thinking man. "Availeth" means to acquire, or demonstrate, so we might say in the modern metaphysical language: "The dynamic treat-ment of a right-thinking man demonstrates much."

It has been impossible in so short a space to completely explain the Absolute Science teaching. We trust, however, that we have made clear the fundamentals upon which it is based; a foundation so universal that the student may belong to any church, or none, and still avail himself of its good.

ONTOLOGY
BY LILLIAN DEWATERS

Lillian DeWaters. Internationally known teacher, lecturer, author, and practitioner. Twenty or thirty years in the presentation of Truth through her various books. Among her best known writings are: *The Price Of Glory, The Seamless Robe, Science Of Ascension, The One, In His Name, The Christ Within, The Finished Kingdom, The "I Am that I Am," The Great Answer.* Her publishing house, the Hycliff Publishing Company, is located at Stamford, Conn.

SINCE girlhood I have consistently studied the Bible and practiced the teachings of Jesus Christ according to my light and understanding. As my vision and insight increased, my beliefs and methods of practice progressed until I now accept only Ontology as the real Christ principle and practice of Being.

Ontology does not incorporate any system of mental therapeutics but preserves one's health, happiness and prosperity by establishing him in the awareness and understanding of *himself* as the Way, the Truth and the Life, even as Christ exemplified . . . verily, one with the Father.

Although Metaphysics has blessed the entire world, extending its radiance from shore to shore, the full meaning of the Principle and practice of Jesus Christ must now come, whereby the mental effort to heal erring minds and conditions shall be transcended. One must come to know himself to be the same I Am as was Jesus, thus perfect from the beginning.

Ontology proclaims the one Mind, Consciousness, Being and Body to be universally present, here and now. *"There is one body, and one Spirit, even as ye are called in one hope of your calling: one Lord, one faith, one baptism; one God and Father of all, who is above all, and through all and in you all."* (Eph. 4:4-6) We are therefore to perceive that we are this One, and no other.

The revelation that I am not a separate man, student, individual nor idea, but of the essence of Being—the Truth and the Life—is what Jesus taught. Christ did not teach that we are mere man, but set aside such assumption in *Genesis* by declaring, *"Moses gave you not that bread from Heaven . . . I am that bread which came down from Heaven."* Until we renounce the age-long doctrine that we are separate from God, we are unable to come into the full knowledge and realization that we are perfect and complete in Being, Mind and body, here and now. Inevitably, sickness, sin, limitation, war and death shall continue in appearance while the belief remains that there are minds, consciousnesses and bodies which need to be perfected and healed; instead of seeing and accepting for ourself the same Mind, Consciousness and body that Jesus so perfectly characterized. Grasping the great Realism that we are the Truth instead of the student, Mind instead of idea, brings tremendous light and power, joy and activity into everything concerning oneself ; and leads to fuller and deeper insight into all things.

One is your Being; One is your Mind; One is your body, and this One is God. The term man is used in the Bible to denote a state of unbelief, a position of inversion wherein one personifies the prodigal, that is, a turning away from his Reality to assume a personal mind, being, life and body of his own. *"Men of low degree are vanity and men of high degree are a lie: to be laid in the balance, they are altogether lighter than vanity." (Ps. 62:9) "Let God be true, but every man a liar."* (Rom. 3:4) Only because one falsely assumes a human mind does he adopt the mental practice of spiritualizing and perfecting his thoughts: obviously, the Mind of God needs no such renovation. Once it is recognized and understood that really there are no individual minds whatsoever, but only the One, infinite and universal, to which we are all equally entitled, shall true and right thoughts be found to inhere within us: for Mind and its thoughts are one.

Said he who knew all things, *"I am come a light into the world, that whosoever believeth on me should not abide in darkness."* Who is this "I" and "me"? Surely the "I" which is Jesus Christ is the activity of the "I" which is the Father, that is, they are one and identical. Therefore the facts which he taught as true of himself must likewise be true of us all, else how could we be in him and he in us? The time is now at hand for us to disown an assumptive individual mind and body that we may recognize and accept the one Mind and no other to be our own; likewise the one Life and Body. How else could we truly state that "God is all," and that "Jesus Christ is in you"?

Ontology brings Jesus Christ again to the world as Emmanuel, God—Perfection—with us. It instructs us to return to our original estate of Perfection by accepting Jesus Christ, not as a man or person, but as the state of perfection ever existing for us all. *"Ye are complete in him."* (Col. 2:10) In ourselves as separate entities, each striving to achieve and attain perfection, each struggling to overcome limitations for himself, we are nothing: for all the while there is but the one infinite state of Perfection to which nothing can be added nor anything taken away. *"Ye are the light of the world"* . . . *"Whosoever drinketh of the water that I shall give him shall never thirst"* . . . *"Ye are not your own"* . . . *"By grace are ye saved through faith; and not of yourselves: it is the gift of God"* . . . *"Jesus Christ maketh thee whole"* . . *"Come Forth!"* Plainly, then, Ontology is *being* the Truth, *being* the one Mind which is indivisible and eternal, pure and perfect. Understandingly accepting this true Mind and Being, exultingly we declare, *I am the Truth . . . I am the Life . . . I and my Father are one.* Again the great Answer is revealed to this world, that the "I" which is God, the Father, and its perfect characterization, Jesus Christ, *is likewise the* "I" *which is you and me!*

Of course after we accept the Christ-Mind, and see clearly that we are immortal Life and Truth here and now, and nothing less, naturally fuller and deeper insight will be revealed to us on all things, for the immortal Promise reads,—*"The Holy Ghost, whom the Father will send in my name, he shall teach you all things, and bring all things to your remembrance, whatsoever I have said unto you."* (John 14:26)

What greater conclusiveness of the spirituality and immortality of the body could the Saviour ever have furnished than to let it be crucified and put into a sepulchre hewn out of a rock, and later walk forth with it as animated, whole and perfect as before? Ever Mind and body are the eternal "I" which all the ignorance and false beliefs in the whole world can never extinguish nor interrupt, any more than darkness can stop the light or illusion intercept reality. How can our redemption from sickness and disease take place until we behold and accept the truth of the body, that is, that it is the creation of Mind, and so is whole and perfect from the beginning?

Until now we have never been told that Jesus expressed the perfect body. As we have claimed the perfect Mind of Christ to be inherent in us, it is imperative that we now expand our vision and perceive our body to be likewise as perfect as his. Neither imperfections, deformities nor inharmonies of any kind can continue with us, nor approach us, when the supreme fact of our ever-existent perfect Mind and body is fully understood and realized. *Principle and practice are one.* Wherefore, Jesus commanded, *Stretch forth thy hand! Receive thy sight!* Come forth! He viewed the characters before him, not as separate individuals, as they believed themselves to be, but as characters who verily represented their Author, and none else. To him the Book of Life was finished, closed, and these three,—the Author, the characters and the story, are one. Does not any story book of today illustrate the nothingness of the characters as *such* and their total existence, actions, bodies and world to be wholly the mind of their author?

Jesus was the character specifically put into the Book of Life to fully and completely represent our Author to us. Thus he declared, *"He that seeth me, seeth the Father (Author) that sent me . . . I and my Father (Author) are one."* Thus also the reason he admonished, *"Call no man* (character) *your Father upon the earth." "Ye must be born again,"*—you must accept yourself to be of God, our Author, and not of man, the character! Nor will you be able to do so until you see me as I am,— a character who understands his origin to be God; and so, Father (Author) and Son (character) to be one and the same. My mission is to show you that you are not so many separate individuals, as you believe, born to labor for a living, to be subject to sin, sickness and all sorts of limitations, and finally succumb to death. No! ! I am come to exemplify and characterize for you the perfection, wholeness and purity of yourselves as you really are, that you may behold the Author to be the characters, and the characters to be the Author. *"Whosoever believeth on me* (sees me in this true light) *should not perish* (continue in the belief that he is subject to death) *but hath eternal life."*

"He that hath the Son of God, the true and immaculate concept of himself as the Truth and Life, perfect in both Mind and body, *hath Life*, immortality; *and he that hath not the Son of God*, he who interprets himself otherwise, *hath not life,"* is without the true concept, thus necessarily without the true experience of Being. (I John 5:12) Ontology therefore again presents Christ Jesus as our Mediator; and as our Saviour and Redeemer: for he portrays the steps we are to take in order to return to Paradise. That is, that we do not need to leave any world to be in Heaven; nor heal any body in order to express the perfect one; nor exchange any personal mentality for the Mind of Christ, since our Perfection is always wherever we are. Everything we need is already within us, and at hand. When we come to see who we really are, and accept our true Mind and body to be one perfect whole, then shall it come to pass that *"death is swallowed up in victory."*

THE SEARCH FOR TRUTH
BY JAMES E. DODDS

James E. Dodds, Pastor and Founder of the Church of The Truth, and Dean of the Academy of Spiritual Science, Portland, Oregon, obtained his early Metaphysical training in New York City. Coming to the West Coast in January 1919, he founded the Church of the Indwelling Master, at Santa Monica, California. Dr. Dodds, ordained by the Christian Unity Church, Los Angeles, California, was editor of Mind, Inc. and Mind Magazine from 1931 to 1936. President of the "X" Club of Los Angeles three years. Second Vice-President of the International New Thought Alliance, and District President for the State of Oregon of the I.N.T.A., Dr. Dodds is author of: *Lessons in the Silence.*

WE ARE interested in the search for Truth. I believe that all truth students are sincere in their seeking for something better than what they have. They are seeking for a new concept, a new adjustment with Truth, or with God, or with that Something which is able to help them, able to motivate them into a larger life, a life that means greater satisfaction. I believe that every truth student is sincere in his desire to live a larger life, to make more real, genuine progress.

TRUTH IS OF GOD

When we think of the word "Truth" from the standpoint of Metaphysics, New Thought, Unity, or whatever modern term we wish to use, we agree that Truth in its ultimate is God. Truth in its ultimate is absolute good. We are in search of that which is our good, the good of that man who is the real individual. And if we focus our attention, our vision, too far away from the self, we are liable to miss the mark. We are instructed that Truth dwells within us. "Ye are the temple of the living God." Ye are the temple of Truth. Truth resides in you as a self-conscious active unity, and if you look elsewhere for it, you overstep the mark, you fail.

A NEW CONCEPT OF GOD

Unfortunately, we have been brought up to feel that God is somewhere beyond our reach. Some have been taught to surrender their right to deal with God directly—to think that only the few were so privileged. There are two aspects of God which I believe most of us have had to consider before we could know the one we are enjoying today. The idea of God as a great Being sitting on a throne, dealing out justice, and the idea of God as an intangible Principle. But today we have the concept that God is the actual livingness of the individual, that God dwells in each soul, that each is privileged to know Him; that God is the actual true or real livingness of man, not far off, but close at hand. God has chosen to express Himself as man. The Truth of man is God. That is, the *real self* (Christ).

It is this idea, I feel, that Wm. Ernest Hocking, Professor of Natural Religion at Harvard, develops in his book "Living Religion and a World Faith," in which he says: "The Worldfaith-to-be is a belief in obligation, in a source of things which is good in some kind of permanence; for what is real is selfhood." The author places his hope more on the common people throughout the world than on the theologians, finding in mankind a universal sense of the presence of God and the intuition of the truth in which the will of God lies. In this optimistic faith we are face to face with the reality that truth lies at our very door. Those of us who are fortunate enough not to have been overloaded with fixed concepts, with traditional ecclesiastical ideas, find ourselves closer to God than those who are limited by theological barriers. It is essential then that we shall endeavor to return to a greater sense of simplicity in order that we may proceed more definitely in this consciousness of infinite goodness or truth, which we call God, and as we do, we enter into new measures of life and here we find new values. We discover that all those things that are real, those things on which we can depend, those things that constitute real, genuine, and eternal security all lie within the individual being. They are eternally waiting our recognition, appreciation and acceptance. And it is living in the consciousness of those values that gives life a new worth here and now.

THE STUDENT FOLLOWS THROUGH

At this point it is necessary that we recognize one certainty. So long as we are in search of a Truth it is apparent that we have not found it. That is very much the same as the saying used in the far East: "The man who says 'Oh, Allah! Oh, Allah!' be sure he has not as yet found his Allah, for he who has found Him is calm and full of peace." Which is to say, we are enjoying peace and security, or in other words, we are satisfied only when we have actually found truth. You see, we are not satisfied until we feel right about God. When we have moved into the position where we feel right, there is rest, there is no longer a struggle or concern, and in that rest each is refreshed and renewed and prepared for the next step. It is quite necessary for us to recognize too, that there is no end to the search for Truth. "As veil after veil is lifted, there shall be veil upon veil behind." There is always more life. There are always new vistas of spiritual vision and understanding. Truth is that which unfailingly produces satisfaction. If the things you value no longer satisfy, then you need a new vision, a new concept of Truth. You need a new measure of understanding.

TRUTH CANNOT FAIL

Truth cannot fail you. We fail Truth and often think we have accomplished when we haven't. This is due to our relative, wishful thinking.

To be absorbed in the outer aspects of things is the peculiar nature of the relative mind. Sir Arthur Eddington of Cambridge, England, made this point clear when he said men's minds move, not from truth to truth but from approximation to approximation of truth. You see, we never grasp the whole truth, the inner essence, in our relative thinking. One's Hunger is never satisfied. We are always dealing with something that isn't finished, isn't complete. Why?—because the relative mind is inadequate. Truth is delivered by the mind of Christ, the immortal mind. Only when Its Truth is established, is there satisfaction, fullness, and rest. The comprehension of this point is, I feel, the first step in progress.

SELF-ANALYSIS

I think, then, we need to look to ourselves and say, "Now, to what extent am I being satisfied? To what extent are my prayers being answered? To what extent is my meditation satisfactory? To what extent am I dealing satisfactorily with God or with my Good?" When we put ourselves in that place we demand greater fidelity to purpose, a greater love, a greater unity. Then we are real seekers.

NO UNIVERSAL REALM OF ABSOLUTE TRUTH

Another point we need to comprehend is that there is no vast universal realm of absolute Truth. Many have thought that there is a realm in which all the answers lay ready for delivery to all Beings. If that were so, free will would have been completely wiped out. We would just be copyists, automatons. But we are not that. Remember, you are a child of God. You inherit the very wonderful faculty of being able to think. And I would say this, the real you, the God of you, indwelling you, thinks dynamically. The true self has wisdom and thinks according to its need for growth and progress.

THE CHILD OF GOD IS NOT A FINISHED PRODUCT

The child of God is not a finished product. The children of God have all potentialities and are in the process of understandingly becoming that all. And for each one, every step taken in growth and progress is a perfect step, in perfect sequence. Consequently, the real of you thinks that which is true for you, and places that truth at your objective disposal. "Before you ask I will answer, and while you are yet calling I will bear." The Christ of you has placed at your disposal that which is essential for your objective growth, and, therefore, your lesson is to appreciate this and never feel for a single moment that God has forgotten you. God cannot forget His own, for every Being is God in action. Every Being is an extension of God, endowed with the character and nature of God. It is for us to cultivate the remembrance of this vital truth and accept the self as a Being whose home is in the Kingdom of Heaven. By our manifestation of the attributes of Christ we announce out citizenship in this Kingdom. The Kingdom of Heaven's citizen announces his citizenship by his living. This we need to realize. Real knowing always produces a positive certainty. You think that which is true for you. You think it. You do not just think about it.

BELIEF AND KNOWING

Intellectually you may accept what I say, and believe it, but it isn't true for you until you really think it and understandingly grasp the full significance of its meaning. Then you know it to be true for yourself and take possession of it, and it is no longer a belief—man believes, Christ knows. This constitutes true and real thinking. The idea produced represents an absolute; it brings peace and power to your soul, order and rest throughout your "consciousness" Kingdom. That is Truth and therefore an absolute.

THE TRUE WORD OF GOD IS NEVER SPOKEN

The true word of God is never spoken. You see, a word is only a symbol of an idea, or a feeling. But while we cannot speak orally the word of God, the thing that we experience within, we either consciously or unconsciously announce by our living. We are privileged to announce the Word by being it. Then only is one the conscious embodiment of Truth.

LOVE IS OMNIPOTENT

Love is the strongest force in the universe. It is for us to appreciate our good as waiting our acceptance, as waiting our love. This absolute "love" is the Word and nothing can defeat it. A Truth understandingly grasped represents power; an intelligently handled force that nothing can defeat, because it carries within itself the power to correct and change everything essential to its own fulfillment. We must know that we are endowed with the capacity to accept and use these positives. But positives are not dominant, arrogant forces. A reality, a truth, always functions according to the law of the Kingdom of Heaven. The law of the Kingdom of Heaven is peace and harmony, the very essence of graciousness. Whenever a Truth functions, it benefits everybody concerned; wherever it appears it adds to the value of life. It never in any sense robs anyone of anything. That is why the great men and women of all time have been gentle, gracious and loving, though commanding persons. And in them you find announced that man is just as strong as he is gentle. To be truly gentle is to be truly noble and able.

TRUTH IS FOR MAN WHAT HE NEEDS WHERE HE IS

Truth is for man what he needs where he is in order that he may grow and be more than he has been. That is the aspect of Truth that we are interested in—anything that will deliver to us a measure of value that makes it possible for us to give a better account of ourselves right here today. That is the thing to which we should apply ourselves. I am not so much interested in being good a hundred thousand years from now. I want to be good for something today. Being good for something today and every day will take care of the future. I choose to live consciously in that experience in which I find myself able to meet and handle each little and big experience peacefully and victoriously. And I know this, that whatever is essential for me to have in order to do this, is at my disposal. If I do not have the use of it, it is because I do not know how to have it. I have not learned how to be receptive to the guiding and motivating influence of that good. For it is the nature of Truth to teach me how to accomplish peacefully and victoriously. Then, too, we must recognize that we are never a finished product, there is always more to know, we shall always grow.

THE VICTORIOUS TRUTH STUDENT

The Truth seeker is one who is always at home to his good, always at home to God. The Indwelling Christ is the true thinker; there is no other thinker or source of absolute Truth. No one can progress for another, each must do this for himself. Progression is, after all, our own personal responsibility. We cannot expect any outside agency to do for us what we are not willing but able to do for ourselves. If I do not think enough of myself, of my life, of my possibilities as a Being to so organize myself that I may give a good account of my stewardship and live a life of self-reliance, how can it be done for me? That, my friends, is the way of the Kingdom. We as individuals are called upon to rise to the place of spiritual intelligence wherein we know and understand for ourselves and in that understanding we receive the power, the ability to live victoriously where we are, and in that we have found our security and we are free to enjoy the fruits of the Kingdom, because then we know how to call them forth. Everything in the Kingdom of Heaven is subject to your call. But this Kingdom, so far as you are concerned, is only as large as you have made it by your own thinking. The Kingdom of Heaven is within you. You are that Kingdom and it is for you to rise to this vision and know that by true spiritual thinking you are able to have at your disposal everything that is essential to your well-being that you may give consistently a better account of yourself.

THE SIMPLE METHOD OF ATTAINMENT

There is a way by which one may bring this about, providing he is willing to apply himself. This is where the difficulty lies as a rule, we are not always willing to *do* something about it. It is by way of the law of Love—for Love is the way of acceptance. *I will love my good and take possession of it and live in the fullness of Heavenly abundance. Thus I will glorify God by my living.* Remember, love is the fulfilling of the law. Love is omnipotent. That which you learn to love, you take possession of. Therefore, I say those things you feel you need, remember to love them for what they are, and let them take their legitimate place in your immediate life and serve you. After all, you as a child of God are the thinker, and remember the thinker is greater than the thoughts he thinks. The creator is greater than his creation. You are greater than anything in your life, in your world, in your Kingdom. Therefore, live accordingly and as you do this you will find yourself in the Kingdom which I shall define as that state of consciousness wherein you find at your disposal everything essential to your well-being where you are, now and forever.

WHAT OUGHT TO BE, IS
BY MURREL POWELL DOUGLAS

Rev. Murrel Powell Douglas of Indianapolis, Indiana, is a native Hoosier. For twenty-two years she has served in the capacity of minister of the Unity Truth Center of Indianapolis; President of the International New Thought Alliance in 1928 and 1932. Nationally known as teacher and lecturer from coast to coast in the interest of the I.N.T.A.

"In the beginning was the Word, and the Word was with God, and the Word was God. The same was in the beginning with God. All things were made by Him; and without Him was not anything made that was made."

IN ACCORDANCE with this instruction, we believe this to be a spiritual universe which exists only by virtue of the Word of God and that it is sustained and governed by His power and wisdom. The Apostle Paul also tells us:

"By faith we understand that the worlds have been framed by the Word of God, so that what is seen hath not been made out of things which appear."

Since there is no other source or origin of anything other than God and His Word (which is Himself) all things must of a necessity be perfect, because that which proceeds from God cannot subsist or exist other than as God Himself, or as He disposes.

In some of the ancient Scriptures God is spoken of as "He Who Is" and also "That Which Is." In the Book of Revelations we read:

"I am the Alpha and the Omega, saith the Lord God, who is, and who was and who is to come, the Almighty I am the first and the last, the beginning and the end."

The action of reason establishes the axiomatic consciousness whereby man perceives that that which is, is necessarily all there is, there being no such thing as that which is not. Therefore, He Who Is, God, is acknowledged to be all the presence there is, all the power there is, and all the consciousness there is. This also establishes His indivisibility for there is nothing besides Himself by which, or with which He can be divided; His unchangeableness, for there is nothing besides Himself into which He can change; His eternality, for that which is all there is, can have no cause, nor is it an effect.

This premise establishes the fact that the universe is the Lord's meditation, and that man, being the image and likeness of God, is the idea of it as a united whole. As God created the several kingdoms He pronounced them "good and very good." Solomon has said:

"The generations of the world are altogether healthful, and there is no poison of destruction in them."

Again we read:

"God made not death, neither hath He any pleasure in the destruction of the living."

Strict adherence to the Word of Truth in belief and utterance delivers the vision of immortality and the kingdom of heaven at hand in accordance with the saying of Jesus Christ:

"Keep my sayings and ye shall never see death."

There is no source or foundation for the belief in evil, for the word "evil" signifies the sense of lack. Disease is the belief in the lack of health. Poverty is the belief in the lack of wealth. Ignorance is the belief in the lack of intelligence, and so it is with all we might call evil. The omnipresence of God in His absolute goodness disproves such beliefs and the illumined consciousness finds them unthinkable.

We confess that the Word of God is "forever established in heaven" and that His perfect universe remains "unspoilable and unkillable." Man, through his ignorance, has superimposed over the perfect creation, a counter-creation, which is supported only by his beliefs, and therefore is not substantial. God does not lend Himself to falsity, and only substantiates those creations which are in accord with His word, therefore we pray:

"Let the words of my mouth, and the meditations of my heart be acceptable in Thy sight, 0 Lord, my strength and my Redeemer."

It is therefore not our opinion of truth that we are to accept, but God's own infinite universal Idea; not what may be so, or seems to be so, but what is so in the final analysis.

If we were to speak in purely metaphysical terms we would say that the functioning of man's mind to certain ideas and beliefs is responsible for his experience, and that if he is not living the abundant life, which God has ordained, the cure would not be in the manipulation of his affairs but in the change of belief; however, we are to be reminded of the fact that the change to a true belief does not make truth true, but it is merely the acceptance of that which is unchangeable and eternal. The allness and omnipresence of God is the guarantee of this.

Often when one asks for help on a problem, he uses the expression, "know the truth" about this. The rationalized mind does not deal with the problem, but turns immediately to meditations upon pure being and hears again the authoritative word of the Almighty, "Good and very good." It is as though the entire universe, with all of its apparent differences, were melted into one gloriously resplendent whole, and brought forth again in the wondrousness of "the pattern given in the mount." It is purged of the evil supcrimposed by the mind of man and is seen to be a paradisiacal world; it has received a baptism.

In the twinkling of an eye this change takes place. "In the twinkling of the eye" does not necessarily indicate the passing of time. We might express it this way: "In the batting of the eye lid" or "in the taking of another look." In other words, we are to see it as God sees it—see it as it is, in Truth. It is written of God, "Thy eyes are too pure to behold evil." We can be assured, however, if evil were a reality, God would hold it eternally in His vision, for He Himself is the knower, the act of knowing, and the thing known. He is the "all and the in all." As it is, He looks through these superimpositions and sees His perfect creation, just as we look through a shadow on an article and see the perfect article, knowing the shadow-spot to be a shadow and not a spot.

Jesus Christ said that we have ears to hear and hear not, eyes to see and see not. Our prayer, then, might well be—O, that we might see what we see.

Every prayer is made in the presence of the answer, the answer suggesting the prayer. Jesus Christ instructed His followers in this manner: "Whatsoever ye desire when ye pray, believe ye have received it, and ye shall have it." Treatment, or prayer, therefore, is not a method to bring something about, but an acknowledgment of the truth, the acceptance of God's own word, the confession of the way it is. It is written:

"As it was in the beginning, is now, and ever shall be . . ." good
and very good.

This irresistible language of inevitable truth clears the mist from the mind, destroys doubt, contradicts and corrects erroneous beliefs, denies false appearances, revealing the presence of the perfect as the absolute and only life and being.

One does not find the world resistant and unyielding but responsive and obedient to the chaste language. This word of God "rusheth through the universe" and demonstrates that,

> "All things respond to the call of rejoicing, All things gather where life is a song."

The word of truth is not merely the means for the alleviation of temporal trouble, but is an eternal cure for all past, present, and future ills, by the deliverance of the perception and vision of permanent freedom.

A TRIBUTE TO JAMES A. EDGERTON
FORMER PRESIDENT OF THE I.N.T.A.

Excerpts from President Edgerton's address to the 1921 Congress of the International New Thought Alliance at Denver, Colorado.

IN THE Alliance are many different schools—Unity, Divine Science, Homes of Truth, New Thought, etc. The Alliance is a federation. In it we believe in the largest possible liberty. We have conceived the idea that it is possible to have organization with the blessings going out from cooperative effort without restrictions and limitations and we are hoping to realize that ideal in this International New Thought Alliance.

The Alliance is founded on the Christ principles. In my opinion, the first of these principles is Spiritual Healing. I say that because Jesus Christ not only by word but by deed repeated this commandment perhaps oftener than any other. His last charge to His disciples was that they heal the sick, and a very large portion of His ministry was given to healing. There is another reason why I would place this first, and that is because it has been neglected for 1,600 years of church history. It was practiced by the disciples and in the early church up to the time of the Council of Nice, but after that to a greater and ever greater extent was ignored and forgotten. "The stone rejected by the builders becomes the head of the corner."

Like unto this principle is that of Divine Supply. Jesus said, "Take no thought for the morrow." You are familiar with His repeated commandments to His disciples of like import. Now, the world has interpreted that, in times past, as being a commandment of poverty and in so doing has lost the great lesson that He intended to convey which is a lesson of faith.

Take no thought of the morrow because the Father knows what you need and will supply you. "The laborer is worthy of his hire." This principle is being practiced today by all the field workers of the Alliance. It is being practiced successfully by the field workers of Unity and by teachers of this truth in many different organizations. I say to you it can be practiced not only in spiritual things but it can be practiced in business. I know whereof I speak, for I have applied these very principles successfully in business and I know of many other men who have done the same. We can work for God in business as well as in any other line, if we look at it in the right way. The more service you give, the more riches will come back to you. This spiritual law goes all the way through life, and so we believe in the Divine Supply.

We believe in Christ Service, that is the third principle. "I come to you as one that ministers." A man who has true nobility does not need to fear any service no matter how menial so long as it is given for the help of others. Jesus Christ was not in any wise abased by washing His disciples' feet or by any other service that He rendered. We are coming to learn that lesson.

The fourth of the Christ Standards is Love. "God is Love." "As I have loved you, love one another." The last and the greatest is Faith. "As your faith is, so be it unto you." There was no limit to His faith. His faith did not waver even at the removal of mountains. He knew the law—the law that we are now learning.

The word of the Christ is universal. "I, if I be lifted up, will draw all men unto me."

I have heard many healers complain that they took on themselves the symptoms and conditions of the patient. I wonder why? They must have thought they were doing the healing. That alone would account for such result. Jesus said, "It is the Father in me that doeth the works." If we approached our patients from above with the idea that God was doing the healing, we would not take on any of the conditions or symptoms, do you think? Whatever task we approach and whatever endeavor we approach—whether it be of salesmanship or what not, we never make a mistake by approaching from above.

In this Alliance work we not only teach healing and practice healing, but our one great object is to teach people how to heal themselves and how to keep well, so they will not need healing. We are aiming for a permanent result.

Man is infinite in possibility; man is infinite in quality; and all of the resources of the Universe are open to his command when he learns the law. We are only at the beginning of our development. It is now in this age our privilege to discover the inner world. We have discovered the powers of nature. It is now for us to discover the powers of mind and of the soul. We are spiritual beings here and now and it is for us to create the kingdom of heaven on earth. If we ever expect to be in heaven, it is well to get in the habit of holding heavenly thoughts.

The Alliance has been more concerned with being right than it has been in making a stir in the world. We believe in founding our house upon a rock, even the rock of Truth. We were much more concerned as to quality than quantity, for we knew if we were right, if we did found our house upon the Rock of Christ, that not only the storms might beat against that house and it would not fall; but that having found the Kingdom, all other things would be added unto us—even numbers and influence.

Having founded our work in the Truth and on the Rock of Christ, we go forward confidently knowing that this growth will increase; that this message will go out until it creates a new civilization, even the civilization that was in the vision of the greatest man that ever touched this planet—the Man of Nazareth.

THE SCIENCE OF BEING
BY IDA B. ELLIOTT

Ida B. Elliott, President of California Divine Science College, received her education at the High School of Des Moines, Iowa, and at the Iowa College; was graduated from and ordained by the Denver College of Divine Science in 1907. Miss Elliott established her work in Oakland, California, in 1908. In 1913, The California College of Divine Science, was incorporated and the First Church of Divine Science organized, later called Divine Science Fellowship. Miss Elliott is author of: *The Teachings of Divine Science, Living by the Law, How the Fairies Won Their Wings, The Great Realities.*

DIVINE Science is based on a belief in the Omnipresence, Omniscience, Omnipotence and Omniaction of God—One Presence, Knowledge, Power and Action. In other words: God is all, both invisible and visible. One Mind, Intelligence and Substance. One Spirit, Life and Law. This Mind is the source of all wisdom, love, knowledge, understanding and power. Its action is the expression of these inherencies which man calls the "Law of the Lord." This Law is also called the "Will of God" or, "God in action."

Man is the expression of God and is forever one with his Source. But, believing in two powers, he thought himself separated from the true Source and came into the bondage of his false beliefs. Hence the basic statement for class work is: "I accept the Omnipresence *without any reserve.*"

THE APPLICATION

This premise includes within it the Universe, expressing all forms according to law, and embodying the intelligence of an upward push, generally named evolution. What is evident in the realm of form bears witness to the process of soul enfoldment or spiritual evolution.

Since it is true that man as an *expression* of God is inherently perfect, it is logical to accept that as such he must partake of the nature of the Substance out of which he is "pressed." Yet believing for generations in separation he comes into *full consciousness* of identity with his Source only through the process of soul unfoldment or evolution.

Hence, man's constant application of the basic Principle, or fundamental truth of the Allness of God (accepting the Omnipresence without any reservation, acknowledging but one Power working always according to Perfect Law) frees him from the belief in separation and duality. He thus realizes identity with his Source, or the Christ consciousness that "I and my Father are one," and proves the Law, "As a man thinketh in his heart so is he."

The strong appeal of Divine Science to most students is that it is not an *exclusive* but an inclusive presentation of this Truth, including in the basic statement the highest deductions of science, psychology, philosophy and religion.

MEANS OF ATTAINMENT

1. The Psychology of Divine Science

In acquiring knowledge of Divine Science the student may take one of three ways. He may name the basis "One Mind," and from this premise approach the application of Infinite Intelligence in the visible universe. In the psychological interpretation the student learns the different phases of Mind action, both objective and subjective; the power of thought and the result of negative and constructive thinking; the effect of his thought on his emotions; and the effect of resistance, resentment or any negative attitude toward people, circumstances, conditions or events of man's everyday experiences.

He may learn with the aid of the microscope that every cell of the body is intelligent, hence is responsive to his thought; that wherever man searches, be it with microscope or telescope, he finds evidence of this Intelligence. Thus his conclusion is the same as the leading natural scientists of today: "In the final analysis *all* is Mind." And the intelligent, constructive use of that Mind means mastership in self-control and dominion in all his affairs.

Moreover, he learns that all the resources of that Mind are available to man. In the words of Emerson, "There is one Mind common to all individual men. Every man is an inlet to the same and to all of the same." I like to transpose that statement somewhat and render it thus: "There is a Mind common to all men. Every man is an inlet and may be an outlet to the same and to all of the same." In this acknowledgment, we learn there is an unfailing Source of supply for man's every need. As man learns to be an inlet and an outlet to the "Mind common to all men" all the devices that go to make the sum total of ease and comfort are brought forth in form for his use. The more perfectly man identifies himself with this Mind the more he finds the true Source of opulence to be rich ideas through which he may draw from this exhaustless store.

In right thought and controlled emotions are the security of his health and harmony of environment established, and an ever increasing awareness of oneness with a great Force, working according to infallible law, for his highest good.

II. The Philosophy of Divine Science

Another way of approach to the study of Divine Science is the science of philosophy.

Man has long accepted a universe, but what is the truth of this universe?

What principles and laws govern it? Can a universe have diverse principles, forces or laws governing it? What is the reality back of all visible manifestation? Where did man come from? Why is he here? What is his destiny?

With the premise, "I accept the Omnipresence without any reserve" the student proceeds to investigate the principles, laws and forces of the universe to prove for himself that the Principle of the universe, the fundamental Truth is One Infinite Good. Everywhere, by the aid of the telescope, microscope or the seeing of the eye he finds a Something expressing Itself intelligently according to the law of each form. Every form, whether mineral, insect, bird or animal having a definite purpose in the general scheme of things.

This "Something" we call the Presence, and in Its contemplation man literally "lives, moves and has his being in God." In this great Unity is found the love that holds all within Itself unto Itself.

The highest form in this marvelous manifestation is Man in the "image and likeness" of the Limitless. He is here to learn dominion over himself and all lower forms through this unity and to manifest the purpose and power of the invisible God.

III. The Religion of Divine Science

Some students with a superficial understanding of Divine Science say, "Divine Science is not a religion but a philosophy." What they mean to convey is that Divine Science formulates no creed. But we do maintain that in our basic acknowledgment, "I accept the Omnipresence without any reserve," is the essence of the truest religion.

The real meaning of the word religion (re-ligio) is to bind back. And that is just what the student does in his application of the Omnipresence. In the allegory of the Garden of Eden is a portrayal of the Omni-presence; One Presence, Mind or Intelligence creating or coming forth in the visible out of Its own substance. And it was said of each manifestation, "good and very good." Man in "the image and likeness of God" with every good provided for him was commissioned to have "dominion over all things." There was just one thing he was not to do—to "eat of the tree of good and evil," or conceive for himself a world of duality.

Throughout the remainder of the Bible we find man, through the power of his own choice, working his way out of sense delusion and illusion into conscious oneness with his Source made manifest by the man Jesus. Man, always the "image and likeness," the perfect Idea in Divine Mind, but coming into the knowledge and understanding of his sonship through his *acceptance* of and fidelity to the One Presence and Power. The history of the soul in its journey from sense delusion to the *realization* of its sonship is set forth in the Bible narrative. In the various stories, experiences and parables related in the narrative we find the laws and principles governing man's emancipation clothed with personality. In the journey, many Christ types develop until the perfect type emerges in Jesus the Christ. In this marvelous manifestation man finds "the Way, the Truth, the Life." Jesus *accepted* his Sonship, *identified with* the Father ("I and the Father are one"), *proved* it by his words and works and *identified* man with the same Source. He declared: "I am the Vine, ye are the branches;" "I am the Light;" "Ye are the Light of the world;" "The works that I do shall ye do also." The law governing this life was simply stated by the Master in these words: "The Lord our God, the Lord is one; and thou shalt love the Lord thy God with all thy heart and with all thy soul and with all thy mind and with all thy strength. The second is this: Thou shalt love they neighbor as thyself." (R.V.)

Hence we find the law governing the realm of Reality or the Kingdom of Heaven is love or *conscious oneness with the Father and with humanity.*

We find in Jesus' teaching the truest psychology as he emphasized the power of thought, the effect thought has on the emotions, the right use of the imaging faculty and the sure working of the law. "If thine eye be single thy whole body shall be full of light." "Love your enemies and pray for them that persecute you." "Agree with thine adversary quickly, while thou art with him in the way; lest haply the adversary deliver thee to the judge and the judge deliver thee to the officer, and thou be cast into prison."

For the student of philosophic trend a perfect code of ethics is provided in the Sermon on the Mount and I Cor. Chapter 13.

In the course of training carried on by this College there is the constant blending of the three ways of approach. The different terms used in the different methods meaning the same thing are harmonized into a practical, workable science for everyday needs. The logical conclusion of the whole matter is: There is one Principle or Fundamental Truth, invisible and visible. Call it Infinite, Spirit, Mind, Energy, God or whatever man conceives it to be. It is unhindered by name for It is that which Is; undefeatable, undefilable, imperishable, Infinite and Eternal, always working according to the law of Its own nature.

Thus man finds in the Science of Being a Principle of Life as unfailing as the principle of mathematics. Moreover, in the eternal pronouncement, "Let him have dominion" he knows that he is fully equipped to exercise that dominion. And he will do so as he learns to work according to and with the perfect Law.

GO FORWARD
BY WILLIAM FARWELL

William Farwell, born in Alameda, California, in 1866. Grew up on a stock ranch. In 1888 became a business man. Went to Home of Truth in Alameda for healing in 1895. Was converted from agnosticism instantly, while walking, by a strong influx of Holy Spirit which had the effect of clearing away doubts, affording a conviction that God is Spirit indwelling, and that Jesus Christ is all that the New Testament declares. Became a Truth student; in 1898 entered the work of the Home of Truth in Alameda. In 1900 went to San Jose to establish a center that would exemplify New Testament Christianity. In 1912 he became a member of the New Thought Alliance. From a small beginning the work, which is now called the Christian Assembly, grew steadily. Branches have been established in Gilroy, Willow Glen, Palo Alto, Redwood City, Burlingame, West San Jose, and Oakland.

IN THE history of the New Thought movement there has never been an opportunity for proclaiming the good tidings, like that which presents itself today. The present state of Christianity as a whole is comparable to that which existed when Jesus sat by the side of Jacob's well in Samaria and asked the Samaritan woman for a drink of water. The religions of that day had run their course, and in their decadence they were unable to satisfy the hunger and thirst of the soul for truth. The saying, "When that which is perfect is come, that which is in part shall be done away," described the situation then present. Therefore Jesus said to the woman, "The hour cometh, and now is, when the true worshippers shall worship the Father in spirit and truth for such cloth the Father seek to be his worshippers. God is spirit: and they that worship him must worship in spirit and truth." (John 4:23, 24)

The world-wide decadence of man-devised systems of Christianity today is sufficient cause for a return to the pure, primitive type presented by the record of the New Testament. The disparity between the standard of the Christ and the present day forms is due largely to a want of faith in and obedience to the will of God. The Savior of the world, in the days of his flesh, was not a friend of formalism. He had been sent from the Eternal to perfect the plan of salvation hidden within the letter of the Old Testament, and to establish in the inner life of mankind the new creation of God, called the kingdom of heaven.

The divine Teacher spent little time explaining the nature of God to his disciples. The many great miracles which he wrought served to establish the faith of mankind in his God-given authority, and to prove that he was the Messiah for whom the people of Israel had long been waiting. Everything that the Christ said and did led up to a great climax which was reached on the day of Pentecost when, in fulfillment of the prophecies of the Old Testament and those of the Christ, God poured forth his Spirit upon the waiting apostles and other disciples. Through them three thousand, and later other thousands, were anointed by the influx of the same Spirit that had descended upon Jesus after his immersion in the River Jordan. By the forthpouring of Holy Spirit the risen and ascended Lord became the Leader and the Teacher of all those born again of water and the Spirit.

In his explanation of spiritual life to Nicodemus, Jesus said, "Except one be born of water and the Spirit, he cannot enter into the kingdom of God. That which is born of the flesh is flesh; and that which is born of the Spirit is spirit." (John 3:5, 6) In this statement a line of demarcation is fixed between the once-born and the twice-born natures. Everything depends upon God's gift of Holy Spirit. The rebirth of a disciple of Jesus

Christ begins with the influx of the light of the Spirit of truth in his soul. Today the regeneration of the understanding requires about three years, during which period the mind of a student of the inner life is transformed by interior contact with the mind of Christ. Following this, a real disciple puts into practice the truth that he has learned in the light of the indwelling Spirit, and in due course he is born anew in the will. The regeneration of the understanding and of the will, when complete, brings the disciple up to the level of the divine Teacher, as indicated in the words, "It is enough for the disciple that he be as his teacher, and the servant as his lord;" "Ye therefore shall be perfect, as your heavenly Father is perfect; " "Whosoever is begotten of God doeth no sin, because His seed abideth in him: and he cannot sin, because he is begotten of God." (I John 3:9)

This goal of complete regeneration was reached by the disciples of Christ in the first and second centuries of the Christian dispensation. During the intervening centuries Pentecostal gifts have never been withdrawn. In every age God has had His witnesses in those who received the gift of Holy Spirit and regenerated in the understanding and in the will. The history of Christianity shows that about the third century the Christian religion, which had been fugitive and unpopular, became acceptable and popular in the Roman Empire, with the result that it became more formal than spiritual. Today the average Christian is regenerate in understanding only, which signifies that he is like a house divided against itself; for, in regard to many essentials, he knows the will of God but does not do it. The record shows that periodically during the last sixteen centuries new movements have arisen, some inside and some outside of the old forms of religion. These were due to the spontaneous action of Holy Spirit. The following are some of the leaders of such movements: St. Francis of Assisi, St. Theresa (the patron saint of Spain), George Fox, and John Wesley.

In our own day and age the New Thought movement from its beginning has been a spontaneous work of the Spirit of truth working in the hearts and souls of many men and women who are receptive to the influx of the Spirit. As was the case in other movements, the Lord began with one soul, the soul of Phineas P. Quimby, and multiplied and increased and replenished the earth from that small beginning. A review of the record of the New Thought movement shows that the Spirit of truth, which comes in the name of Jesus Christ, accommodates himself to the situation of the hour; that from the vantage point of the Godhead in the inner life of humanity he works with all kinds and conditions of men without respect to persons. This is in accordance with the revelation of the attitude of God which we find in the words of the Christ in his last prayer when, in referring to his disciples, the Son said, "And the glory which thou hast given me I have given unto them, that they may be one, even as we are one; I in them, and thou in me, that they may be perfected into one; that the world may know that thou didst send me, and lovedst them, even as thou lovedst me. Father, I desire that they also whom thou has given me be with me where I am, that they may behold my glory, which thou hast given me; for thou lovedst me before the foundation of the world." (John 17:22-24)

From observation it is evident that the Spirit of truth is sent to one who is ready for regeneration, to illuminate and guide him in the rebirth of the understanding. The beginner is dealt with as a child, and the Spirit accommodates itself to his limitations; but when the regeneration of the understanding is completed, more is expected of him. Then God demands a life in obedience to his will: such a life as Jesus outlined for himself when he said, "Man shall not live by bread alone, but by every word that proceedeth out of the mouth of God." (Matt. 4:4) The progress of the soul in regeneration is from darkness to light, weakness to strength, imperfection to perfection, and from mortality to immortality, to the glory of God. In the progressive steps of soul unfoldment one who continues to regenerate is led by the Spirit of truth closer and closer to the standard set before him in Jesus Christ. The attitude of the divine Teacher is expressed in his words,

"To whomsoever much is given, of him shall much be required: and to whom they commit much, of him will they ask the more." (Luke 12:48)

The progressive soul learns from experience to depend more and more upon the leadership of the living Christ for direction, and more and more upon the Holy Spirit for inspiration and leading. One who comes into the truth a liberal, is in course of time, if he progresses, due to become a devout follower of Jesus Christ. Having passed beyond the primary degree in soul enfoldment one discovers that these words of the Lord are true, namely: "All authority hath been given unto me in heaven and on earth; " "Without me ye can do nothing."

Spiritual movements which have a visible head, or leader, have the advantage of regimentation, and the disadvantage of having an intermediary between themselves and the real Leader, Jesus Christ. Whereas, movements like the New Thought which do not have a visible leader, in the form of a prophet, have the disadvantage of being scattered in their efforts because of the want of regimentation under the leadership of a visible head or prophet. At the same time such movements have the great advantage of coming under the direct leadership of the invisible, but very present, Leader, who says, "Lo, I am with you always." There is no question but that the divine plan of salvation calls for allegiance to the one Lord and Savior, who, by the Holy Spirit indwelling, is the Good Shepherd: the Teacher and Healer of his followers.

The strength of the New Thought movement lies in the freewill allegiance, without human regimentation, to Jesus Christ. The appeal of the movement is to those who love freedom, who are interiorly open to the leading and guidance of the Holy Spirit, and who are not given to following a personal leader in a personal way, or to following a man-made plan of salvation. This type has an open mind, and a receptivity to the influx of Holy Spirit, which is desirable in the sight of the Lord. In order to progress in the regeneration of the will, this type of soul should pay heed to the words of the Christ, "Except ye turn, and become as little children, ye shall in no wise enter into the kingdom of heaven." (Matt. 18:3) Their desire for freedom can be realized only by doing the truth that Jesus taught.

In the nature of things it is necessary for one who desires to make a complete success of his spiritual life to put all his faith in Jesus Christ, and follow the one who said, "I am the way, and the truth, and the life: no man cometh unto the Father, but by me." (John 14:6) The one who has an innate love of freedom is assured that as he comes to know the truth through doing it, the truth will make him free in the true sense of the word. A natural love of freedom, together with personal initiative which is allowed to interfere with true discipleship to the living Christ, results in inhibitions. Those who will not surrender to the leadership of the One appointed of God for all mankind will not progress beyond a certain point, for they will have isolated themselves to such an extent that they will not be membered in Christ. Whereas, one who becomes as a little child, and follows the Lord Jesus by doing what he says, is due to arrive at the goal. He shall be perfect, not only as his Leader is perfect, but as his Father in heaven is perfect.

The New Thought movement today has a great opportunity. Whether it will make the most of it or not, depends upon the attitude of those who make up the movement and give it its character. A spontaneous trend in the direction of real discipleship to Jesus Christ, and the cancelling of everything that interferes with this, should result in another immersion in Holy Spirit, such as blessed the first disciples on the day of Pentecost.

Much has been made of the subject of thought in the teaching of New Thought, while the subject of feeling has been neglected. This results in a lack of balance. The truth is that thought and feeling constitute human life, and that the rebirth of the feeling nature is of first importance. Man is a creature of habit, because originally he was created to live according to the will of his Creator. While in the fall man lost the habit of thinking and feeling in unison with God, he continued nevertheless, to be a creature of habit, and here in the world his mental habits determine the tenor of his life, and also his end. Mental habits are the result of repetition in thinking, willing, and doing, which culminate in a state of the will affording a facility almost automatic in repeating the same acts. A disciple's part in the regeneration is largely that of overcoming habits which are detrimental, and acquiring habits founded upon divine truth. The formation of new spiritual habits demands mental and moral effort in learning to think, feel, and act in cooperation with the divine mind. In this vital work God provides a Helper by sending the Spirit of truth to guide and lead each follower of the Christ in the formation of mental, moral, and spiritual habits that are acceptable to God. Concerning the divine Helper the Teacher said, "He shall take of mine, and shall declare it unto you." This signifies that the mind of Christ is the pattern from which the regenerate mentality of a disciple is formed. As Moses in constructing the tabernacle made everything according to the "pattern in the mount," so the heavenly Helper teaches each disciple how to conform to the ideal which is in divine mind. What this ideal amounts to in its fulfillment was revealed to the disciples on the Mount of Transfiguration when they saw Jesus transformed by the intense interior work of Holy Spirit, until his face shone like the sun at noon day, and his garments were white with a supernatural light.

Hitherto in the New Thought movement there has been little advance beyond the things of beginners. The primary teaching, as it is called, is not sufficient to lead souls to perfection. Recruiting is always going on, and every year thousands of beginners start for the goal, while at the same time there is small provision for the advancement of those who have been a long time on the way. To make good the promise of their initiation into the mysteries of the kingdom of God within, it is necessary for those who have been born anew in the understanding to regenerate in the will. When these two phases of the new birth, referred to by the Christ as being "born of water and the Spirit," are complete, a disciple is ready for the crowning work of God: namely, the redemption of the body. The regeneration of the understanding and the will gives the Redeemer a foothold in the humanity of a disciple, which he can gain in no other way. It is then that the real significance of the words of the Christ at the Last Supper, when he presented the symbol of life to his disciples in the form of a cup of unfermented wine, is known: namely, "This is my blood of the new covenant, which is poured out for many unto remission of sins." (Matt. 26:28)

The redemption of the body of Jesus Christ, made evident in the resurrection and his ascension bodily into eternity, completed the plan of salvation which the Son of man worked out in his days on earth, as a demonstration of his power to redeem the human body. The blood which was poured out at the crucifixion was an antitype of the life-giving Spirit which was poured forth upon the waiting disciples on the day of Pentecost. This is our quest today.

HEALING METHODS BASED UPON THE NEW TESTAMENT RECORDS

The Healer's Authority:
"Verily, verily, I say unto you, He that believeth on me, the works that I do shall he do also; and greater works than these shall he do; because I go unto the Father. And whatsoever ye shall ask in my name, that will I do, that the Father may be glorified in the Son. If ye shall ask anything in my name, that will I do." (John 14:12-14)

The Healer's Preparation in the Silence:
O Lord, uphold the word which I speak in thy name, and to thy glory.

The Healer (addressing silently the one seeking healing):
Have faith of God.
All things are possible to him who believes. Do not doubt in your heart.
Believe, only believe.

JESUS CHRIST HEALS YOU.

According to your faith it is done unto you. Amen.

Note:—There should be an interval of a few minutes between each of the above statements.

In the cases of diseases that are the after effects of sin or lawlessness in any form.

The Healer's Authority:
"Peace be unto you: as the Father hath sent me, even so send I you. . . . Receive ye Holy Spirit: whose soever sins ye forgive, they are forgiven unto them; whose soever sins ye retain, they-are retained." (John 20:21-23)

The Healer (addressing silently the one seeking healing):
Thy sins are forgiven.
JESUS CHRIST SAVES YOU. Amen.

Variants:
The blood of Jesus Christ cleanses you from all sin.
The holy healing hands of Jesus are upon you.

PRACTICAL RECIPES FOR MEETING TODAY'S PROBLEMS
BY EMMETT FOX

Dr. Emmet Fox has what is said to be the largest congregation in the world. At Sunday services in the Manhattan Opera House, he speaks to between five and six thousand people; and on Fridays at noon, the Grand Ballroom of the Hotel Astor is filled to overflowing. A highly intelligent group, his listeners include leaders in New York's business and professional life. For many years, Dr. Fox was a successful electrical engineer in England. Having a natural philosophic bent, he discovered in Emerson what seemed to him the Key to Life. But Emerson, with his academic detachment, seemed like "an electric motor running by itself, not geared to the machine." Then Dr. Fox came across some little pamphlets of the American Metaphysical Movement which seemed to him to supply the belt between the electric motor of Emerson and the machinery of everyday life. Ten years ago Dr. Fox came to the United States for a two-months' vacation, but liked this country so well that he remained and decided to devote his whole time to teaching this Metaphysical religion which, he claims, is really primitive Christianity. The large and unusually intelligent audiences he attracts signify the vitality of his message. He is the author of the widely circulated book "The Sermon on the Mount."

SCIENTIFIC prayer will enable you, sooner or later, to get yourself, or anyone else, out of any difficulty on the face of the earth. It is the Golden Key to harmony and happiness.

To those who have no acquaintance with the mightiest power in existence, this may appear to be a rash claim, but it needs only a fair trial to prove that, without a shadow of doubt, it is a just one. You need take no one's word for it, and you should not. Simply try it for yourself, and see.

God is omnipotent, and man is His image and likeness, and has dominion over all things. This is the inspired teaching, and it is intended to be taken literally, at its face value. Man means every man, and so the ability to draw on this power is not the special prerogative of the Mystic or the Saint, as is so often supposed, or even of the highly-trained practitioner. Whoever you are, wherever you may be, the Golden Key to harmony is in your hand now. This is because in scientific prayer it is God who works, and not you, and so your particular limitations or weaknesses are of no account in the process. You are only the channel through which the Divine action takes place, and your treatment will really be just the getting of yourself out of the way. Beginners often get startling results at the first time of trying, for all that is absolutely essential is to have an open mind, and sufficient faith to try the experiment. Apart from that, you may hold any views on religion or none.

As for the actual method of working, like all fundamental things, it is simplicity itself. All that you have to do is this: *Stop thinking about the difficulty, whatever it is, and think about God instead.* This is the complete rule, and if only you will do this, the trouble, whatever it is, will presently disappear. It makes no difference what kind of trouble it is. It may be a big thing or a little thing; it may concern health, finance, a lawsuit, a quarrel, a house on fire, or anything else conceivable; but whatever it is, just stop thinking about it, and think of God instead—that is all you have to do.

The thing could not be simpler, could it? God Himself could scarcely have made it simpler, and yet it never fails to work when given a fair trial.

Do not try to form a picture of God, which is, of course, impossible. Work by rehearsing anything or everything that you know about God. God is Wisdom, Truth, inconceivable Love. God is present everywhere; has infinite power; knows everything; and so on. It matters not how well you may think you understand these things; go over them repeatedly.

But you must stop thinking of the trouble, whatever it is. The rule is to think about God, and if you are thinking about your difficulty you are not thinking about God. To be continually glancing over your shoulder, as it were, in order to see how matters are progressing, is fatal, because that is thinking of the trouble, and you must think of God, and of nothing else. Your object is to drive the thought of the difficulty right out of your consciousness, for a few moments at least, substituting for it the thought of God. This is the crux of the whole thing. If you can become so absorbed in this consideration of the spiritual world that you really forget for a while all about the trouble concerning which you began to pray, you will presently find that you are safely and comfortably out of your difficulty—that your demonstration is made.

In order to "Golden Key" a troublesome person or a difficult situation, think, "Now I am going to 'Golden Key' John, or Mary, or that threatened danger"; then proceed to drive all thought of John, or Mary, or the danger right out of your mind, replacing it by the thought of God.

By working in this way about a person, you are not seeking to influence his conduct in any way, except that you prevent him from injuring or annoying you, and you do him nothing but good. Thereafter he is certain to be in some degree a better, wiser, and more spiritual person, just because you have "Golden Keyed" him. A pending lawsuit or other difficulty would probably fade out harmlessly without coming to a crisis, justice being done to all parties concerned.

If you find that you can do this very quickly, you may repeat the operation several times a day with intervals between. Be sure, however, each time you have done it, that you drop all thought of the matter until the next time. This is important.

We have said that the Golden Key is simple, and so it is, but, of course, it is not always easy to turn. If you are very frightened or worried it may be difficult, at first, to get your thoughts away from material things. But by constantly repeating some statement of absolute Truth that appeals to you, such as *There is no power but God, or I am the child of God, filled and surrounded by the perfect peace of God, or God is Love, or God is guiding me now,* or, perhaps best and simplest of all, just *God is with me*—however mechanical or dead it may seem at first— you will soon find that the treatment has begun to "take", and that your mind is clearing. Do not struggle violently; be quiet but insistent. Each time that you find your attention wandering, just switch it straight back to God.

Do not try to think out in advance what the solution of your difficulty will probably turn out to be. This is technically called "outlining", and will only delay the demonstration. Leave the question of ways and means strictly to God. You want to get out of your difficulty—that is sufficient. You do your half, and God will never fail to do His.

Whosoever shall call upon the name of the Lord shall be saved.

*   *   *

Everything in your life today—the state of your body, whether healthy or sick, the state of your fortune, whether prosperous or impoverished, the state of your home, whether happy or the reverse, the present condition of every phase of your life in fact— is entirely conditioned by the thoughts and feelings which you have entertained in the past, by the habitual tone of your past thinking. And the condition of your life tomorrow, and next week, and next year, will be entirely conditioned by the thoughts and feelings which you choose to entertain from now onwards.

In other words, you choose your life, that is to say, you choose the thoughts upon which you allow your mind to dwell. Thought is the real causative force in life, and there is no other. You cannot have one kind of mind and another kind of environment. This means that you cannot change your environment while leaving your mind unchanged, nor can you change your mind without your environment changing too.

This then is the real key to life: if you change your mind your conditions must change too—your body must change; your daily work or other activities must change; your home must change; the color-tone of your whole life must change—for whether you be habitually happy and cheerful, or low-spirited and fearful, depends entirely on the quality of the mental food upon which you diet yourself.

Please be very clear about this. If you change your mind your conditions must change too. *We are transformed by the renewing of our minds.*

This may be called the Great Cosmic Law, and its truth is seen to be perfectly obvious when once it is clearly stated in this way. In fact, I do not know of any thoughtful person who denies its essential truth. The practical difficulty in applying it, however, arises from the fact that our thoughts are so close to us that it is difficult, without a little practice, to stand back as it were and look at them objectively.

Yet that is just what you must learn to do. You must train yourself to choose the subject of your thinking at any given time, and also to choose the emotional tone, or what we call the mood that colors it. *Yes, you can choose your moods.* Indeed, if you could not you would have no real control over your life at all. Moods habitually entertained produce the characteristic disposition of the person concerned, and it is his disposition that finally makes or mars a person's happiness.

You cannot be healthy; you cannot be happy; you cannot be prosperous; if you have a bad disposition. If you are sulky, or surly, or cynical, or depressed, or superior, or frightened half out of your wits, your life cannot possibly be worth living. Unless you are determined to cultivate a good disposition, you may as well give up all hope of getting anything worth while out of life, and it is kinder to tell you very plainly that this is the case.

If you are not determined to start in now and carefully select all day the kind of thoughts that you are going to think, you may as well give up all hope of shaping your life into the kind of thing that you want it to be, because this is the only way.

In short, if you want to make your life happy and worth while; which is what God wishes you to make it, you must begin immediately to train yourself in the habit of thought selection and thought control. This will be exceedingly difficult for the first few days, but if you persevere you will find that it will become rapidly easier, and it is actually the most interesting experiment that you could possibly make. In fact, this thought control is the most thrillingly interesting hobby that anyone could take up. You will be amazed at the interesting things that you will learn about yourself, and you will get results almost from the beginning.

Now many people knowing this truth, make sporadic efforts from time to time to control their thoughts, but the thought stream being so close, as I have pointed out, and the impacts from outside so constant and varied, they do not make very much progress. That is not the way to work. Your only chance is definitely to form a new habit of thought which will carry you through when you are preoccupied or off your guard as well as when you are consciously attending to the business.

If you will do so, it is safe to say that your whole life will change for the better. In fact, nothing can possibly remain the same. This does not simply mean that you will be able to face your present difficulties in a better spirit; it means that the difficulties will go. This is the scientific way to Alter Your Life, and being in accordance with the Great Law it cannot fail. Now do you realize that by working in this way you do not have to change condition? What happens is that you apply the Law, and then the conditions change spontaneously.

Now, in order, if possible, to forestall difficulties, I will consider them in a little detail.

First of all, what do I mean by negative thinking? Well, a negative thought is any thought of failure, disappointment, or trouble; any thought of criticism, or spite, or jealousy, or condemnation of others, or self-condemnation; any thought of sickness or accident; or, in short, any kind of limitation or pessimistic thinking. Any thought that is not positive and constructive in character, whether it concerns you yourself or anyone else, is a negative thought. Do not bother too much about the question of classification, however; in practice you will never have any trouble in knowing whether a given thought is positive or negative. Even if your brain tries to deceive you, your heart will whisper the truth.

Second, you must be quite clear that what this scheme calls for is that you shall not *entertain*, or *dwell upon* negative things. Note this carefully. It is not the thoughts that come to you that matter, but only such of them as you choose to entertain and dwell upon. It does not matter what thoughts may come to you provided you do not entertain them. It is the entertaining or dwelling upon them that matters. Of course, many negative thoughts will come to you all day long. Some of them will just drift into your mind of their own accord seemingly, and these come to you out of the race mind. Other negative thoughts will be given to you by other people, either in conversation or by their conduct, or you will hear disagreeable news perhaps by letter or telephone, or you will see crimes and disasters announced in the newspaper headings. These things, however, do not matter as long as you do not entertain them. In fact, it is these very things that provide the discipline that is going to transform you. *The thing to do is, directly the negative thought presents itself— turn it out.* Turn away from the newspaper; turn out the thought of the unkind letter, or stupid remark, or what not. When the negative thought floats into your mind, immediately turn it out and think of something else. Best of all, think of God as explained in the *Golden Key*. A perfect analogy is furnished by the case of a man who is sitting by an open fire when a red hot cinder flies out and falls on his sleeve. If he knocks that cinder off at once, without a moment's delay to think about it, no harm is done. But if he allows it to rest on him for a single moment, under any pretense, the mischief is done, and it will be a trouble-some task to repair that sleeve. So it is with a negative thought.

Now what of those negative thoughts and conditions which it is impossible to avoid at the point where you are today? What of the ordinary troubles that you will have to meet in the office or at home? The answer is, that such things will not affect you provided that you do not accept them, by fearing them, by believing them, by being indignant or sad about them, or by giving them any power at all. Suppose you witness an accident or an act of injustice let us say—instead of reacting by accepting the appearance and responding with pity or indignation, refuse to accept the appearance at its face value; do anything that you can to right matters, give it the right thought, and let it go at that.

People often find that the starting of this right thinking seems to stir up all sorts of difficulties. It seems as though everything begins to go wrong at once. This may be disconcerting, but it is really a good sign. It means that things are moving; and is not that the very object we have in view? Suppose your whole world seems to rock on its foundation. Hold on steadily, let it rock, and when the rocking is over, the picture will have reassembled itself into something much nearer to your heart's desire.

The above point is vitally important and rather subtle. Do you not see that the very dwelling upon these difficulties is in itself a negative thought? The remedy is not, of course, to deny that your world is rocking in appearance, but to refuse to take the appearance for the reality.

*   *   *

The Bible promises that on certain terms the wayfaring man, you and I, may see God. Of course, you will understand that there is no question of "seeing God" with the physical eyes as one sees a man or a house. With the physical eyes one can see only physical things, and God is Spirit, and spiritual things have to be spiritually discerned. Also, spiritual perception is not a matter of apprehending outlines and surfaces as physical sight is. Spiritual perception is direct spiritual experience in which the subject and the percipient become one. Therefore, to see God means— as far as our restricted and crippled human speech can express the thing at all—a realization of perfect essential unity with Divine Goodness Itself.

To believe in God as Omnipotent Cause, and absolutely to reject any claim for a lesser cause of any kind; to refuse to concede the power of causation to such things as climate, germs, manmade medical laws, or laws of poverty or decay; to refuse to concede reality to the race limitations of time and space; in the face of appearances, to judge righteous judgment, and hold unswervingly to the One Cause—this is a purity, that which guarantees to man that he shall see God.

Courtesy of Mr. Fox's publishers, Harper & Brothers.

OUR CONTRIBUTION TO THE WORLD'S THOUGHT
BY JOHN SEAMAN GARNS

Dr. John Seaman Garns, founder and president of the School of Psychology and Divine Science at Minneapolis, Minnesota, graduated from the Drake University of Oratory; received his Bachelor of Arts Degree from the University of Minnesota and, later, honors from the Curry School of Expression, Boston. Dr. Garns was for ten years head of the department of public speaking at Lawrence College, Appleton, Wisconsin; fourteen years on the faculty of the Public Speaking Department and the Extension Division of the University of Minnesota, and for years in charge of the Dramatic and Public Speaking Departments at the MacPhail Conservatory of Music and Dramatic Art. In 1933, he received the Degree of Doctor of Divine Science from the Divine Science College of Denver, Colorado. Only rarely does he leave his school in Minneapolis for brief lecture tours.

WHATEVER we may believe about the importance of this present moment we cannot fail to see that our civilization is at the crossroads and that there is only one of two ways it can take—one up, the other down. The downward road keeps man's consciousness pointed outward toward the material world, and the struggle for things and powers. The upward turn centers attention even more sharply upon man as Mind and Spirit, and keeps his attention upon his subjective significance.

Do you remember the arresting words of Dr. Kaarlo Valkonen, the Finnish scientist in Robert Sherwood's play, "There Shall Be No Night"? In the first scene of the play, in a broadcast being made from Helsinki to America, he emphasizes the danger of man's present tendency to trust the outer as over against his own inner mental and spiritual resistances.

"We have counted too heavily upon pills and serums to protect us from our enemies, just as we have counted too heavily upon vast systems of concrete fortifications and big names to guard our frontiers. Of what avail are artificial protections if each man lacks the power of resistance within himself? . . . The greatest of all adventures in exploration is still before us—the exploration of man himself—his mind—his spirit . ."

And again toward the end of the play, when Dr. Valkonen knows that his own hours of life are numbered, one of the men quotes the words of the Seventh Angel of the Apocalypse:

"And they shall see his face, and his name shall be in their foreheads. And there shall be no night there, and they need no candles, neither light of the sun, for the Lord giveth them light; and they shall reign forever and ever."

And the famous scientist replies:

"That unknown Jewish mystic—somehow, unconsciously, knew that man will find the true name of God in his own forehead, in the mysteries of his own mind. . . . I have seen it in all kinds of men, of all races, of all varieties of faith. They are coming to consciousness. We have the power within ourselves to conquer bestiality, not with our muscles and our swords, but with the power of the light that is in our minds. What a thrilling challenge that is to all Science! To play its part in the ultimate triumph of evolution, to help speed the day when man becomes genuinely human, instead of the synthetic creature—part bogus angel, part actual brute—that he has imagined himself in the dark past."

And if this is the challenge of our time to *natural science*, how much more must it challenge us who are teachers of the New Age doctrines in *religion!*

The objective universe is forever unfolding before our very eyes, from lower to higher, from "less differentiated to more differentiated"; the up-welling fountain of creativeness, forever functions life and mind in forms and organizations of ever increasing beauty and significance.

Not only forms and organizations unfolding in the objective but in that most highly evolved product on this little planet, earth—the creature called Man. The unfoldment still goes on in his mind and in his ideas of the eternal truth regarding himself and the universe. So though there may be a Finished Kingdom already established in Idea-Patterns in the Absolute, Man and his objective universe seem forever unfolding in a series of changes which we call progress, development, evolution.

This process of creation still goes forward before our very eyes, in the hurrying events of our time. Now, at its apex, in the mind and spirit of man, we must look for increasing change, for new methods, for new ideas, new beauties, new modes of manifesting Truth. The body of man may change little, but his techniques of controlling nature will change with ever increasing rapidity because his mind gives him mastery in this field. Methods in mathematics and mathematical procedures are established and have changed little in three thousand years; but at the very peak of conscious life, in man's awareness of his relationship with the Infinite Universe within him and around him, we may expect change to be rapid and increasingly significant.

In this time which so challenges our philosophy of life, we must expect to see religion and religious thought and practices increasingly important, intelligent and significant. They are the very point of articulation where the new and living Word is ever being spoken. Therefore man will look less and less to the past for his methods of thought and his practices and techniques of living. He will, like the modern scientist, look more and more within himself to the concrete data of experience, to the inner reality of mind and spirit.

Where, in the past, men have attempted to fixate religion or to pour these vast and living experiences into molds, we may now expect that these stoppages will be swept away in this new outpouring of creativeness on the mental and spiritual planes. We must expect that when the molds are broken, this great upwelling fountain of creativeness will find continually new and more beautiful methods of incarnating itself.

This is the reason that the hour of destiny has struck for the whole New Thought and Metaphysical field of service. We have the message free of the forms of the past. Will we drop our nonessential differences in methods and speak our word with power to a world so much needing its life-giving ministrations?

The first step in the evolution of religion was from the superstitious worship of Gods many, to the worship and recognition of the One God. The second movement has stressed the importance of beholding God concretely and realistically incarnated in man, as Jesus the Christ, the Wayshower, the first perfect incarnation of the man idea. But the second step began to deteriorate when it moved into the *worship of the Man himself* in place of pointing to the *principle* and the *ideal* which he was functioning. The third step has been the recognition of the deeper implications of Jesus' message, and that it may be expressed in the significant phrase, "God-in-me." This realization of God power in every individual is certainly the very essence of the forward movement of religion in our day.

The whole metaphysical field of religious and philosophic thought has its reason for being in the emphasis of this new phase of religious development—God self-realized and incarnated within each individual who will learn to handle creativeness for cosmic ends. It was very natural that when this tremendous, this all-inclusive idea of creativeness in Man began to dawn upon the minds of individuals here and there, they should feel it a prophetic message. It was very natural also that groups following the emphasis of some leader should unify themselves about the one new aspect of Truth he was giving. So we find different organizations known as New Thought, Unity, Divine Science, Religious Science, Absolute Science, Mental Science, or groups under any other one of a dozen different labels. The central purposive drive of each of these schools of teaching is ways and means of making Mind or Spirit operative in the creation of a new world—personal, social, economic and political.

The shadings of thought and the techniques in which these schools of thought differ are of minor importance; *the points of agreement are fundamental and basic* and all draw from a few simple principles. It might be said that the points in which they differ, move about two different centers of approach; the one a religious approach, putting emphasis upon Jesus and his teaching of the Christ Principle; and the other making a scientific approach, with emphasis upon the power of mind to create. Yet any thorough-going appraisal of the teachings of Jesus and of the Christ Principle lead one inevitably to a realization of the creativeness of mind and the techniques by which this process goes on. And, on the other hand, any complete and adequate use of mental law as a means whereby man joins himself to the universal creativeness, must inevitably move one back to a new concept of man—man as perfect Man—incarnated and created under Law, as the Christ Principle.

So the whole New Thought and Metaphysical field is rapidly moving closer and closer together, exchanging thoughts, accepting views from one another, assimilating as good scientists should, all contributions to a field of thought in which the final test is after all pragmatic. Essentially, this field is one army of workers and world servers moving toward the New Age in which individual Man shall recognize the God Principle within himself and shall know exactly how to make it operate creatively to the establishment of peace, power and plenty, not alone for the individual but for the building of a new society in which there shall be absolute brotherhood and in which war shall be unknown.

The New Thought field as a whole in all its branches is making available the most marvelous principle in the universe, *the creativeness of Mind or Spirit*, and whether one describe it in terms of the Son, the Christ Consciousness, and the Jesus Christ Principle on one hand, or as the Law of Creative Mind in Action —the law of the universe in creative operation through man—it matters little.

The natural scientist is in some ways wiser than we who work in a more intangible world of mind and spirit. The biologists and chemists do not quarrel with one another because different individuals in their field are experimenting with or are in process of discovery of some differing aspects of their science. They are saying implicitly, "Here before us is the universe, the truth is in it, we are forever probing to find new aspects of that truth and to record them. It is a universe of law and the test after all is not any individual's *opinion*, not any set of *authorities* that draw from the past, or from organizations of the present. The test of truth is after all the recognition that Truth IS, and that our only proof that we are thinking and living in tune with this universal order is after all the pragmatic test. If we are true to the truth as we see it, if we constantly test it out in the laboratory of life, we shall each and all of us be making our contribution to the race knowledge and to this particular field of thought, and shall be one with all others as the universe we work in is One."

If we in the New Thought field increasingly take this scientific attitude, if we will be clear that there is only one essential essence in the universe, only one system of truth within it, only one set of principles, only one perfect way for operating it, then we shall have an essentially scientific approach to religion, and what is more important, *be making our contribution in this age to the science and art of living*, in tune with the Infinite Order.

Our purpose is a common purpose. We are all describing the same thing; we are all attempting to state the truth in so simple a fashion that it may be made available to increasing thousands of people. Our one purpose held in common is that we may serve humanity by revealing to men the secret of their being. Whether we describe these deep truths in terms of mind or in terms of the teachings of Jesus, we are all approaching the same set of laws; we are all realizing that they are already inherent in man and need only to be recognized and manifested to make possible the building of this new society and a marvelous new world order.

We must furthermore see that there is room for each one of the many differing points of view; for it is one of the principles of teaching that *we must teach in terms of the listener's experience*. The men and women who need this message differ in their degrees of development, in their levels of consciousness, in their backgrounds of experience. Some people with a religious background have been saturated with the symbols and the thought of Christianity; they quite naturally must receive this message' in terms of that with which they are familiar. Many other people think they have rejected Christianity, not understanding its true inner significance; they imagine that they are through with all religion; they will therefore more readily receive this great message of Man and his relationship to the universe in terms of the symbols and techniques of natural science. The New Thought field is therefore now seeing that each one of the varying schools of thought and each one of the approaches to this great Truth has its place for it is attracting and serving certain people whom no other group could perhaps serve. Our points of agreement are always in principles; our differences are merely differences in the language and the techniques which we use for the imparting of these principles to others.

What the world needs in our day as much as any other one thing is a unified and an enlightened teaching as to the nature of Man. Dr. Alexis Carrel has made that necessity very apparent from the point of view of natural science in his wonderful book, "Man, the Unknown." The teaching of the New Thought field, if it could be unified, would furnish the keystone in the arch, which is wholly wanting in the very enlightened teachings of modern science. We have a contribution which should be unified, correlated and presented with power to a world in great need of this message. In order to do this, there should be a stronger central organization which could systematically forward the teaching by field lecturers, radio programs, books, and strictly modern educational methods.

This whole field of thought is rapidly realizing that the central thesis of its teaching is the oneness of God, the divinity of Man, and the availability of limitless power through certain definite techniques of creativeness by which man joins God in the unfoldment of the creative process and the building of a New Order here upon the earth. The minor differences of approach merely enrich us all with tools, if the individuals behind these teachings will but realize *that we are all one even as the Source from which we draw is one.*

Our first great need today is the realization by every one in the field that we are all one, one because we are subscribing to the next great forward movement in the unfoldment of man and his powers.

Second, we need an organization strong enough to forward in business-like and systematic fashion the broadcasting of this great message to our world.

Third, we need schools which will without fear or favor and from a wholly impartial point of view represent *all aspects of this thought.* We should prepare workers and teachers for the age that is now upon us, who shall know and be thoroughly grounded in

(a) A religious approach based upon the teachings of Jesus and a broad knowledge of the relationships of our thought to the religious thought of the world.

(b) Courses which approach this teaching from the point of view of the science of mind and the laws of creativeness, as constituting a new field of spiritual psychology.

(c) Courses in personality integration showing how these laws of mind may be correlated with the teachings of Jesus and with the accepted ethical and moral teachings of the past and present, revealing how individual man may reeducate the whole self, dissolve the old instinct life and the race consciousness, and ridding himself of prejudice and intolerance, place himself in living relationship to the world of mind and spirit.

(d) A science of society and government based upon the principles which Jesus enunciated and which are so evidently embodied in the very nature of man himself and in his relationship to his God. Certainly any new society must be built upon these principles. Equally surely the modern teaching of sociology will not reach and help people as it might until it accepts the teachings of the Nazarene.

(e) The teaching of a science and art of meditation, of prayer and treatment. There is here from the psychological point of view a real science. If we are to help other people to get the best out of their own minds and find easily and quickly a dynamic relationship with the Mind and Spirit of the Universe, there must be training based upon law.

(f) Last of all, a broad and undogmatic correlation of the many approaches to metaphysics, as related to philosophy, theology, psychology, and the natural sciences, and a final theory of how the Word incarnates itself in Action.

The New Thought field has made a great contribution to the world's thought. The time is here when this contribution must be made available to millions of seeking souls. It must be systematically broadcast, not alone to the few but to the multitudes who are hungry for some practical method of approach which shall make available a new type of living—a life deeply aware of its devotional and operative unity with the One. This is one of the greatest moments of need in the history of the world. We have the message that meets the need. Are we big enough and selfless enough to deliver it?

SEVEN STEPS TO SELF-FULFILLMENT
BY J. B. GOLDSTONE

J. B. Goldstone is National Secretary of the Canadian Metaphysical Alliance, at Winnipeg, Manitoba and editor of its official journal, *Triumphant Living*. From 1926-31 lectured on religion, health and psychology in the principal Canadian cities. Elected National Secretary of the C.M.A. in 1936 which office he still holds. Ordained by the Church of Advanced Thought, Winnipeg, 1938. Is a member of the faculty of the Institute of Metaphysics, Winnipeg, and Fellow of the National College, Toronto.

IT is not metaphysicians alone who hold, with Emerson, that "the key to every man is his thought." There is a universal acceptance of the fact that the deeds of men, whether performed individually or collectively, find their source in the thoughts (or principles) which motivate them. This is a rather formal and elaborate way of saying what Solomon said far more appealingly: "As a man thinketh in his heart, so is he."

The following principles seem to be universally valid, universally true, and therefore universally acceptable.

1. That God is Omnipresent, Omniscient, Omnipotent law or good;
2. That all men are divine;
3. That Truth and Reality are never contrary to science and reason;
4. That "as a man thinketh in his heart, so is he";
5. That Divine Healing is the result of definite and unfailing laws;
6. That good can be furthered on earth by studying, rewarding and exalting goodness;

7. That the Church should be an institution for service to humanity in every way that humanity needs service.

(Article 6, paragraph b of the Memorandum of Agreement and By-Laws of the Canadian Metaphysical Alliance)

FROM PRINCIPLE TO PRACTICE

How and why will the clear understanding and persistent application of the seven principles stated above contribute toward the realization (or demonstration) of Life More Abundant? I have arranged my answer under seven headings.

1. Identification

When man really knows who he is, and can affirm from a deep spiritual consciousness that "the Father and I are one," all things become possible to him. All power is given to him who is attuned to the source of All Being. This identification, this affirmation of direct relationship to Divine Mind, is the very first step toward participation in the Divine Life. Some call it the *Good Life Universal*, others the *Godly Life*, and still others the *Kingdom of Heaven*. The important thing is not the term used for it, but an intense consciousness of our kinship with the Father and of our part in the establishment of His Kingdom. A truly inspired writer, Dr. C. F. Potter, has said: "If you can feel yourself a child of the universe, or as some put it, a son of God, you'll never feel unrelated anywhere." You will cast off all sense of separateness, and will know the joy of being one with "all there is." You will know what it means to "be still, and know that I am God." Your demonstrations on the plane of everyday living will be successful in direct proportion to your concept of Ultimate Reality. *"We never get what we long for until we have a sense of belonging."*

2. Recognition

To affirm your own kinship with the Father, and at the same time to doubt or deny its existence in your fellow man, is to miss the whole essence and the major purpose of Christ's teachings. All of us, regardless of color or race, creed or caste, are children of the same Father. All of us are participants in the same Divine Life. Without this recognition of the Fatherhood of God, we have no valid or lasting foundation for the Brotherhood of Man. And Christ knew that without the Brotherhood of all men there could be no Kingdom of Heaven on earth.

3. Knowledge

It seems to me that every branch of the modern metaphysical and New Thought movement accepts the principle that "knowledge is a function of being." The New Thought leaders were great pioneers in urging their followers to "lay the foundations in Wisdom for the Affirmations of Faith." They were among the first to turn their churches into classrooms for mental culture, as well as "houses of devotion." They took the view that all education was, in the larger sense, Religious Education. Their advanced thinking in this respect is endorsed in the practice of nearly every liberal church in the world today, regardless of denomination. No longer does the charge hold good that the church is an enemy of education. There is scarcely a church to be found in the larger cities, which does not sponsor courses in cultural subjects—that does not have its discussion groups, and other adult educational activities, such as lectures on literature, sociology, psychology, and current events.

The message of New Thought has always been: *to improve our circumstances, we must first increase our knowledge and enlarge our consciousness.* We must learn to use our powers of thought and of creative imagination (which have been rightly called "Divine faculties of the human mind") for the achievement of all worthy desires. We cannot live up to our highest potentialities until the mind is trained to understand and to use its inherent powers for creative and constructive thinking.

And so we attach deep significance to the admonition: "Be ye transformed by the renewing of your mind," because every day in our lives we behold fresh evidence of the miracles wrought by right thinking. "Right thinking is the father of right doing; and right doing results in happiness."

4. Reason

When we declare it to be a fundamental principle that "Truth and Reality are never contrary to science and reason," it is but another way of saying, "Prove all things; hold fast that which is good." (I Thess. 5:21) Paul would surely not have said this, had he not regarded research and reason as important avenues leading to Truth. That there are higher truths and subtler realities than can be perceived by the senses (even when aided by the most powerful of microscopes, the most sensitive of scales, or the most accurate of measuring devices) no one will dispute. Today many of our scientists frequently refer to the superphysical, and for the most part concede the interaction of spiritual law in the natural realm, and natural law in the spiritual realm.

The eminent British philosopher, Havelock Ellis, expressed our viewpoint when he declared: "If at some period in the course of civilization we seriously find that our science and our religion are antagonistic, then there must be something wrong either with our science or with our religion."

We believe it is possible for modern man to live a Christlike life without being compelled to accept any doctrines or dogmas which he feels do violence to his reasoning faculties. There is nothing in the Bible which indicates that Christ demanded the surrender of man's reason as a preliminary condition to his salvation.

"Prove all things" implies a warning against the placid assumption that no effort need be made by the individual to discover Truth for himself. Many are they who would not mind receiving the vital Truth about Life, if they could secure it from a single book, lecture or conversation. But a

lifelong search for the Truth does not appeal to them.

While the fundamental principles of metaphysical Truth can be very quickly stated, they are seldom as quickly assimilated. No truth can be said to belong to us by virtue of the fact that we have heard it stated. *No truth actually becomes our own until we have made it our own*—by weaving it into the very fabric of our lives. Before we can do this, we must feel the need of "educating the whole man throughout his whole life," by a process of continuous research, earnest meditation, prayer for guidance, and the careful testing of vital ideas and ideals in what Dr. Alexis Carrel has so aptly termed "the laboratory of our own lives." As we progress in our quest for genuine self-fulfillment, we keep on adding to the hard won and experience-tested truths of everyday life, those higher truths wherein we perceive "the mystical union of the soul with the integrating Principle of all being." Having done this, we have at last won through to the Truth that sets us free from all bondage, all limitation.

5. *Healing*

In affirming the healing power of spiritual Truth, the Canadian Metaphysical Alliance declares that "Divine healing is a result of the use of definite and unfailing laws." To understand the essential meaning of health, we must think of it as *harmony*. You must think of good health as a combination of mental, physical and spiritual harmony. Otherwise, you are apt to seek health through the cultivation of just one type of harmony, at the expense of the others.

Modern psychiatry recognizes that many mental ailments tend to masquerade as purely physical disorders—and they know that any attempt to treat a mental disease by means of surgery, drugs or diet, is utterly futile. On the other hand, we think it is also true that even though the laws of mental and spiritual health be observed, if the laws relating to sound physical health (balanced diet, sufficient exercise, air, sunshine, rest, etc.) are grossly neglected, the offender is bound to pay for his violation of what is truly another aspect of Divine Law. For good health is a state of harmony, achieved through Right Thinking, Right Eating—in short, it is a compound of every physical, mental and spiritual factor that comes under the heading of *Right Living.*

"Mind not only makes sick, it also cures." All health finds its origin in the mind of man, rightly attuned to the definite and unfailing laws of God. It is the considered opinion of one of America's foremost psychiatrists, Dr. Karl A. Menninger, that "religion will long continue to supply the healing of the nations to a far greater extent than will psychiatry."

In the matter of health, as with every other vital concern of Life, the law of Sowing and Reaping cannot be evaded. One cannot sow the mental, physical or spiritual seeds of disease, and expect to reap the rich blessings of radiant health. On the other hand, one cannot escape possessing God's Gift of perfect health— if he is intent upon achieving the state of Harmony from whence all health proceeds.

Man's body is indeed his holy temple, and it is equally certain that "every function of it, every cell of it, is intelligent, and is shaped, ruled, repaired, and controlled by mind."

6. Life More Abundant

The New Thought Philosophy is "the philosophy of the Good Life," translated into terms which give it a direct bearing upon the individual's conduct in everyday life. It is a philosophy which affirms that man was made to rejoice, not to mourn—and that the real test of any religion or philosophy is in what it adds to the health, the happiness and spiritual advancement of the individual who bases his life upon its fundamental principles. *"By their fruits ye shall know them."*

The New Thought philosophy does not picture man as innately depraved, an object of celestial wrath, or a plaything of the gods. It derives unlimited inspiration from the Psalmist's declaration: "I have said, Ye are gods; and all of you are children of the Most High." It therefore looks upon man as a Creative Force in a friendly universe, ever evolving from the lower to the higher, ever reaping in accordance with his sowing, and ever aspiring toward that Christlike consciousness from whence is derived the manifestation of the Kingdom in the here and now.

7. Salvation Through Unselfish Service

The source of the Kingdom of Heaven is in the Great Within. For Heaven is not a place on the map, but a condition of one's consciousness and cooperation with the Divine Plan. The demonstration of this high degree of Heaven-consciousness is achieved through the Law of Giving. Just as man is enjoined not to live by bread alone, neither is he to attempt living for himself alone. Nor is it enough for him to be a passive hearer of the Word; he must also become an active doer, else the words he hears (or uses) are just so much sounding brass or tinkling cymbals. The words we speak and the deeds we perform must never contradict each other. They must be made to harmonize to the *nth* degree. How else is the Word to be "made flesh" and to dwell among us, unless we make a genuine effort to incorporate what we believe into what we do?

The supreme Law of Life is not that of Getting, but of *Giving*. Rev. E. Stanley Jones once sought to express the very essence of Christianity in a four-word sentence: *"Be Christlike—give thyself!"* Jesus gave himself, unstintingly and without reservations, to the service of all mankind, that by his example we might know and understand the full purpose and the true meaning of his ministry, namely, that "Love is the fulfilling of the law."

When we say that the Church should be an institution for the service to humanity in every way that humanity needs service, we feel we have expressed the only valid reason for the existence of the Church. For, in our view, the Church is not a building, but a fellowship of devotion to the service of humanity. The true spirit of service is immortalized in the following couplet by Edwin Markham:

> "Do something, brother, to befit
> An offspring of the infinite."

You can have no better reason than that for being (or becoming) identified with any church, with any branch of the great Truth movement, or with any movement that is soundly and sincerely dedicated to the betterment of human life through the rendering of Christlike service in a Christlike manner. The Christlike manner is clearly suggested in Matthew, Chapter 23, Verse 11: "He that is great among you, shall be your servant"—the servant of *all*, including the "least of these."

In keeping with its happy and affirmative philosophy of Life More Abundant, the New Thought movement does not think of "service to humanity" in terms of painful and unprofitable self-sacrifice, but rather in terms of joyful and infinitely profitable self-fulfillment.

This glorious attitude is illustrated by an incident in the life of the late Sir Wilfred Grenfell, famed for his selfless devotion to the humble fisher-folk living on the bleak coast of Labrador; his founding of their hospitals; his establishing of their nursing stations, orphanages, schools, and even their cooperative stores.

Once, after Dr. Grenfell had concluded a lecture in Philadelphia, a wealthy woman exclaimed, "Oh, Dr. Grenfell, how *noble* of you to sacrifice yourself for these poor people!"

Dr. Grenfell drew himself up and said: "Sacrifice? Oh, no! Let me tell you, my good lady, that I am having the time of my life!"

Such, then, is our ideal of joyous service. And we think Dr. Grenfell was equally right in his belief that the final judgment of an altogether righteous Judge would be based, not upon "Well Believed," but upon "Well Done."

MY VISION OF THE TRUTH
BY ALBERT C. GRIER

Reverend Albert Cotton Grier, best known as the founder of "The Church of Truth," at Spokane, Washington. Graduate of the University of Michigan. For years teacher of the sciences, botany, chemistry and physics also author of a laboratory manual in physics. Now prominent in national religious circles having been twenty-five years a minister of the Universalist Church and later connected with the Oxford Group. Also he established churches at Coeur d'Alene, Idaho, and New York City and from 1912-31 he published *The Truth Magazine*, and is author of the books: *Truth and Life, Truth's Cosmology, The Truth Way, and The Spirit of the Truth.* Now living at Redlands, California.

I WAS born in a very promising field, religiously. My parents were Universalists and I came naturally into it. I never can get *out* of it. It was not a seat for my soul but an arrow pointing the way. It not only told me of God's love for all of His children but that He was concerned with each individual's unfoldment, and *that* came from the within and not from the without in men or things. Then when I learned the relationship between my thoughts and my well-being, everyman's thoughts and his health, I naturally went on to everyman's affairs and his destiny.

At first, I saw the implications for earthly things but it would not end there. The great sweep of eternity was its only limitation. I saw, as Herbert Spencer had said, that nothing was true that was not eternal, and that everything of the world-expression vanished with time and experience and entered into a field without limitation. And so the answer for Time is Eternity, the answer for the three dimensions is in the fourth dimension, or rather in the dimensionless realm of the Spirit.

So now I could no longer put my faith in the temporal. Not from teaching but from necessity I must put my faith in that which is not only the good of life but the origin of being. I now saw that religion (so wonderfully named "rebinding") was not a separate and subliminal thing but was simply the right understanding of Life. That its laws were not things we merely hoped were right, but I found that obedience to them was a laying hold on the very nature of Reality, which alone could be found in Eternality.

When this discovery came to me, through many experiences which had soul-awakening power to me, I established *The Church of The Truth*. I was like a chick just emerging from the shell which material philosophy had built around my soul and which was destined to be broken by the process of Life. I felt I had never lived before and I was right, except for those premonitions of Eternity which had stirred within me. It would be hard for a chick to relate the new life to the old but I tried to do it. But it was only as I saw that the Spirit of the New had always operated in the Old that my life became oriented. I saw that by right thought I could obtain, or rather realize, health and all the good my life required. *But I soon learned that I could have right thought only as I lived my interior life in the very atmosphere of the Abiding Presence.* That I must act and think in the atmosphere of the Eternal; in other words I must give my very being over to that Spirit which brought the Universe into being.

It followed that the All could know no evil, could think no error and so if I were to enter into His way, that secret way of thinking and living must be mine. Some *Contract*, but I made it and gave my life to introducing this way of thinking and living to every living soul. A glorious work and I have lived to see an age in which countless thousands are so thinking and living. Emerson had caught a great part of this heavenly vision and he had led many to the Higher Level. Then, more in the line of conduct than of spiritual perception, Abraham Lincoln lived this vision out. And when he told his wife, when she would have kept him from signing the Emancipation Proclamation, "I must. I am a man under orders," he simply declared the Way.

It is obvious that this, The Truth, is a matter not of teaching but of revealing. Not an artificial revealing, but rather of the nature of that which comes to the inventor when he has made himself ready for the knowledge that comes to him, or as Emerson has said, "when due preparation has been made." One can make due preparation by certain methods which we proceeded to teach. First, a giving of ourselves to the higher life. And this is vital and must be complete, a complete surrender of that lower self which eventuates in failure, sickness, wars and broken human relations. As daring as it may seem, we are impelled to recognize and proclaim that as the path to those human failures is the breaking of the oneness of the soul with God, the freedom from them can come by no other means than through that reunion, rebinding, at-one-ment of the self with its Source. And this the voluntary and glad action of the soul.

Healing is not the whole of Truth but is a clarion call to the Truth. And so we boldly claim healing power for Truth and risk our all in the claim. But Truth is so much bigger than bodily healing. It is a circle without circumference but not without a center. God is that center. Nothing short of God can contain the Allness that the Universe contains. To see healing as all of Truth is to miss the great vision.

This is true of every element of the soul, success, education and every conceivable attribute of the nature of man, God-sized man. Jesus can only be understood as we see him. as he claimed--- "I and my Father are One." Not *like* his father but *one with Him*, and he takes another step that goes with it—"I and you are One." He seldom made use of the God-claim but many times called himself the Son of Man. To say that Jesus revealed God is true, but even more true it is that He revealed man.

So while it is true that healing is a result of psychology it has its origin in the Spiritual nature of the Universe, which is to say in the unity of man with God. Men seek to find a union between a man's thoughts and his business. Perhaps that is the next step in the evolution of man's consciousness. But man does not succeed by psychology but through psychology and the true psychology is, as its name indicates, the speaking of the soul. And as in the final analysis health is primarily soul wholeness, business is soul activity. This same line of procedure is applicable to every department of man's activity.

War, which seems so far from the soul, is now being seen to be the soul out of harmony with itself and so with others. In our private relationships this great sequence is now being seen. And so we to whom it was given to discern the fundamental sequence did a noble but very daring thing. We abandoned all of the lesser ways of peace, prosperity and health and took the subliminal one of the soul. And the day of this administration has but begun. Things beyond the scope of human sight are in the offing. We see that every quality of the soul has its field and method here.

The story of the Tower of Babel is no fancy. Man with his tremendous power has tried to build "the house not made with hands" with tools that fail. No power of body, of heart or mind can build that house. It will fall to pieces unless it is builded of soul and by its laws. Not only is it impossible to build it otherwise but the qualities it must display are of a beauty, a strength and a perpetuity that transcend our finite comprehension.

Yes, we gladly set man free from his illnesses by its power. When we witness the hospitals and pain of the human body it would seem that no greater joy could come than to set man free, but there is a field of such exquisite fineness that we breathe again the scripture words— "eye hath not seen nor ear heard." Not even the allurement of man's peace needs, when peace means simply non-fighting, can compass the peace that Jesus knew as he said, "Peace, my peace, I give unto you. Not as the world giveth, give

I unto you." And it embraces every relationship, all discord, all conflict, all friction, individual and class and nation in its scope.

Our eye beholds a new picture, not the old one polished up but a new one that cannot ever be covered or destroyed. This is the Kingdom of Heaven which Jesus tried to make clear to man but it can only be seen by eyes baptized by Truth. And it is to the supreme task of causing man's eyes to be thus anointed and so his life to be thus glorified that we of The Church of The Truth have dedicated our lives. Not just to cure all diseases or to quell all quarrels or to stop all wars or to build everyone a beautiful home or to fill all mouths, *but through the demonstration of Truth's Power to do these things, to bring to man the means of the supreme things which are the goal of all life.* As we know that it is not a match alone that kindles a fire but the combustibility of fuel combined with it, and as we see how eager the souls of men are for this vision, as shown in the vast multitudes that embrace it, we are made to know the truth of the Truth and to see the fulfillment of the promise of Jesus Christ, the Master Man of the Universe, that "Ye *shall* know the Truth and the Truth *shall* make you free."

THE PATHWAY OF SPIRITUAL PROGRESS
BY AGNES BARTON HASKELL

Reverend Agnes Barton Haskell, leader of Unity Truth Center, Holyoke, Mass. for the past sixteen years. President of the New England Federation of New Thought Centers for two years. Member of the executive Board of I.N.T.A. 1936 to 1938. Twenty years active service in Truth work teaching, preaching, and healing.

I FEEL I can best explain what I teach and why, by telling you first of my own healing experience which brought me into this work we love so much.

This experience taught me many lessons which I now teach to others. One lesson was the power of right thinking; others the power of the spoken word, the value of persistency, and the realization that "with God all things are possible."

For nearly two years I remained the most of the time in bed, in the little town of Rockport, Massachusetts. About eighteen years ago I had become a hopeless, helpless, incurable cripple in the home of my father and mother. During the time that I was going down hill in consciousness, growing weaker in body, having my limbs draw up and joints stiffen, in bitterness and discouragement I was separating myself from God. Before I had reached this helpless, hopeless condition and was up and around the house, I had torn my Bible in two and thrown it away, for I was angry at God! Then it was that I grew weaker and at last was confined to my bed, for you see I had willfully separated myself from God, the source of all life.

Perhaps many of us must go to the extreme limit of apparent separation from our good before we give God an opportunity to help us. This need not be so. "An ounce of prevention is worth a pound of cure;" therefore, I teach that to know the only true God, and to understand Jesus Christ and what be taught, is life eternal HERE AND NOW. "There is but one God, the Father, in Whom are all things, and we in Him."

There came a night when I forgot that I had said I would never pray again. I found my dear, unselfish mother was to be rushed to a Boston hospital the following morning for a major operation. I prayed! This was my first prayer for months and months, although I had been brought up in a minister's family. I had been a teacher in Sunday School, a leader of young people's meetings, and I was called by my father his pastor's assistant. Now, as I prayed, I seemed to have a mental moving picture. I was carried back to a little country church in Maine where I was standing on the platform behind the pulpit, looking down into the corner of the room where my Sunday School class used to meet. There I saw myself with the other girls of ten to twelve years of age. I saw the beautiful face and snow white hair of the teacher, as she seemed to close a book. Pointing her finger at us she said, "Now remember, girls, the point of the lesson is this, Jesus Christ gave thanks BEFORE He raised Lazarus from the dead." Then the picture faded, and I wondered why I should have gone in thought and vision back to the Sunday School class of my childhood. All at once it dawned on me that the Spirit was showing me why my prayers have not been answered. And right then and there, I prayed not only for my mother's safe return to health and strength, but for my own also. From that time on, until I could walk freely and return to a normal life once more, I did not have the help of medicine, massage, or any kind of outside help. It was seven months after the time of my prayer, and thanksgiving to God, before I could walk without a limp and say that the demonstration had been made.

In looking back over that seven months, I find I did three things: first, I made my request known; I gave thanks for the answer; and then I made "decrees." The spirit of truth within me called to remembrance every helpful Bible verse, poem, or motto I ever knew that could help me.

I made my request for health, strength, and happiness. Then I recalled "judge not by appearances," "if you are weak declare you are strong," "decree a thing and it shall be established unto you." In making my request I used the verse, "Send out Thy Light and Thy Truth; let them lead me." For a decree, I used one a friend sent me in a letter, "The Spirit goes before and makes the way plain, easy, happy and successful." Many times the words of Emerson were a help to me: "Do the thing and thou wilt be given the power."

At one time during the convalescent period, I felt discouraged because I could not see that any progress had been made for some little time. Then because I continued faithfully to make my request known, to make my decree, and to give my thanks for answered prayer, encouragement came to me in the gift of a Truth hymn book in which I found the words, "Unanswered yet, but do not say ungranted. For God will finish what He has begun." With fresh courage I went on until the perfect manifestation.

And so I teach the request, the decree, and praise with thanksgiving, as a method of procedure for those that need, as I did at that time, something to hold to, something to work with.

In time, we all find that we work free from a method, as we do from the repeating of our multiplication tables, because it becomes a part of us.

I believe the highest type of prayer is the contemplation of God. "God is spirit." "Do I not fill heaven and earth? saith the Lord." "For in Him we live, and move and have our being." "He that cometh to God must believe that He is." "The Lord is good." "God is love." "Is there anything too hard for the Lord?" "With God all things are possible." After meditation along this line, I treat in the same way any and all conditions needing treatment, either for myself or any one else who has asked my cooperation: "God's glorious, wonderful, joyful, loving will be done in you, through you, for you, by you and as you, now and always."

If we can say with all our hearts, "Thy Will be done," knowing that God's will for ALL His children includes all the blessings we are seeking, then we truly can rejoice. "Delight thyself in the Lord, and He shall GIVE THEE the desires of thine heart." God gave us free will, but the most wonderful thing about that gift is the privilege we have of surrendering it to His Divine Wisdom and Divine Love. In the words of the old hymn, "Our wills are ours to make them Thine."

Instead of adding to your list of worries the fear that your faith is not equal to the overcoming of some seeming problem, you may take the words, "I believe, 0 Lord, help Thou mine unbelief." You do believe in the Power, Wisdom and Love of God. Your fear is, that you will not understand your part and therefore will not cooperate in bringing the desired results to pass. "I believe, 0 Lord, help Thou mine unbelief."

Often meditation with words, followed by meditation without words, brings a realization of fulfillment. The demonstration is finished. I think most of us find it sometimes takes more meditation with words before we can realize the omnipresence of Good, than it does at other times. This again, is a procedure which becomes a part of ourselves and we shall know "the fullness of God" in every area of our lives.

It is for *all* to know "the love of Christ, which passeth knowledge, that ye might be filled with all the fullness of God." How do we know that *all* shall "know the love of Christ"? and "be filled with all the fullness of God"? I think the stories of the prodigal son and the ninety and nine give us that assurance. It is our separation from God (in consciousness) that causes lack of any good thing or condition. Our return to our Heavenly Father in prayer and meditation, brings us to the door that always stands open for "no man can close it." And there we find Divine Love and all the "added things," as food, raiment, and even the golden ring. For those who are unable to find their way back to the fold of rejoicing with all its added blessings, the story of the ninety and nine is given us. The good shepherd will never be satisfied with ninety and nine, but will go forth and search for the last one and bring him home. *"All* the kindred of the nations shall worship before thee." *"All* shall know me from the least to the greatest." "If I be lifted up . . . will draw *all* men unto me." And Jesus *was* lifted up!

How wonderful to know we may be freed from all the results of our many past mistakes, by calling for and accepting the government of our own indwelling Christ, in our lives and world. We have our choice, Christ or Karma—"Choose ye this day whom you will serve." I remember my great joy in finding the following Bible verse, for I believed we had this choice, but I had never found the verse that proved it as I wished it proved. I found it in the Thirteenth Chapter of Acts: "Be it known unto you therefore, men and brethren, that through this man (Jesus Christ) is preached unto you the forgiveness of sins (our mistakes). And by him all that believe are justified from all things, from which ye could not be justified by the law of Moses."

The dear Sunday School teacher of my childhood days knew God as a Power and Presence in her life. One evening, while seated in the alcove on the second floor of her home, the electric lights went out. She waited for them to come on, but finally she noticed that they were also off in the street. Then she started from her desk in the alcove toward her chamber where there were matches and a gas jet, but before reaching the door she made the mistake of stepping off the first step of the stairs and pitching head first to a landing half way down the stairs. Her two daughters, who were elsewhere in the house, heard the fall and realized their mother must have tried to walk in the dark and had fallen downstairs. By the time they reached her the lights returned, and they found their mother with a smile on her face, brushing off her clothes, and unhurt. Knowing their mother's great faith and her understanding of God, they asked her what were her thoughts when she found herself falling head first down the stairs. Laughingly she replied that her first thought was, "I am falling down the stairs," but her second thought which she carried with her from stair to stair was, "I am falling into God, I am falling into God."

Here was one who realized that she lived, moved and had her being in Him. In this particular instance did she not find God as divine protection? We may learn to know God not only as protection, but as divine guidance, as healing power, as abundance, as peace, joy, love and wisdom.

I heard of a young mother who has been a faithful follower of the Truth teachings for many years. Not only does she hold her own daily Silence for all her needs and desires, but always includes her husband and his affairs, and, of course, the health and protection of her baby girl. One morning she placed the baby in the carriage where the little daughter often had her nap on pleasant days. She pushed the carriage close to the back door of her home, saying over and over, "I clothe you safely round with Infinite Love and Wisdom." An hour later, while making a bed, the mother felt the urge to hurry from the room, leaving her work unfinished. Then, without apparent reason, she went out and moved the carriage back under an apple tree quite a distance from the house. When she turned back to the house, she heard a loud crash, and saw a large number of bricks fall in the very place where only a few minutes before the baby had been peacefully asleep. She did not know that the landlord had sent a man to repair the top of the kitchen chimney and had not heard him on the roof. The little one *was* "clothed safely round with Infinite Love and Wisdom."

"For He shall give His angels charge over thee, to keep thee in all thy ways." "Who so hearkeneth unto Me shall dwell securely, and shall be quiet without fear of evil."

Jesus Christ never taught that we must wait until after our birth into the next expression of life, before we can be healed of evil, error, inharmony, failure or lack. "Now is the accepted time, now is the day of Salvation," were His words. Surely God's work is finished in us now. What we acknowledge and persistently declare is done now, we shall see fulfilled.

The Divine Power that dwells in us and is called by some "that something within," is a Master Mind and an Almighty Power. "Let that mind be in you which was also in Christ Jesus." "Christ (acknowledged) in you, your hope of glory." And Jesus said, "The Father in me, he doeth the works" and "The Father and I are one." "The works that I do shall ye do also." "Make your request known unto me." No one can say "me" for us. We are to make our requests known unto the Life, Power and Intelligence that enables us to speak the word "me."

Indwelling Mind sees to it that we have "Conscious Omniscience, Direct Knowledge of Truth, Spiritual Perception, and Perfect Intuition." Thus we unfold into the power of the Perfect Life, and the Kingdom of Heaven Consciousness brings us the outer manifestation of the Kingdom of Heaven with all its added blessings.

Our pathway of spiritual progress brings us into the realization that God the Good is ALL and in ALL. His will for us is something Wonderful and Joyful now and always. "Prove me now herewith . . . if I will not open you the windows of heaven and pour you out a blessing, that *there shall not be room enough to receive it.*"

The Lord IS our strength and our power. He maketh our way perfect.

NEW THOUGHT THE MODERN ACTION OF THE INDWELLING CHRIST
BY DANIEL BOONE HERRING

Daniel Boone Herring, Dean of Religious Philosophy of the College of Universal Truth of Chicago, Ill. For over forty years he has devoted special study and research to the Christine dialogues of the Four Gospels of the Christian Bible. The result of his studies, have been such books as: *"Mind Surgery," "Arise and Walk," "Key to a New Life," "The Thirteenth Man."* Now residing in Los Angeles and continuing his writing and healing.

MODERN metaphysics has a tendency to turn the minds of its students entirely away from the world. This taking of untrained minds and directing them away from the obvious, apparent, and present is not making for permanent results, for the student who does this flies back to the visible world with greater tenacity than ever, as soon as he discovers that mind is to be used for thinking, and that the obvious, the apparent, the present and the physical and material world are just as useful as ever.

Another erroneous idea with which I have had to deal all through my work is that the student seems to think that there is some mysterious Law which the practitioner can invoke, which will relieve the student of responsibility, and which will make him free from the obligations of life and its problems. As far as I know, *there is no law which will enable any man or woman to escape the responsibilities of life.*

The sum of all Jesus taught may be summed up in these words: "The Father and I are one." God is not one person or thing and you another person or thing—you are one in essence and fact. There is nothing in all the teachings of Jesus indicating that he at any time considered the Mind of God or the mind of man in any terms other than unity. It was this understanding of the complete unity of God and man that enabled Jesus to become the Christ.

Life does not mean to "have and to hold." Life means to *be* and *become*. Man is limited only by his mental concepts; God has placed no limitations upon his creations or his resources. To discover this, means to be born again, born into freedom out of bondage, born into health out of disease, born into abundance out of limiting poverty, born into manhood and womanhood out of automatic robots who jump and jerk and die when others speak the word of command. We may learn through the experience of others, but we grow only through our own.

Let us cease then from seeing limitation in any direction. Let us cease from the senseless effort to get things and begin to act like gods instead of robots. Let us begin to see what we can give, and start the limitless well of refreshment within our own souls to flowing outward.

Did you ever hear of an oak tree going back into an acorn? Well, our effort to get things and put things inside of us is just the same kind of a violation of the law of growth as it would be if the oak tree tried to "get" what was outside of it inside of it, and then crawl back into the acorn. The law of life is expression of the livingness at the center to an ever-widening circumference without.

The work of Jesus was to address the ever-radiant son of God in every one—here was the secret of his power to heal. He judged nothing save the wholeness, the superlative degree of spiritual completeness in every one. His vision was so fixed upon the Father's presence in every atom of matter, in every point of space and in every instant of time, that his word acted instantly upon all substance. Even the waves obeyed his strong words of command. Even the apparently dead Lazarus stood forth, radiant and alive, at his strong recognition of the Allness of Life. The man with an apparently withered arm, had merely a withered spot in his mind, and Jesus vivified that atrophied brown spot with his strong realization of the presence of God there. If this living presence of God Almighty is in every atom of matter, how can a single cell of your body be filled with anything less than that living presence? Can you locate that Presence and find its activity in your body if your mind demands of the universal servant that it find germs, parasites, causes of disease?

You can see that it is no longer necessary for you to be acted upon by the hypnosis of suggestion from those who seek the causes of disease. *To hold this mental image of this living, radiant Life in every cell of your body causes all other conditions to drop out and off your body; because this living presence of God's wholeness is a cosmic fact of your being and has more power than the hypnosis of ignorant men.*

This instant of time, as you read these words, this radiant, risen, Son of God stands within every cell of your brain calling, "Awake thou that steepest, and arise from the dead." Life is ever calling you to arise from the grave and experience the cosmic fact of the resurrection. The Resurrection is not a historical fact of one man only—it is a continuous and constant fact of the entire universe. Everything is being resurrected all the time; not an instant in time when something or someone is not being resurrected from the grave of non-recognition.

New Thought is the modern action of the indwelling Christ. It is calling hundreds of thousands of people everywhere to awake, to stand forth, to awaken themselves from the hypnosis of fear, to "see" with the inner eye of mental understanding the folly of fear; to see that doubt itself is a hypnosis; that the whole universe is a living, throbbing, intelligent presence, awaiting the strong words of command and authority of its children.

It is the nature of Infinite Intelligence to flow outward into expression; and you were created for the purpose of letting it do just that. Let things be done for you. Let Life happen. Let your thoughts flow outward and no harm can come to you either from within or without. This is the Divine protection. God cooperates with man when man cooperates with God. All life is this cooperative interaction between God and man.

Life is a great economist; it never duplicates; it tolerates no atom which is not and does not fulfill a cosmic need. Think of it *You* are as necessary to God as God is to you; He needs you—YOU. The cosmos depends upon *you*. Have no fear then of what men may say about you—God is saying: "Thou art my beloved son in whom I am well pleased."

To unify yourself with this Power through mentally seeing it and acknowledging it, is the work we are presenting herewith. Reduced to a mental formula, it amounts to this: I recognize nothing save the superlative degree of the one and only supreme Intelligence in every atom of matter, every point of space and every instant of time, within and without my physical body and all physical bodies. Intelligence cannot act in any manner save intelligently. Therefore, the whole universe serves me and recognizes me as its image and likeness. Intelligence includes order, harmony, poise, balance, abundance, health, happiness, and power and dominion.

* * *

A Description of How I Give A Treatment
"He sent his word and healed them"

I am writing down my manner of "giving a treatment," hoping that it may inspire others to give descriptions of their systems of work, to the end that we all may be helped in the work to which we have consecrated our lives. First, I have given my work a name—"Mind Surgery"—details of which are completely outlined in my book of the same name. This name seems to fit and actually describe my methods of work; seems to describe fully how I give a treatment.

It is fundamentally different from any other method I have ever heard of at any time; different because it utterly ignores any form of diagnosis. I am not interested in what is wrong with the one I am treating. *I know what is right.* I ask for and read the story the student sends in describing his or her problem—but I refuse to let that picture register on my mind, because I am told by Jesus that the law of mind is: "If two of you *agree* as touching anything on earth, it *shall be done of my Father.*" The student is coming to me to be *freed* from that picture which is so indelibly impressed upon his or her mind; hence I cannot afford to *agree* with him if I wish to help him. I do not "deny" the picture, nor mentally claim it to be a dream or an illusion. I know only too well (from personal experience) that it is neither dream nor illusion (to him). I am not afraid of it and I do not recognize it as having any power over either me or the student. I simply look at it for what it appears to be to the student—a very real active thing now present with him, from which he wishes to be free.

Then I enter into a consciousness of *oneness with the Father (in me)*—then I extend this awareness to include the student   (for, the Father is *one*)—thus I mentally locate the living, radiant, risen Christ in the student. The Christ (in him) has overcome the world. The risen Christ (in the student) has more power than the picture he sent to me. My work is done—*I loose him and let him go*—not back into the picture he gave of himself, but I loose him into the *living presence of the risen Christ (in him)*. My work is done. I am joyous because I have practiced with this thing until I can do it in the face of any or every situation and KNOW that the work is done.

I can trust the *Christ*—I have introduced a mental activity in the student which is a *light—a power* greater than the supposed power of the picture he held of himself as being in bondage. I take no burden upon myself, assume no responsibility and ask for and claim no credit. *All glory be to God, radiantly alive*, and about his Father's business in the life of that student. This quickening of the Living Christ in the student through my ministry *cuts out his old picture*, as a surgeon cuts out a diseased tonsil—hence *Mind Surgery*. I forget the written picture the student sent me because I do not let it register in my mind substance. Hence I eternally *salute the risen Christ in all I address.*

I do this and simply this—and do it simply—no more—no less.

At this place I *let go* and *let God* do the work. I do not choose to deal with the problem in any complicated manner, but reduce the whole thing to the utmost simplicity. I refuse to assume the prerogative of telling God just what to do for this student —or how to do it.

I have but this *one treatment*; I use it for anything and everything, from the itch to poverty, loneliness, sin-soaked sensitiveness, inflated egos or deflated egos. I am assured within my own heart that *God knows what He is about* in every one of His children.

I recognize God as the *Absolute*, and each one of us as a "relative" to that Absolute. I recognize that God as the Absolute is consciously and alertly alive in every one, although that one may not be aware or alive to His presence—hence I *know* that the infinite love and tenderness of God overshadows every living creature.

I can utterly and do utterly trust God to do all things, and recognize no situation or negative condition as being too difficult for Him to heal and handle perfectly—regardless of how hopeless the student may appear to be at the time. I feel a sense of total satisfaction after each treatment. God has spoken— it is done. "He sent his word and healed them." My decision upon the matter is final. I will not compromise nor adulterate it with any suggestion from any source whatsoever. God either is or He is not—I choose to assume that He IS.

Life proves He is. My own living experiences have piled almost mountain high the evidences of the efficacy of this method of healing and freeing people from bondage. I rest securely in His love and send forth His word *of healing power* in perfect *peace*, knowing that God *cannot fail.*

"He sent his word and healed them."

(Much of the above material has appeared in my books, "Mind Surgery," and "Arise and Walk.")

AS I SEE IT
BY HARRY GRANISON HILL

Harry Granison Hill, pastor New Thought Temple, Cincinnati, Ohio, since 1927, was born in Indiana. A.B. Bethany College, West Virginia, 1897; A.M. 1900; post graduate work University of Chicago, Indiana University and Columbia; D.D. Austin College, Effingham, Ill., 1904; ordained Christian Ministry (Disciples) 1897; pastor successively at Hebron, Ind., Fergus Street Church, Cincinnati; First Church, Omaha, Nebraska; and Third Church, Indianapolis, Indiana, until 1912; also National Secretary of Education, Disciples Church; Chautauqua lecturer; president Indiana College Music and Fine Arts, Indianapolis; consulting psychologist. A member Delta Tau Delta, Mason 32 Degree. Club: Torch. Author: *Rational Religion, Paradox and Principle, Heart to Heart Talks*. Contributor to philosophic, psychological and religious periodicals. Temple address: McMillan & Woodburn Sts., Cincinnati, Ohio.

IT is not altogether a matter of regret that New Thought resists a clear and concise definition. Definite definition would tend toward dogmatism, and all creedal statements confine and restrict freedom of thought. Those who have taken leading positions in the movement have been, almost universally, independent individualists. They had to be, to be brave enough to rebel against the orthodoxy by which they had been surrounded and conditioned in earlier years. The fortitude of their new found faith tended to strengthen their highly individualistic natures and make them independent in thought and expression.

For these, and perhaps other reasons, anyone who attempts to briefly explain New Thought must of necessity give only his own conception of its philosophy and practice. This must be said, however, that there has never been any considerable effort to standardize New Thought beliefs, and yet the entire movement has automatically reached a considerable unity in diversity. We have all been willing to think and let think. What I shall write is merely my own thoughts, and is not binding upon any others. I have often wished we could hit upon some other more inclusive name because I am so much in harmony with many of the tenets of Unity, Divine Science, Churches of Truth, and Science of Mind that I long for some inclusive designation which would be acceptable to all these schools of metaphysics, and thus allow us to present a common front to the world which is often confused by these varied titles, without knowing their real similarity and mutual agreement.

While many, both within and without these various bodies, may be led to believe that New Thought, and its related movements, are to be distinguished as principally concerned with the healing of physical ills, I am led to believe that our purpose and scope is much wider. If our distinguishing characteristic is merely that we are interested in mental and spiritual therapy, we will fall far short of being a completely satisfactory religious movement. Let it be distinctly understood that I am in wholehearted sympathy with mental and spiritual therapy, but I believe these results are the legitimate by-products of a much larger thing than the mere connection of physical disabilities.

It was Jesus' evident idea that seeking of the kingdom would lead to all other desirable ends. This endless and age-long quest of the human heart to relate itself harmoniously to the totality of the universe on all its spiritual, mental and material levels, is the ageless effort of humanity which ever has been and ever will be.

An acceptable religion must do something much more than merely substitute for medicine and surgery. And I am profoundly convinced that wherever religions have failed, it has been because they left men and women intellectually dissatisfied, spiritually starved, emotionally maladjusted, and in many cases suffering in body. Only that religion which can stand the test of the most searching investigation, rigorous experiment and demonstrable results, will have more than a temporary existence. I became a New Thought follower and advocate only after I was led to see that in it alone of all religious structures, I could harmonize and adjust the valid views of philosophy, the evident findings of modern psychology, and the reconciliation of all the implications of science. One more influence prompted me, and that was the fact that in accepting and following the principles most commonly announced by New Thought, I found my own life and the lives of others led into complete satisfaction and happiness. All these things I have had added unto me, and have seen added to others, through the practice of the great truths and principles we have learned to adopt and apply. New Thought has answers for the great questions which trouble men. It has an acceptable rejoinder for doubts and fears.

One is tempted to tell what New Thought is, by telling what it is not. The temptation is all the stronger because we need to unlearn so much of superstition, pseudo-science, mythical theology and fear, before we can commence the construction of a clear and convincing philosophy.

It requires considerable consideration and a definite act of will to decide to eliminate from one's mind all these preconceptions, and make the resolution to believe only that truth which can vindicate itself and extend over every phase of knowledge and of life, without promise or exception.

To drive out errors, however, is not enough. Jesus' parable of the room cleansed of evil spirit applies here because nature abhors a vacuum, and constructive and creative thoughts must be allowed to overcome the evil with good.

We can start from this point with the author of Genesis who wrote, "In the beginning God." The most natural and perhaps the most common cornerstone of New Thought philosophy is a clear concept of What, Where and Why is God. God of course is the immense assumption of any rational religion. Into the concept of God we consign all that is necessary to account for cause, method, power, purpose and plan of the Universe. He becomes then the First Cause, the Eternal Energy, the All Power, the Universal Intelligence, and the Ultimate Reality in which everything else finds its being and existence.

God, then, becomes that process in the Universe which when known and complied with, brings the world and men into the highest and most abundant life. But we cannot think of Him as a dictator, a vacillating tyrant, a vindictive autocrat, or merely a much larger edition of man. While super-personal, we must not entertain the idea that He is personal and anthropomorphic.

Since Spirit is absolutely independent of the limitations of time and space, there is no place where the Presence and Power of God is absent. He must be wherever His work is manifesting, and wherever He is acting, and so God is immanent in man, and around and beyond the farthest star and in all the inter-space between. In Him all that is has its being. God is undoubtedly much more than we can fully comprehend, but He is at least all we are declaring. Since He is All in All, there is none beside or outside Him. In Him as Mind, all things have their origin by the action of His thought—"the Spirit of God moves on the face of the waters"—and from the formlessness all that became material was manifest. Thus all things began in Mind, were created by thought, and became manifest as material.

Thus man's mental powers, being individualized expressions of Universal Mind, are now able to work with God, and by the same methods and powers. Jesus explained his astonishing demonstrations by declaring (in substance), "I observe the way God works, and then I work in the same manner." Wherever man becomes Christ conscious, as Jesus did, there and then, he too, is able to accomplish what is to the world remarkable works.

The key to successful living, therefore, lies in the realization of the power of the mind, its laws of action, and in the application and compliance with these immeasurable powers and laws.

The true New Thought student is able to reconcile Jesus to a perfectly natural and reasonable category, who while He is unique in accomplishment, spells not an exception, but the norm of what all men can be, and should be, if they fully appreciated their divine birthright and developed their own potential privileges and powers.

Far from accepting the old dictum that we are "conceived in iniquity and born in sin," and are therefore heirs of the mistakes of our ancestors, and alienated from God and predestined to condemnation and eternal torment; the follower of New Thought claims his birthright as a Son of God and a joint heir with Jesus, in whom was incarnate all power in spirit, and in mind, and in matter.

This conception of himself immediately emancipates the individual from a sense of inferiority, and enables him to lift up his head, and throw back his shoulders, and gives him a consciousness of capacity, power and ability. Thus he becomes master of himself, his affairs and his environment.

The example of Jesus inspires us with the conviction that what one man has done and become, others may do and be also. Indeed this seems to have been the burden of Jesus' teachings. He entertained a deep and abiding idea of God, and his own relation to Him. He was conscious of the divine spark within, which was his real self, the I Am which is impervious to evil and empowered with mighty capacity.

The prologue to John's gospel is a concession to the lofty Greek idea of the *logos*, the Word, the first begotten, the direct emanation from the Divine Creator and Father of us all. This *logos* of the Greeks, became the Christ of the early church, and is the best word we can find to convey the thought of the Divine Indwelling in every human heart. This we might say in passing is only one of many instances where New Thought lays tribute to many ethnic religions and wide-spread schools of philosophy, which orthodoxy refuses to recognize, to its own loss. Truth is truth to us, and we make it ours if it can validate itself. We are under the same duty to reject error, however ancient or respectable it may have become. But New Thought is bound to be loyal to Truth as it would be loyal to God, because in the last analysis, the two are identical.

New Thought does not believe in the traditional habit of the ostrich which denies all evil and attempts to escape reality by ignoring it. We believe, however, that we possess the means and capacity to overcome, control and conquer all apparent enemies to our health, happiness, and the ample provision for all our needs.

Mind is master and whoever learns to use this tool is capable of meeting every circumstance and mastering every condition.

Thus New Thought is a complete cover for all of life's supreme issues. Through it, we can successfully adjust our spirits to the Universal and Ultimate Reality. By the methods suggested, we have developed a technique of satisfaction. When we become attuned to the Infinite, we have entered the Kingdom of God and all desirable things become our available possessions.

Spiritual adjustment to God is Man's first and last concern, and when this becomes a surety, everything else follows in its train, and we become more than conquerors through the inner power of the indwelling Christ, who is the eternal possession, and the potential power in every person.

At a very early stage in its history, New Thought made friend and ally with modern psychology, and has grown and expanded with this latest and most important of all sciences. Although reluctant at first to admit modern applied psychology to the family circle of science, the recent tendency of even the most materialistic scholars is to yield to it a place near the head of the table.

Physicians—the best of them—are today availing themselves of the consultations, advice and cooperation of psychologists, and of the competent New Thought practitioners who are themselves broad minded enough to recognize that a fact discovered by a physician or a surgeon—if it be a fact—is every whit as valid as if it were stated in a verse from the Bible, or were the conclusion of the most respected religionist. I am bound to respect every conclusion of the laboratory as I would respect any other creditable declaration of Truth.

I have made it a practice to cooperate in the fullest degree, and the most cordial manner, with the ethical and capable physicians whose knowledge, skill and devotion to humanity I most sincerely admire. Together we have worked for the restoration of many who were ill, and I believe I can truthfully say that our respect has been mutual.

I often avail myself of their advice, diagnostic ability and of both their medical and surgical skill. Even more frequently they have referred their patients to me for the reason that they recognize the source of the complaint is some maladjustment in the mental, emotional or religious life of the patient. From my viewpoint, and in the light of many years experience, I believe this practice will not diminish, but greatly increase, and I can most heartily say, "God hasten the day."

How can we afford to be anxious or jealous for credit in a cure? It is not the agency but the result that is of primary importance, and in every instance God is, in the last analysis, the Power that heals.

As I think of healing, it goes far beyond the treatment of merely physical afflictions. Sick bodies may excite pity and concern, but none of them are in number and degree as awful as the sickness of mind and heart. Statistics of all our institutions for the mentally ill reveal the fact that calculating on the unit of "daybed," the mentally ill exceed all those who are in hospitals from every other known affliction. This indicates that more people stand in need of mental treatment than need medical attention, when all are added together.

When we add to all these institutional cases the number of "out-patients" not yet committed to institutions, the proportion of mental patients is vastly augmented. Here is the field for New Thought counsellors and practitioners. Men and women need to be adjusted domestically, economically, emotionally, socially, intellectually and spiritually.

They are not always easily adjusted. They cannot be intellectually fooled. They must be given common sense advice, rational answers, sincere encouragement, lofty inspiration. There is no side-stepping, no mere quotations of self-appointed authorities, no false grounds for hope, no compromising with Truth, that will permanently satisfy and adjust and rehabilitate such heart-sick and heavy-burdened or confused people.

I know of no other religious principles which can withstand the searching questions such individuals ask out of their dilemmas. I can truthfully say, however, that in all my experience I have never had a tough-minded and intransigent patient put his finger on a single inconsistency in our principles and practices.

It is in this contact that my own faith is strengthened in the invincibility of our approach to a philosophy of life. Whatever stands the test of every day's experience is worthy of trial and testing.

Constructively and creatively, I have witnessed even greater demonstrations of the power of thought and of conscious cooperation with the great Reality of the Universe.

I have seen mediocrity develop into almost sheer genius. I have seen men redeemed from poverty, failure and despair into prosperity, success and almost ecstatic happiness. I have seen homes threatened with wreck and ruin, become radiant with love and affection.

All these I have seen, and many other effects, as a result of the sincere application of Truth principles. Words fail me when I attempt to tell all I have seen in others and experienced in my own life. This philosophy is the power of God unto salvation to all who accept and practice it.

Out of the noise and confusion of our day, out of wars and rumors of wars, out of hate, strife and bitterness, out of error and untruth, out of the ineffectualism of ecclesiasticism, out of ignorance and unhappiness, there is emerging and will emerge a universal solvent with healing for all woes, and so far as I see at the present time, New Thought is its nearest exponent.

SCIENCE OF MIND
BY ERNEST HOLMES

Ernest Holmes, founder and dean of the Institute of Religious Science, and founder of the Science of Mind Magazine, Los Angeles, California, is the author of "Science of Mind," "The Bible in the Light of Religious Science," "Creative Mind," "Creative Mind and Success," "It's Up To You," and "Your Invisible Power."

LET us approach the Science of Mind and Spiritual Psychology with its vast possibilities, without fear; in true humility, happily, willing to accept, eager to experiment.

There is nothing supernatural in metaphysical laws. That which today appears supernatural, after it has become thoroughly understood, will be found to be spontaneously natural. We know that faith has worked miracles in the lives of men in all ages, and to those who follow different religious convictions, its wonder-working power has produced amazing results.

We know that the prayer of faith has healed the sick. Naturally, we ask ourselves how such results are brought about. If we were to ask the average person who teaches the principles of Spiritual Mind Power, no doubt we should receive an answer similar to the following: "We believe in God as the Infinite Spirit permeating everything. We believe that there is a Law of Mind which responds to our thought, faith and conviction. We believe that the universe in which we live is a Spiritual System and that the Kingdom of Good is ours and is present with us now." Such declarations as these, meaningful as they are, are statements of one's conviction, but a declaration of faith in certain principles is quite different from the conscious use of such principles. It is not enough for an electrician to say he believes in electricity, that he believes it to be an ever-present reality or energy, or that it can run all the machinery in the world; it is necessary for him to apply his understanding of electricity for the definite purpose of producing light, heat and motive power.

Too many people in our field mistake a declaration of belief in Spirit for an effective mental treatment. No greater mistake can be made. We must not only believe that God, or Divine Reality, is all Power, we must use our belief in a definite way. This is what constitutes correct mental practice. Man's thought is creative because his thought is God-power flowing through his individualized will and imagination.

A spiritual treatment, to be effective, must be spoken from a consciousness which knows itself to be the presence, the power and the activity of God. This Spiritual Power can and will heal, accomplish, demonstrate, answer prayer. It not only will but It must, for this is Its nature.

Spiritual Power is of no particular value to us until we use It. We must not only be conscious of this Power, we must be *actively* conscious of It. This is one of the first lessons we learn in spiritual science. It is written that Jesus, standing before the tomb of Lazarus, said, "Father I thank Thee that Thou hast heard me. And I knew that Thou hearest me always." Afterwards he gave the command, "Lazarus come forth." Jesus first *recognized* the Power, "Father I thank Thee that Thou has heard me," next he consciously *unified* himself with It, "And I knew that Thou hearest me always." Following this, he made a declaration, an affirmation, a command; he told Lazarus to come forth. This was *conscious acceptance*. We could not find a better method for our own mental use of spiritual thought power. Since the whole process of a spiritual treatment is an activity of thought, it follows that the one thinking must consciously be aware that his treatment will be effective.

Although we are surrounded by Divine Intelligence, Love and Wisdom, we may lack an actual higher guidance because we lack the higher acceptance of such guidance. Daily we should state that we are guided and directed into right action; we should know that there is an Intelligence which goes before us and makes perfect, plain and immediate our way. Divine Guidance is as definite a Principle in the universe as is the law of attraction and repulsion, but the use of Divine Guidance is what we make it. Its use is through the activity of right ideas. Our acknowledgment of good becomes the good which we acknowledge—"His word runneth very swiftly."

The greater the conviction, the more power our word will have. We should act as though we already have dominion over evil. We should declare the truth by stating that there is nothing to be afraid of; Good is omnipotent. Good, instantly, effectively and permanently destroys both fear and the effect of fear. The freedom of God is our freedom; the Power of God is our power; the Presence of God is in us now. The Mind of God is our mind and the Joy of God is our joy.

Spiritual mind treating is not day dreaming, and it is more than meditation. *Meditation is for the purpose of inbreathing the Essence of Reality; treatment is for the purpose of using this Essence in definite constructive ways.*

Because the Spirit is personal to each, then each individualizes God and no two persons are alike. Thus God as Infinite Person is not only real to each one of us, but real in a unique sense. Treatment should be filled with an atmosphere of this Reality. We should make statements similar to this: "Because God is infinite in His capacity to know, there is a Mind within me that knows exactly what I should do today. Realizing that the Spirit with me is God; being conscious of the Divine Presence as the sustaining Principle of my life, I let that Mind be in me which was also in Christ Jesus. This Mind guides me today in my every decision. I declare the same guidance for all people."

Our true inheritance is self-sufficiency, perfection, peace and wholeness. This certainly includes abundance, self-cxpression and happiness. The Will of God and the Nature of God are identical, since God could have no will opposed to His nature. Hence, if God is wholeness, peace and joy, then the Divine Will for all is wholeness, peace and joy. The Will of God is always toward the more abundant life. We have misdirected the energy which is already for us, hence the importance of reeducationg the mind to a more direct perception of its relationship to God.

The Science of Mind deals with a Principle in Nature which acts like other principles. If we wish to use this Principle as a science, rather than to use It merely in a hit-and-miss method, we must make a scientific approach to, and a conscious use of, spiritual power. We need not go outside ourselves to do this.

The Principle of Truth, of Mind and Spirit, or whatever term one wishes to designate It by, is the Actor, thc Doer—"Be still and know that I am God." The Creative Principle acts upon thought. We should call upon this inner Intelligence, in belief and in confidence, knowing that It will respond to us.

God as Spirit is the Divine Presence, while the Principle of this science is the Law of Cause and Effect. The Divine Knower operates through mechanical Law. This Law is Mind in action. When you give a treatment you should feel that all the power there is in the universe is flowing into your word. Believe that Truth swings instantly into manifestation through your conviction, for this is the power of your treatment. Be simple and direct.

This has nothing to do with will power, mental concentration or suggestion. There is that within each one of us which is conscious of its unity with Good, with all the Power there is. Upon this Power, Presence and Light, we must depend with complete confidence. Thus faith passes into experience with scientific certainty. Faith is the most dynamic power known.

Effective treatment must be independent of any existing circumstances, for the Divine Creative Spirit knows no circumstances, It is the Creator of them. Here is the crux of the whole matter. This is why we are told never to count our enemies but to "Look unto me and be ye saved."

When you say "There is One Life and this Life is God," you have made an abstract statement about a Universal Principle, but when you add, "This Life is my life now," you have consciously connected this Principle with your own experience. In giving treatments one should use the words and thoughts which convey the desired meaning to his own mind. Treatment should be simple, unlabored, calm, and designed only to convince the thought of the one who gives it. All treatment is self-treatment. The manifestation of the treatment is in the Law of Cause and Effect.

It is impossible to divorce a true concept of God from the most powerful mental treatment, merely because God, or the Creative First Cause, constitutes our entire being in Reality. The act of self-knowing, which takes place in our thought, is in Reality the One Mind recognizing Itself. The action of this Mind, through our thought, creates our experience. Spiritual mind treatment is an active thing, but its activity is a mental and spiritual recognition either in the form of spoken words or of a deep inner realization of the truth, applied for some particular purpose.

The Power that creates exists before we use It. However, It can give us only that which we mentally take, and often our unbelief becomes our acceptance, our fear a misplaced faith. We bind ourselves by the very power which could as quickly free us. We should increase our receptivity and have a greater faith, if we wish to experience a larger degree of Iivingness. Our bowl of acceptance must be held up so that the outpouring of Spirit may be measured into our individual experience. It is self-evident that the Creative Spirit must express Itself in the terms of the instrument through which It flows. So far as we are concerned, this instrument is faith, belief, acceptance. We should lift our thought upon the cross of Unity and here, where the winds of God blow free, accept the Divine Givingness and the

Divine Forgiveness, which are eternal in the nature of Reality.

All treatment is for the purpose of stimulating an interior awareness. If we are treating for physical or financial betterment for ourselves, or for someone else, inwardly we should become aware that the good we desire is now manifest. All of Spirit is wherever we center our thought. Truth in Its entirety is forever with us, ever available. Spiritual Power awaits our recognition, and Divine Guidance our consent. The Spirit flows through us as an outlet for Its own self-expression.

To dwell upon lack is to create it. To think of disease is to perpetuate it. To remain unhappy is to attract more unhappiness. Deliberately we must turn from that which hurts. The Law of Mind exists in a formless state and can only take the form for us which our thought gives It. When we think within ourselves, we think upon It; when we direct our thought, we are directing It. It is in this way that our word becomes the law unto that thing whereunto it is spoken. We should sense this Power which is at the point of our word, while being careful to realize that we need not put power into our word, for as a matter of fact, we really take it out. This is not concentration, it is conscious belief definitely directed.

The particular form of mental procedure in this practice is unimportant, the all-important factor is whether or not one believes in, and understands, the spiritual nature of things. We must believe that love, goodness, truth and beauty are at the center of everything, therefore at the center of the person, the condition or situation which we designate in our treatment. We must believe that Love is God, infinite, eternal and ever present. We cannot escape Love. We exist in Love and are One with It. We live by, through and in It. It motivates our entire thought, purpose, plan and action. Everything we see, we see with the eyes of Love. Everything we hear we hear with the ears of Love. We see God everywhere; wherever we look we see Him, wherever we go, we find Him.

The process of reasoning which one uses in a mental treatment, must establish his thought upon a spiritual basis, enthrone him in a Kingdom of Good and give him dominion over evil. Thoughts and things are not separated, they are identical. When the practitioner uses the word "elimination" he must believe that something is being eliminated; when he uses the words "right action" he must believe that the entire right action of the universe is centered, through that word, upon the object which he designates, or for the purpose which he has in mind. In this way, business is an activity of consciousness and the business of Mind is never inactive. Man's business is God's business and God's business is man's business, which is the business of life.

We do not deny the physical universe, we affirm that it is *Mind in form*. The physical body exists that the soul may function on this plane. Body is not an unreality; quite the reverse. It is a divine and perfect reality when rightly understood.

We are compelled to think of Spirit either as apart from us or within us. If apart from us, there is no way to find It. If within us, there is no escaping the divine fact. *Unfoldment and not search is what we need.* Unless mind healing becomes spiritual, it degenerates into the process of exchanging one negative idea for another. How can we expect any result to rise higher than its cause? Hence, all true mind healing is spiritual; it rests upon a deep inner realization of the Divine Goodness.

The Creative Principle can operate for us only by operating through our belief, hence we limit It to such belief. *We must know that the body of God, the body of our patient and the body of our affairs are one and the same thing.*

The winning or losing of what we call a demonstration, lies entirely in one's state of thought or consciousness, in whether or not he is able to perceive more good than evil. For since the Divine Spirit and Law is the only Actor, the true Saviour, the All in All, It has no opposition, no competition, no otherness. A consciousness of God should run through our entire treatment. Thus we may say, "I baptize all people in the essence of love; I pour the spirit of joy upon all occasions; I throw mental peace around every form. There is that within me which proclaims `Behold, I make all things new.' "

Our work rests entirely upon demonstration. If the thought is not manifesting rightly in our experience, we should work until it does. We should have a deep realization of the Divine Presence, and out of the spiritual power generated in this realization speak our word with complete conviction. When we give a treatment we must believe, for this is the power of the treatment.

The following is a suggested outline for treatment. There is no magic in any particular words. Words are effective only in so far as they stimulate a corresponding recognition of their meaning in the mind of the one who uses them.

A Suggested Outline of Treatment for Health and Prosperity.

This word is the Presence, Power and Activity of the Infinite Mind in me. Therefore It is the law unto the condition or the person for whom It is spoken. It is perfect in Its action and permanent in Its manifestation.

Infinite Intelligence governs, guides, directs, sustains and animates my life (if treating for someone else mention his name). The Infinite Mind knows no mistake. It is never discouraged. This Mind is my Mind now. All belief in fear, discouragement, disappointment or failure is erased from my consciousness.

I am forever supplied with every good thing, forever happy, radiant, well and complete. This word establishes the law of wholeness and harmony throughout my entire being and in everything I do, say or think (or the person for whom or the condition for which I am working). My life represents that which knows no limitation, is forever manifesting complete joy and freedom through me.

Spirit daily provides me with everything necessary to my happiness, to my wholeness, and to my complete self-expression. I represent the Principle of Divine Activity which never tires, which is birthless, changeless and deathless. I know that the Infinite Intelligence which sustains all things, and the Perfect Law which holds everything in its proper place, governs my life and action (or his life and action).

My whole being responds to joy, to peace, to truth and to abundance. Only that which is good can enter my experience. (At this point one may definitely state that the particular good he seeks is now accomplished.) I know that as a result of this word, happiness, health and prosperity immediately spring into action and manifest through me (or through him). I know that the action of Spirit in me (or him) is always complete, perfect and enduring.

Every organ, action and function of my physical being represents this Divine and Perfect Life, manifesting within me. I am aware of my Partnership with the Infinite and I know that everything which I do shall prosper.

(Enter into a silent realization and acceptance of what you have said.)

It is done. I accept. I believe. I know.

THE PRINCIPLE AND PRACTICE OF METAPHYSICS
BY E. V. INGRAHAM

E. V. Ingraham, now a resident of Los Angeles, California, was associated with the Unity School of Kansas City for about thirty years. Personal student of Emma Curtis Hopkins. Spent thirty-seven years in study of comparative religions, ancient and modern. He is the author of: *Ladder to the Sky, Wells of Abundance, Winds of Heaven, The Silence, The Magic Formula of Success, Prayer, Its Practice and Its Answer, Incarnation and Re-incarnation, and Fourth Dimension Plus.*

METAPHYSICS, according to the dictionary, involves "the systematic study or science of the first principle of being and of knowledge." Metaphysics, therefore, approaches spiritual things as the scientist approaches the world of form. The material scientist devotes himself to research and experiment in an effort to determine the nature and possibilities to be derived from the visible creation. The metaphysician devotes himself to investigation and application in the realm of Universal forces from which the visible creation is derived.

Science long denied or disregarded the existence of an Infinite and Intelligent Cause for the material universe. Religion has, in many instances, denied or disregarded the importance of the material world. In modern times, scientific and religious efforts are broadening their research to include both the visible and the invisible aspects of the Universe. The chief difference today seems to be that the scientist is seeking the cause through studying the effect; the religionist is seeking to understand and control the effect by studying the Cause. Pure metaphysics is most effectively working to unite these two phases of human knowledge and experience.

THE PRINCIPLE:

To state the principle upon which metaphysics builds its science would be to restate the oldest doctrine in religious philosophy; namely, that God is Omnipresent, Omnipotent and Omniscient. All of the religions of the world, in one way or another, have accepted this definition of the origin and nature of the Universal system as most adequate. In fact, according to the Bible, this is God's own revelation of Himself, for He said, "I am that I am and beside me there is no other." This literally means that God is the sum-total of the entire Universal system, the Creator and the created. Pure religion and pure science of the future must take this fact into account since there is no science complete until it takes into account both cause and effect.

If God is Omnipresent, He is the only presence there is and there can be no presence, visible or invisible, but the presence of God. Furthermore, He is equally present at all points in the Universe; the life, substance, and intelligence not only of space but of form as well. This concept places man himself actually within the nature of God. He was literally created within the image of God. Not only within the image of God but since he is created of the very essence of the Creator, he is also in the "likeness of God." Creator and created must be one, just as all cause and effect are one. The created must contain within itself the elements of the Creator, since like can produce only that which is like unto itself. Therefore, man and the manifest Universe are but the visible aspect of God Himself. What seems otherwise is the result of man's own short-sightedness; his failure to see all things in their entirety. Nothing but ignorance could have any existence outside the realm of Truth and ignorance is a mere lack of intelligence, life, power and substance.

If God is Omnipotent, man is literally surrounded by and interpenetrated with an Infinite Spiritual Power which is the only power there is. This Power is the central motive force animating all creation including man and his affairs. Therefore, there is no degree of power that is not available to man. Adjusting his thought, feeling, and action to fact would be all that is required.

If God is Omniscient, He is all-knowing. Everything that has ever been known or ever will be known exists in the spiritual ethers in somewhat the same manner that radio music exists in the electrical ethers as it is sent out from broadcasting stations. Since we are created from the surrounding ethers, Omnipotent Creative Intelligence is inherent within us and every created form as well. Creation is, therefore, intelligently designed and directed. Back of every person, thing, or situation is an intelligent design; this design is the "Word" or "Christ." This is the "personality" of God existing as the foundation structure of man's outer nature. It is the "Father within," or the Lord *YOUR* God.

The next point for the metaphysical student to take into account is that God is Spirit, or a *self-active Presence*. So often, people pray, affirm, or declare as though the Creative Law of Life had to be aroused in some manner and induced to act in their behalf. If this were the case, there could not have been a creation in the first place. Jesus always "lifted his eyes unto heaven" to "see what the Father was doing." What He saw the Father doing, He did likewise and perfect results were forthcoming. This was the practice of sages before and after him.

Since the operations of the Law of Life created all things, the Law must move to perfect all things according to its own standard. If perfect from the viewpoint of the Creator, it must be entirely satisfactory to the created also. Therefore, to be within the operations of the Law is to be within a current of Infinite Power which moves to perfect every element of creation. Here is the hope of illumination, healing, success and supply.

No procedure of man either intellectually or physically is vital and effective until he has trained himself to proceed with relationship to the foregoing facts. To proceed without a conscious relationship thereto is to discover that both he and his affairs "run down," so to speak. Man and his affairs cannot survive without conscious contact with his Source any more than vegetation can survive without contact with the forces of nature.

Ignorance, disease, failure and poverty are sins against the Law. Therefore, the Law moves to destroy and convert these false structures into perfection. That which seems to be an opposing force in our experience is only our opposition to the underlying "trend" of life; we are not moving in harmony with the creative purpose. "A man's enemies are those of his own household"—his own reactions against the trend of creative power.

Metaphysics does not accept the foregoing as a final and completely understood fact but as a foundation from which to proceed. From this point, the individual begins an endless search into the mysteries of Omnipresence. What he discovers, he seeks" to prove for that which is true in any principle must prove itself in manifest results.

THE PRACTICE:

There are two distinct phases of metaphysical practice. They are interrelated and are to be followed in the order referred to. They were emphasized by Jesus Christ in explaining his mission on earth. He described the first when he said, "I came to preach the gospel." Therefore, what He *taught* was the gospel. But the gospel is more than talking in generalities about God and reciting religious doctrines. The literal meaning is "Godspell." To preach the gospel means to awaken men to the realization that they are engulfed within the actual presence of God; that they are in the presence of God and influenced or governed by God.

You have, at times, felt completely entangled with and influenced by conditions in your world. In that state, you were under a "world spell"; a spell of ignorance about yourself and everything around you. The God-spell is being aware of your relationship to the Infinite Presence and conscious of its governing influence upon your life and affairs. This state is as encouraging and exalting as the "world spell" has been discouraging and depressing.

The second phase of metaphysical practice was also given by Christ when he stated, "I came not to do mine own will, but to do the Will of Him that sent me." Therefore, what He *did* was a revelation of the Will of God—the objective toward which the self-operative origin of life moved. Following this plan, He healed the sick, corrected the inhibitions of their minds, fed the hungry, produced money to meet the demands of the commercial system of his time and even raised the dead. According to his own statement, all of these acts were revelations of the objectives toward which the Law of God moves. We must then conclude that *the Will of God is the will to perfect every element of His creation.* This must include man and his affairs, for if either man or his affairs are imperfect, the purpose of the Creator is not fully manifest.

Since, as the Scriptures teach, "the Law of God is written in your inward parts," there must be a moving force in you that is the personalized activity of the Universal force. Study yourself and you will find there are some tendencies in you that you cannot change. Such tendencies as the innermost desire to gain perfect knowledge, power, life, health, wealth and success. Jesus habitually consulted this unalterable tendency of his innermost nature to find out how the Universal forces worked. "The Father within" is the manner in which He described it. The word "Father" as translated in our Scriptures literally means "first mover, or fundamental action." This perfectly coincides with the teachings of more ancient mystics that the "highest and inmost God are ONE." Once we realize that the operations of the Universal Law are toward the same objectives as our innermost ideals, we have tangible ground for an infinite faith that every high objective is completely attainable. To be completely under its "spell" is to find the fires of genius burning in our own nature.

TREATMENT:

Metaphysical Treatment is not a matter of developing thoughts and imposing them upon our bodies or our world to produce results that we imagine will be more satisfactory to our cultivated habits. Science involves the systematic and orderly arrangement of facts and the science of mind demands the systematic and orderly development of consciousness. Thought and feeling are the elements involved in metaphysical science. They must be developed from the study and analysis of the moving forces that animate creation, rather than from the material forms alone. Treatment involves turning the mind "in" to comprehend the unchangeable tendencies of your ideals, for they are the inner or personal counterpart of the Universal Creative Power.

The mind has two phases, the power *to think* and the power *to feel*. The power to think is masculine in its nature and its action is within. The mind must first comprehend, see, or understand. Once the mind grasps the meaning or action of anything, the feeling nature is automatically aroused. With the awakening of feeling, the process begins to turn outwardly toward results in the world of form. The stronger the feeling, the greater the outer pressure is exerted on the world of form. This outward tendency of emotion is a natural and automatic function and is not an act of the will. Notice how your face awakens with a smile when inward joy becomes great enough.

Feeling is the feminine principle of the mind and only through feeling are our hopes and ideals manifest. It is as futile to attempt to produce outward results by thought alone as it is futile for the male of a species to attempt to produce offspring without the female. If you do not believe this, by a process of reason, try to convince someone that you are happy when you have no inward feeling of joy.

Scientific treatment is designed, first, to awaken the mind to fully understand that health, success, wealth, etc., are basic operations of the Law of Life; second, to awaken the feeling, or realization, until one's whole nature is aflame with the passion of health, success, and wealth. When this becomes the habitual state of consciousness, outer results are sure and automatic.

Study your method of progress in mathematics for a moment and the foregoing technique will be clear. First, you would not take up the study of mathematics as a profession unless you had a desire to be a mathematician. *Desire is the revelation of inner and potential capacity*. You *study* mathematical rules with the motive that your mind may grasp the meaning. You *press* the mind *"IN"* to understand. By meditating upon the process of the rule which you have discovered, or which you "see," you begin to *feel* the impelling force of its activity. The stronger the feeling of its operations, the greater power you possess. When your thinking and feeling natures clearly coincide with the processes of the rule, then you proceed to act, or turn outward. The outward act is not merely to solve the problem, but to bring the rule into the problem. The answer is the automatic effect of the rule itself. In other words, the answer comes "not by might nor by power, but by the spirit" or activity of the rule. Once the mind has grasped the fact that this is the scientific approach to spiritual dominion, one has the right procedure in attaining every abiding desire of the heart.

In studying a mathematical rule, you have found that a slow, thoughtful, and often audible repetition helps to "press the mind in" to understand. For this reason, it has been found that an audible analysis of your ideals, hopes and aspiration, coupled with the fact that they are the inward activity of Universal Law, is most helpful. This practice continued until you have developed a strong feeling, or realization, is scientific treatment whether of yourself, another, or any of the affairs of life. The operation of the Law is the same at every point in creation and treatment is only bringing these operations out through the mind and feeling nature so they come into contact with flesh and events in the outer.

The foregoing thoughts are not to be merely read or accepted. They are to be challenged, analyzed, meditated upon until they are clearly comprehended by your mind. When this plan has been followed they will become your own. This practice will form an unshakable foundation upon which you may build a new life for yourself, a life that was ordained from the beginning and which springs from the foundations of the world. But you must first study until you *KNOW* and meditate until you *FEEL* these facts as living Truth in your nature before giving any undue attention to results.

The time has come for us to cease taking spiritual things as an escape. Life is more than "rest" from struggle or "peace" that is merely passive. The challenge of the times demands heroic action and if we would find peace that is enduring and success that is satisfying, we must arouse ourselves; "quit ourselves like men." We must become as dynamic and scientific in our spiritual procedure as science and war have become in developing ways of destruction. Spiritual things are not weak and divine things are not for those who would be lulled into a hypnotic lethargy of mere quietness. Spiritual attainment involves actively linking yourself with the Power which created. To be ONE with Omnipotence is to be endowed with power from on High and to regain the dominion over your flesh and your world which was assigned to you at the dawn of your creation.

"Be not weary in well doing, for you will reap in due season if you faint not."

THE SCIENCE OF PRAYER
BY W. FREDERIC KEELER

W. Frederic Keeler, who for many years was pastor of Divine Science Church in New York City, as well as London, England, and Los Angeles, California, is one of the best known teachers and lecturers in the New Thought field. Thirty-six years in practice of Christian Healing. At one time he published: *The Constructive Thinker*, in New York and *Christian Victory*, in San Francisco. At present he publishes *Keeler's Comments*, and resides in San Diego, California.

THE one method of Christianity is prayer. Method is procedure. The science of Christian procedure is given us in the Lord's Prayer itself and in the manner in which we are to perform that prayer.

It is to be secret.

"And when thou prayest thou shall not be as the hypocrites are for they love to pray . . . that they be seen of men," and even "when thou doest alms . . . thine alms may be in secret . . . otherwise ye have no reward of your Father which is in heaven."

Not only are all prayers an act in mind, in consciousness only, but we are told specifically that this is the one way of prayer.

Ralph Waldo Emerson left the ministry of the church because it required him to pray audibly.

The first thing a Truth student is called upon to do is to lay aside many of his old patterns of thought. It is undesirable patterns and paths of thought that cause our troubles. The sole design of thought processes is that brought to us in our text book, the Bible. The great originality of Quimby lay in his discovery and teaching that the cause of sickness lay in wrong thought patterns.

We are to ask ourselves, "Are we to follow what 'people say' and do or are we to follow the very key to Christian teachings, the Lord's Prayer, and of all things the *manner* of its use?"

When you pray for *direct results* in your life or in the life of another let it be in the Silence.

Spirit is silent and unseen, therefore the way to, and with, Spirit is silent and unseen.

We are taught plainly that there is a reward to prayer. In present day parlance we call that reward desired results. The reward is to be open, visible, seen by all. "Thy father which seeth in secret himself shall reward thee openly." In the instructions how to pray this statement about results accruing upon the material plane is twice repeated in its simplest and unmistakable terms in verses Four and Six, Chapter Six of Matthew.

Here again we are to change our thought patterns and beliefs from the old thought to the New Thought. Yes, we pray for things, visible things, Jesus the Master knows. It is perfectly logical that we are to change our ways of thought if we are to change our lives.

Note how definitely we are to enter upon our silent work in this new and secret Kingdom wherein we are to rule all circumstances in unification with God and His Law.

We are to enter the "closet" of our mind. "Enter into thy closet" are the words used and we are to "shut" out the whole world from our consciousness for only "when thou has shut thy door, pray to thy Father which" note again "is in secret."

We use no world methods in prayer. This is utterly scientific. We ask nothing of personalities, we explain nothing, we do not demand, we do not even appeal. We very, oh very simply ask and we do so in childlikeness. When we do so in the peace of our consciousness that is silenced against our worldly troubles "the Father knoweth what things ye have need of."

You have needs and you are eminently entitled before doing anything else to bring them to the Father whereupon we are promised "bread" fulfillment, not a "stone." How could these matters, this science of prayer, be stated more plainly?

So there is a place called the secret place in which we relate with unseen potencies, with the very powers of creation and do this to the production of visible results and that is exactly what all the sciences do. They bring the hidden and the invisible forces openly into man's use and appreciation. The Science of Christian prayer is the ultimate of all sciences. It is the direct short cut to direct effects. If you shy from such a belief and a doctrine it remains that you are to be converted. Pray then for your conversion to the Truth. God is not a far God.

Further science of method—"When ye pray, use not vain repetitions" or you will be acting as a heathen, not as a Christian. Our instructions are factual, do not do "as the heathens do," hit the mark, do not putter and do not depend upon your own mental wordiness nor your own mental pictures. Directly "ask" by means of the Spirit in you. "Ask" from the depths of your soul. "Ask" in peace, not in personal desperation.

The means we are to use are those of a peaceful, silent, conscious request while in the full knowledge that results are in this manner to be expected, not the results in terms of personal whims but rewards that are of God's kind and these include "daily bread" supply and real needs fulfilled on the plane of substance. The fact is prayer and faith is substance functioning on the spiritual plane. The constant transformations of substance from one plane of expression and activity to another should be very familiar to every one in these days of science.

We drop our worldly worries in prayer. They do not exist in prayer, we know that worry is the cause of despair and defeat, it is not one with life or Truth. To face the facts of one's life without worry while being in the consciousness of God is to solve every problem, and to heal.

Remember the way of prayer is a "manner" not a repetition of memorized rote.

Call upon your Father, your Creator Who is in Heaven, Who is in happiness and dare to ask that the beautiful and harmonious things of Heaven be here upon earth in your life and the life of others. Choose your daily needs for others or for yourself. Choice is with you, you are God's child. Speak. Forgive others and forgive yourself. You have that power. And ask that the glittering things of the world, that mere things, will not lead you from the exercise of life-power itself, that you be not diverted or tempted away from the exercise of prayer and real intelligence. Then give thanks for this higher Kingdom, this great Power that is yours in which you may partake of the Glory here and now.

After doing this be patient and faithful in knowing that there is this Law that never fails and be content to learn its ways. If there is any sign of failure you have not moved aright. Cleanse yourself further in the Silent place of your own selfhood, and ask God to help you do so. Learn, of all things, learn to pray, for praying people know that true prayer never fails. Go over every aspect of the simple instructions and depend upon the Inner Kingdom, this New Power of the New Covenant, this New Testament of God's nearness, that Jesus brought to us. During the moments of prayer, for prayer should never be prolonged, swing your consciousness over, way over, into the ways of Truth.

* * *

HEALING AS I KNOW IT is almost methodless and becomes more so with experience. It is prayer in Faith and the Understanding of the Christ Law ignoring completely all laws of worldliness. Its highest manner of procedure is the Practice of the Presence in which I keep consciously in the Presence of God wherein obviously no untoward thing can occur. And at the same time I bring my patient and his problems out of the world (but not of course out of normal earth life) into the Presence. I remain in stillness unmoved and enjoy both my patient and the Presence. This is clearly and distinctly wholly within consciousness and Spirit.

I find that the more quiet and contained life I lead the more I enlarge my understanding of Truth applied to mankind and the more successful I am in giving treatments. I attempt now to analyze such a treatment, to slow it down, to take it apart, to describe that which is practically indescribable since it is a sharing and a witnessing of recreativeness within the one I am serving. The patient deserves first credit for success of the treatment as it consists primarily of his own acceptance, although innerly and unconsciously performed.

I am largely but varyingly aware of what is occurring during each treatment. The action is a conversion to Truth gently and winningly brought about through prayer, each time a wondrous revelation to me. The child gets out of bed and asks for its toys, the fever has departed into its native nothingness. How I wish everyone could have this Healing Experience. The experience is spiritual, therefore the following can only be read between the lines, as it were.

The procedure is conversational. I silently say to my patient, "How are you?" I am sincere to the utmost possible degree. In answer to this practiced concentration I receive an impression. I seek the inner need now before me in consciousness and in prayer. In response I offer, I display one of God's Remedies. For instance, I hold Freedom in consciousness before my patient. I now read myself. I want to know what I am doing and what is best for me to do in this case. I find that it is easy to offer Freedom. Therefore this patient has Freedom. I now offer Reassurance, God's Reassurance. I sense resistance. She therefore has no reassurance. She is interiorally afraid.

Now comes the healing. I am to aid her to receive that which she lacks.

I enter upon no phase of dominance or struggle. That which I offer is like cool water to the thirsty. I am to succeed in giving God's Good. I stand wholly within my Truth. I am certain that there is Reassurance, and a Lovely Way of Life for this patient.

Should I have further difficulty in doing this and still experience resistance I retreat to utter impersonality. It is God's Business and the patient's own, not mine. Solid Joy is for this patient. It is his particularly. It is like converting one to the beauties of a sunset who had temporarily lost that particular appreciation. All disease, to me, consists of a subconscious pattern or fixation of false ideas which register in correlative physical terms. *My Remedy is God's Design particularized by the use of His Principles such as Love, Peace, Joy, Encouragement and Beauty.*

What has this sensing to do with psychology, telepathy and psychism? Not one thing whatever. It is simply Direct Knowing which finds its Source in both God and the one who is to be healed. I "see" nothing and above all I hear nothing. It is not phenomenal, it is a revealment, a wordless sensing, a recognition on my part of the proper way to present Truth to meet the occasion, definitely an answer to my prayer. Our mind's single function is to Know. True Prayer is always answered. I am interested in being Guided in healing this patient. I desire Leadings, and I receive them.

I am confident that anyone can do this who will persist, be sincere, and of all things impersonally keep his own worldly desires out of it. The Healing Mind pays no respect to the loud torn-toms of worldly conceptions. We are not born to trouble. Hurry, worry, fear, fever and death is a description of an attempt to live life without faith and such practices form a habit which is the very antithesis of Faith and Understanding. In Truth we never judge or condemn. God loves all.

I ask no outer expressed faith of my patient. I have a job to do and I do it. *A treatment is a dedication of Truth made by one person for another.* That dedication occurs in the Peaceful Place of Spirit, the Silence. A physical illustration of a treatment is that of taking a person by the hand and helping him across a crowded street, the practitioner being acquainted with the way. No influence is exerted. It is a sharing of life with God. One shows or teaches the way to the other. And whatever occurs does so with the instantaneousness of Spirit.

THE TRUTH WHICH WE CAN LIVE
BY BROWN LANDONE, F.R.E.S.

Dr. Brown Landone, founder and president of The Landone Foundation, New York City, has been a leader of successful metaphysical enterprises in Paris and London, as well as in this country. Dr. Landone is the oldest leader in Truth work, in point of time of service, both in Europe and America. Formerly Director of an International Institute of Art, in France and Italy. At one time, Director of a New Educational Movement in London, representing educators from twenty-two nations. Feature writer in European capitals; Editor-in-chief of: *Seven Volume History of Civilization*. Among his metaphysical books and brochures are: *You are Chosen, What I Know of Youthfulness, Deep Down in Your Heart, Prophecies of Melchi-Zedek, Super State, My All God, Golden Continent, When Will This War End, How Will This War End, etc.*

It is significant—like to the star of Bethlehem—when conquered nations then were desperate, and Roman armies wrought destruction everywhere.

And now again today, with earth raw-torn and bleeding sore, with war of millions raging far—from Brest to Tokyo and Narvik unto southern seas—it is significant that in this tragic hour, our INTA should lift its light for all to see—and give to men, its first composite message of the Truth.

I shall not write of our ideas, nor yet of our beliefs—for each of them is but a variant flashing light of but one facet of the gorgeous radiancy of that great diamond of a thousand facets which we call the Truth.

I write of what I *treasure* most in Truth—of God, and man e'er manifesting God—and of his search, how best to live the Truth.

I treasure first, the *radiancy* of God—forever shining out— unto the utmost star, and out to you and me!

This radiancy reveals the primal nature of our God. The law of science and of spirit too, are unified in knowing that all radiance fore'er shines *out*, and that it never turns its power back on its source. For if it did, it would destroy itself,—just as the bulb of an electric light—if it should try to draw its rays into itself— would burn its light to darkness.

Since God is radiant, he never draws his power unto himself. This treasured concept solves at once a thousand minor errors in our use of Truth, for since each soul is made in likeness unto God, his radiancy is like to that of God, and is all powerful so long as he but lets it shine.

Man's failures come from vain attempts to change this true out-shining power, into a false in-drawing power. By doing this, man vainly hopes to *draw unto* himself whate'er he wants. It fails; for by this means man shrinks his power. 'Tis wiser far to radiate one's power—to know one can expand without a limit to one's energies, and thus—like unto God—*enfold* whate'er the soul desires.

And secondly, I treasure Christ's ideal of *heaven.*

He tried so very patiently to make it clear to those he taught two thousand years ago. The word he used for heaven—ouranos —means *fore'er expanding to the infinite.*

To make his meaning clear, he told his listeners that heaven is like to leaven, and that is yeast! Again he said that heaven is like unto a mustard seed. And we of northern farms know well that e' en one mustard seed can spread its progeny so fast, that soon an entire field is overrun with mustard plants.

The only hell the soul knows on this earth, is the repression and suppression of its deep desire forever to expand!

And all the joys of heaven on this earth come from expanding, hour by hour, to more and more of what the soul desires.

I treasure too, Christ's teaching that the kingdom of all heaven is within us now. The word, *basilica*—translated kingdom in our texts—means fort or stronghold of all power. 'Tis thus the Christ so simply teaches you that deep within yourself, there is the fort of power of all expansion of your soul—and hence the power to radiate, whate'er you want!

Then third, I treasure Christ's ideal of *life*.

There are, we know, four different words translated *life* in our New Testament. But there is only one that's often used by Christ himself. It means, the e'er *increasing increase of activity*. That is, to Christ,—"I am the bread of life," most clearly means, I am the substance that sustains a *constant increase* of activity. And that should be the test that proves, if we are living in his truth, or not.

I do *not* hold that this activity is limited to action of the physical! But ne'er theless, it is significant, that in Christ's healing of the individual, some action of the body did proceed or was required *before* the healing miracle was wrought.

The woman on the road did crawl through crowds to touch the hem of garments worn by Christ; the blinded man was asked to mix soft mud with spittle, for his eyes; another one, was told to bathe in waters of a pool, another, told to lift his bed, and then to walk.

I know it was not such activity alone, which wrought the healing miracles of Christ.

But this I know; no soul can realize the perfect power of Truth until it feels impelled by soul desire so strong that it full willingly shall turn its faith into activity! And so I hold that this true life—the *increase* of activity as taught by Christ—is e'er the ultimate in every healing wrought.

Then fourth, I treasure Christ's ideal of *faith*.

The word is *pistis* in the Greek. For years, I doubted I might have, whatever I believed I had! But then illumination came, when first I recognized that our word 'piston' comes from that same pistis root. I then saw clearly,— that like the piston of an engine, harmonic action is true faith. A piston is forever active, throbbing up and down, continuously, in perfect rhythm. That gave to me a new ideal of the strong faith which Jesus taught. 'Tis not a faith of mental-mind; but rather ever constant throbbing urge of soul. (The words believed and faith, are our translations of the word *pistis*, as used by Christ.)

When soul pulsates with strong desire, and throbs with love of what it wants, continuously, without a let up or a lag,—then miracles are wrought with certainty that's absolute.

And fifth, I treasure Christ's ideal of *love*.

I know it's true,—we cannot love the Truth nor love our God, unless we first are daily manifesting love unto our brother man. That led my soul to know,—the *more* I emphasize how much my concepts of the Truth are different from the concepts others teach, the *less* of help I render unto those I want to aid.

And also this,—the more I recognize the love in other leaders, here and now and in the past, the more of love I shall awaken in the hearts of those I long to help.

There's naught but love can solve the problems of this earth, for man is torn from man by differing thoughts, and naught but love will ease the conflicts of those thoughts! And love will solve the problems of the body, too, for when its cells respond to love, and love each other more, the body is at peace.

'Tis true I do insist on living in an atmosphere of love. It's not from snobbishness of spirit, but from a right divine. I want as workers only those whom I can love, and only those who love enough to work in harmony. Naught else is worth the living on this earth, for what will be the profit to a soul, if it but sells itself to do great work,—and lives in strife, and finds not love!

These concepts—of the radiance of God, of Christ's ideal of heaven here, of love, and e'er increasing the activity of life, and faith that is a deep and throbbing urge of soul—all these, determine now for me, the means I use in helping other souls. They reach beyond the mental mind, to spirit power.

And since true spirit will not tolerate the limitations of the conscious mind, one must—to heal with certainty—e'er lead the soul to free itself of its own conscious thought about itself. I think that we have used too much of thought, and not enough of love. I think we have too often held a thought for this, and then another thought for that,—much as the old time doctor used naught else except a drug for this, and then another drug for that. And I am sure we can not free the soul of conscious thought, by holding other conscious thoughts.

And so, I use the stars! No soul can walk beneath the stars, without soon losing all its thought of worry and resentment too; and e'en its depths of desperation turn to calmness and to peace. Beneath the stars—gigantic and so vast—the soul can not long think of smaller things about itself, for it is lifted up unto the grandeur and the majesty of its true self.

Then next, I seek a *spiritual expression* of the soul! And in this too, the less of conscious thought, the greater is the end attained,—for it is spirit's deeper feelings of a oneness with all life, which works great miracles.

And so I lead the soul to open unto power,—as ferns unfurl at dawn; to voice its joy of life,—as birds that sing unto the morn; to feel its own stability,—as pine trees stand erect and strong, unmoved by storms; and to adjust oneself to life, as willows Wave with winds, forever bending with the winds, yet e'er remaining willow trees; to feel its youthfulness,—as prancing colts at play; to rise above all pettiness,—as eagles sweep the sky above all little things of earth; to reach to heights divine,—by winging up to stars and their vast realms of space; and then for rest, to gently close the mind, as petals of a rose fold in upon themselves as sun goes down.

I know that these are not the essence of our truth; they are but means I use to free the conscious mind of thinking all too much about itself, and then the spirit works its miracles—without the strain of conscious mind. In choice of *means*,—remember "how the lilies grow."

The seventh factor, I hold dear, is the deep feeling of the *presence* of the radiant God. I know he lives *in* all and everything, and that all lives in him—each moment of life here, and through eternity.

I find my God of Truth in everything—in harmonies I hear from wings of humming birds; in concerts of electrons singing silently; in symphonies of stars within the Milky Way.

I know I live within the power that twirls a mist into a star, and grinds a sun to star dust. I know I live within the energy that shoots through million-miles of space. I know I live within the action that forever moves the sea and turns a billion suns!

I know I live within the Mind that called forth Betelgeuse, and forms the atoms, too. I know I live within the Love that makes true brothers of all molecules. I know I live within the Life that makes all life create more life! Ah yes, I live within the joys of stars, and singing birds, and running waters, rustling leaves! I live in God—no limit and no boundary! I even live within the laugher and the mirth and joy of knowing that I live in all that God creates!

And this *expanded* life is heaven unto me—one glimpse of that great Truth which writers of this book give unto you.

WHAT COMES FIRST IN NEW THOUGHT
BY CHRISTIAN D. LARSON

Christian D. Larson, of Norwegian extraction, was born in Iowa. Attended Iowa State College and a theological school (Unitarian) in Meadville, Pa. Became interested at that time (1896) in Mental Science. Located in Cincinnati, 0. in 1898 where he established a New Thought Temple, owned, published and edited *Eternal Progress* in 1901, carrying it to a circulation of over a quarter of a million. Forty of his books have been published. Among the best known are: *Poise and Power, The Great Within, The Hidden Secret, Mastery of Self, Mastery of Fate, The Ideal Made Real, Thinking for Results, Your Forces and How to Use Them, How to Stay Well, and The Pathway of Roses.* Now living in Los Angeles where he conducts public and private activities and continues his writings.

WHATEVER the mode of approach may be, or the method that we use in metaphysical work, it is absolutely necessary that we go deeper and farther into the soul and the spirit of it all, if we are to have good results, and increasing results. The reason for this is perfectly clear. There is no power out on the surface. There is no power in shallow thinking, nor in words or affirmations that are merely outer forms of expression. Our statements must have depth and soul. Our declarations of truth must be charged and endued with a greater something—an inner power; and this power we gain as we go into the soul and the spirit of it all. The same is true of thought, mental activity, faith, vision and consciousness. They all must have depth and height, and do their work in the inner realms of spiritual reality. This is what comes first in the study, the understanding and the application of

New Thought.

Every metaphysical method gains more life, greater authority, and increasing power and effectiveness, when we deepen our thought, and take our work into the spirit. We give something additional to our regular method when we take this step; we create an inner mode of action that can do more and go farther; and, in consequence, results are decidedly better. We accomplish what we seek in much less time; and when this additional method is used in a large way; that is, when we are *greatly* conscious in the inner realms of the spirit, as we do our work, results become remarkable. Indeed, it is on this road that we meet miracle power.

The statement, the formula, the technique, and the forms of expression, are necessary in the application of this teaching; but they are not of first importance. They should be developed with understanding, and they should harmonize with truth and principle; but we should know that they are vehicles for a deeper and greater something that does the work. We should know that results depend upon the depth of thought and consciousness; or, in other words, our nearness to the Source. Experience proves that any well developed metaphysical method, or system of technique, will produce marked results when we go deeper and farther into the soul and the spirit of it all. We may select our favorite methods, therefore, and formulate our thoughts and statements according to the needs of the hour. Results will become greater and greater, as we deepen our thought more and more, and carry our work farther into the spirit.

The importance of taking our thought and our work beneath the surface, and deeper into the spirit, is well illustrated in every religion and philosophy known. When we examine these varied systems, we find that they all have two things in common. They all have two aspects, or levels of thought. The one is the outer belief; the other is the inner teaching. The multitudes accept the outer belief; and they receive therefrom a small measure of hope and consolation. They have a little something to lean on, or hold to, as they journey through life. They have some pleasant promises to dwell upon regarding the distant future; but that is about all. The few, however, who are spiritually minded, discern the inner teaching. They have found the solid rock. They are safe and secure, no matter what may happen out in the sense world, or, whatever the storms of life may be. They are "safe-fixed on high." They are learning to dwell in the secret places. They are guided and protected at every step of the way. "No ill shall come nigh their dwelling." They live, think and work in the deeper consciousness of the spirit.

We meet a similar situation in the metaphysical field. Millions who have come to take a passing interest in the New Thought, have accepted, or been able to see, the outer belief only. They have been helped, temporarily, in a few small ways—enough to make them feel that there is something there; but they have not found the greater something. Nor could they expect to do so. They have merely touched the surface. The real students of metaphysics, however, have enjoyed a different and a greater experience. They have deepened thought and consciousness, and they have discerned the inner teaching; they have stepped into the vastly more of the spiritual realm; and they have, in consequence, gained the understanding and the power. They have had good results invariably; sometimes remarkable results—even astounding results. And, naturally so; for the power is there; any amount of power; and it is found by those who go beneath the surface.

When we see these things, and note the difference between the outer belief and the inner teaching—the weakness of the one and the increasing power of the other— we come to an interesting conclusion. We conclude that the religions and the philosophies of the ages would have been far more effective for good, if the multitudes had been taught and encouraged to seek the inner teaching. The race would have greatly improved; civilization would have advanced far beyond what it is now; the many ills and problems that disturb the world so much would have been disposed of long ago; and unbelievable progress would have been made in a thousand new directions.

The religions and the philosophies of the ages have been face to face, continuously, with a vast opportunity; the opportunity to enlighten the race, emancipate mankind, and transform the earth. But now, this incomparable opportunity has been transferred to the modern metaphysical movement. It is the one movement of thought, in the world today, that can do this marvelous thing; and it will not fail, as former systems have done, if we help the multitudes discern and understand the inner teachings; if we carry our thought and work farther and farther into the soul and the spirit of it all. But we can not approach this task in an attitude of half-hearted interest. We must be determined to do it with all that we are, all that we feel, all that we know. And we will proceed in that fashion when we appreciate how immensely important it is; when we see, as we all do see, how vital it is to maintain a powerful devotion to deeper and higher thinking—and a soul passion for the inner understanding of truth. It is in this way that this movement will grow and develop, until it becomes so mighty for good, that it will prove to be, what many have declared it to be, "the hope of the world."

When we examine the various methods and factors that are used in metaphysical work, we discover at once how important it is to deepen our thought, and enter into the spirit more and more. The power of thought is, in itself, an outstanding illustration. That power becomes effective to the extent that it has depth and soul, and is charged with the *presence* of the spirit. The same is true of our affirmations and statements of truth. They become highly effective when we are deeply conscious of the spirit; when they become vehicles through which the power of the spirit is expressed. And, when we speak the word, it is remarkable how soon our demonstrations or adjustments are made, and the healing realized, when we give something more to those words; when those words are alive with mighty forces from the spiritual within; and when we speak those words, in such a high state of consciousness, that we actually feel as if God were speaking with us and through us at the time. Which, of course, is true during moments like that. The Spirit does act with us, and through us, when we are near enough to the Supreme.

We meet a similar situation in the use of faith—often called the wonder-power in metaphysical and spiritual work. But faith, if it is to do great things, must be more than ordinary believing. There is a wise saying to this effect: "When your faith does not seem to work, have more faith." Which means, that we are to go deeper and farther into our faith; into the soul and the spirit of our faith; and continue to do so. That is how we will have more, and ever more faith, until we have a great faith. And such a faith will carry thought and consciousness so far that we contact Infinity; and it is on that journey that miracle power is released.

To raise consciousness is said to be the greatest achievement in the metaphysical world. And the reason is, that the more we raise consciousness, the more of the mental and the spiritual we become conscious of. This will mean, that we will become conscious of more and more of life, peace, wholeness, strength, harmony, power, truth, perfection, intelligence, all the wonders of the mind, and all the marvels of the soul. Then when we note that what we become conscious of, we gain possession of, we begin to appreciate what the raising of consciousness can do. But how can we lift consciousness unless we go deep and far and high into the vast domains of the mental and the spiritual; unless we seek the supreme heights of the inner life—and do so with all of our heart and soul. It is deeper and higher thinking that will raise consciousness. It is, through a definite and determined effort to go back to God, and draw nearer to the Source, that this remarkable thing is accomplished.

Spiritual understanding is another wonder-worker. Many believe it to be the greatest of all. It is developed as we move in the same direction—

towards the innermost and the highest; and as we seek to enter the secret places of the most High; furthermore, as we search, eagerly, for the deeper and greater meaning of everything in creation; then, above all, as we seek to know the mysteries of the Kingdom. The development of this understanding is a journey into the Spirit—into the vastness and the allness of the Spirit. We step back of the world of things, into that greater world, which is within everything. Our purpose is to find and understand that which is back there, in the beginning of things, at the Supreme Source of it all—with God. It is a journey to that infinite realm, spoken of by the prophets, where all power is given and all truth is known.

To think on these things, is to bring to mind, the numerous and amazing possibilities that are waiting for those who cease to live on the surface; who are not satisfied with outer belief, but who seek, instead, the real teaching itself; and who carry their thought and work deeper and farther into the soul and the spirit of it all. And the way is not as difficult as it may seem. The mind is most responsive; it will do anything for us, or move in any direction, if encouraged sufficiently. The truth is, that the more we think of, and vision, the deeper and the higher in mind and soul, the greater becomes the tendency, and the desire, of the mind to step into that inner realm. Consciousness will begin to develop in that direction. This development will continue, provided we urge, prompt and encourage the mind to go deeper into life and reality; and those activities will be quickened, if we feel convinced that this remarkable thing can be done—that it is being done. The law is this: that the mind will develop the action, and the power to do, whatever we determine to do, *deeply believing*; and, provided we are constant in our purpose. This proves that any goal can be reached, even the highest, and that all things are possible.

A remarkable method, in this field, is that of growth and progression. It is a method of unbounded possibilities; and the principle is well expressed in the statement: "The way out is to grow out." This is, as anyone can see, fundamentally true. We can come out of everything, overcome anything, and attain anything, if we grow far enough. We can, through the laws of progression, gain freedom from any state or condition, and secure anything, in abundance, that life may require; we can even transform our lives, and reach any height imaginable. But growth is mental and spiritual; and, therefore, is an inner process. It can be furthered only in the deeper realms of thought, mind and soul. And for this reason, it is necessary to take our desires for growth, our aspirations, and our constructive activities, into those deeper realms—if we are to advance and progress.

There is neither limit nor end to what may be accomplished through continued progression; and to further progression, on all the levels of life, should be our supreme desire. It will lead to anything we have in view— and to any distance. And on the way, something special happens that is both interesting and significant. We will, on this rising road, see more of everything; we will see everything as larger, better, greater and more perfect at every step of the way; and so our thought about everything will always be new. Here we discover the real meaning of New Thought. It is a mode of living and thinking that goes farther and farther into life, truth and spiritual reality; ever advancing and ascending into more light. It does not stand still, claiming to believe something that is supposed to be final. To try to stand still, is to fall backward. This fact explains much. This teaching is so constructed that it can move forward, and continue to do so for all time. Its fundamental truth is this: "There is more and ever more to be found, known and realized farther on." Infinity is waiting for the growing mind and the rising soul. The one who lives this teaching, therefore, can say upon every morn: "Behold, all things have become new." His thought about everything will always be *new thought*.

We place much emphasis, in this teaching, upon the statement: "Ye shall know the truth, and the truth shall make you free." And we do so with good reason; for this statement reveals one of the great secrets of life. The vital question is, however, how we may know the truth. Literal interpretations and superficial thinking do not lead us into truth. This great knowing does not develop from anything that we may say, do, think or believe out here in the external. It is only through deep thinking and high thinking that we may find and know the truth. It is only through a penetrating insight, and an inner consciousness, that we may know what truth really is, and understand its marvelous meaning. It is only as we go beneath the surface, and beyond the seeming, and journey towards the innermost and the highest in the spiritual universe, that the truth, in its fullness and perfection, is revealed; not revealed, once and for all, but in an increasing measure as we move, in thought, towards Infinity.

We may go on, and consider all other metaphysical methods, with the same object in view; that is, to ascertain what determines their effectiveness and power; and we will come to the same conclusion in each case. We will find that results, in this field, depend, first and foremost, upon *where* we are, in thought and mental action, as we proceed with our work; whether we are on the surface, or beneath the surface; whether we are working in the field of outer belief, or in the realm of deeper understanding; whether we are close to the person, or close to God.

It is our place in the mind—*where* we are in the mind—that determines, more than any other factor, what we are to accomplish in metaphysical study and application. The question of "where," as to mental position, is the one to be asked and answered first of all. We must decide *where* we are to live, think and act when we use our faith, speak the word, affirm the true, and vision the perfect. And, when we decide to go deeper and farther into the soul and the spirit of it all, we have made a great decision. Then we will actually begin to do good work. We will begin to prove the truth, because we are working in the truth; and we can say, in positive terms, that "our prayers availeth much." The methods we are using will become powerful and effective. They will produce definite and increasing results as we advance. They will become highly effective, and immensely powerful, as we go farther, and ever farther, into the spirit—as we draw nearer and nearer to the great Source.

JESUS CHRIST IN HIS KINGDOM
BY ELEANOR MEL

Eleanor Mel, leader of the Boston Home of Truth was born in San Francisco, California. Academic training in Oakland High School and the University of California. The Light came through San Jose Home of Truth as it was then named, conducted by William Farwell, and later named Christian Assembly. Studied with Annie Rix Militz in University of Christ, Los Angeles, California. First field work in Albert Lea and Minneapolis, Minnesota. Came to Boston to attend Congress of I.N.T.A. in 1918. The Boston Home of Truth established in March 1919. Teacher, healer, radio speaker. Offices held, President of New England Federation of New Thought Centers and Vice-President of International New Thought Alliance.

THE one great need today is that we turn more to Jesus Christ— and know Him as really installed in our lives. It is easy for us to know WHERE the Kingdom is. One strong message of Jesus Christ locates it as "within." The answer came to those who were questioning as to when this kingdom would come. Jesus answered plainly. "The Kingdom of God cometh not with observation, neither shall they say 'lo here, lo there,' for behold the Kingdom of God is WITHIN." It is within us, not as a dimensional spot but as a consciousness of the all-good that has power to draw to us everything that we can possibly need—the consciousness that knows no lack. "Seek ye first the Kingdom of God and His righteousness and all these things shall be added." But it is not enough to know that "the Kingdom of God is within us." Unless we make practical use of this knowledge and see Jesus Christ in His Kingdom, "just knowing" this as the permanent way of solving our problems is of little value in our lives.

When He says "The Kingdom of God is within," He means *within you* and *within me*—the within of each and everyone. We need to understand that the Kingdom of God is a practical installation *in all life*. It is the inner *life* of all warring countries—the Kingdom is even within these people who seem to be making a stand in the dark. It may not seem easy for us, with all the evident turmoil, to even remember that the Kingdom of God is an installation in this world—that there is "no other foundation save Jesus Christ"—that "heaven and earth can pass away but the Word of God shall never pass away." But it is TRUE, just the same. Let Jesus Christ within each of us be the reminder!

To make this knowledge actually practical in our lives means to eliminate all fear. We cannot be loving God with all our heart and soul and mind and strength and at the same time be harboring fear in any degree, way, shape or manner. It is wonderful to feel that our part is merely to develop a consciousness that will admit of no presence but the presence of good and Divine Love in our world. This may seem difficult in a world so full of chaos and with the crosscurrents of fear and anxiety and worry but, if we dare to develop this consciousness and hold to it, our part is done and God will do the rest.

Let us see in our world today that Jesus Christ is really in control. He may not be heard of in this capacity, still He is the One in control. He did not come to this earth to demonstrate Life and then leave you and me to do our own struggling in the endeavor to attain what He attained. We need to realize that *His attainment is ours.*

We need to be more fearless about the situations in the world. Fear will not help conditions. When we realize that it is consciousness of the Kingdom of Heaven that we need in order to live our life—when we realize that Jesus Christ is that consciousness—we will learn to identify ourselves with Him and with His Love that never failed to forgive; with His intelligence that never was clouded by ignorance; with His understanding that never was moved and with His Peace that never was disturbed. How wonderful! To be able to actually appropriate His Peace and Love which have been tested, tried and proven! To be identified with the very principle of Life in Jesus Christ! The Life that still stands after being tested to the limit! These are the Powers which are ours by Divine Right and by Gift of God. Thus can we say with Jesus Christ, "0 death where is thy sting? 0 grave where is thy victory?" His Life and His Love are ours. His words that we so often quote are not only His words spoken two thousand years ago but are His words being spoken today!

All Jesus Christ needs is the "right of way" that He may tell to us His best desire. His *best desire* is like that of the Father— "It is your Father's good pleasure to give you the Kingdom." Jesus says, "Fear ye not," because while you are fearful you do not give God the "right of way" and, therefore, you do not become conscious of the "Kingdom of Heaven that is within you." The Kingdom of Heaven really means "expanding activity" of all the good there really is. If we have found it difficult to raise our consciousness above the disagreeable experiences which have seemed to come into our lives and if we are too moved with fear, anxiety, worry and misgivings, remember this—Jesus Christ is here and *He raises* us to that consciousness that permits of no disturbance—"Only believe." He is One that comes to establish us in fearlessness. He becomes the *"right of way."* Isaiah tells us that "there is a highway, a way of holiness, the unclean shall not walk therein." We need to be cleansed of our fears and doubts and worries in order to walk in the Peace of the Kingdom, in order to be worthy and ready to receive that which we already have—the "Kingdom of God within us"—and in order that we may have this out-pictured in our world.

"I came," He says, "that they might have Life and that they might have Life more abundantly." *We make it seem as if He missed His mission if we fail to live the Abundant Life!* This does not mean elongation of Life in years, unless with the years, we have the abundance of joy, life, radiant health, peace and prosperity always—the riches that give us plenty, "overflowing in good measure."

Jesus prospered in everything He did. Everything He touched prospered. Sight sprang forth to the blind and that only because He was being true to the same thing that is within you and within me. But He makes it easier for us if we understand and identify ourselves with Him, for that consciousness with which He did His works and that influence by which God prospered Him so wonderfully are yours and mine without even asking for them. They are *Gifts of God!* We must learn to turn to Jesus Christ and be true to His Indwelling Presence.

He said, "Unless ye eat My flesh and drink My blood there is no life in you." Some of us think how terrible this sounds—like cannibalism! But the life of Jesus Christ is *Light.* Have not the material scientists proven on examination of the blood of very spiritually minded persons, that a chemical change had taken place which, if continued, would end in electric light? Now this is what happened to the blood of Jesus Christ. He became the "Light of the World"—"the Light that lighteth every man that cometh into the world." Later, He said, "I leave the world and go unto My Father."

Just as the air can become vapor, then water, then develop into a block of ice and finally, under the shining sun, evaporate and be drawn upward again, so can we understand the great demonstration of Jesus Christ—His ascension. "In the beginning was the word and the word became flesh." This makes true today His words, "Lo, I am with you always," and they are true for each and every one of us. Let us realize that in turning to Jesus Christ we are not turning to personality but to Divine principle; hence His words, "No man taketh My life from me but I can lay it down of Myself and of Myself I can take it up again." When you and I can say these words in full faith, really believing them, they will become true to us. Remember this: Jesus Christ is consciousness, a faith that never fails, a "peace that passeth all understanding." To eat of His flesh and drink of His blood means to be identified with His Life and Light.

Let us make use of Him and give thanks to God for Jesus Christ! He is the power to demonstrate for us; He is our power to love in the all-forgiving way; He is our power to heal! He is the greatest thing we can turn to, for He is Omnipresent and can speak at all times, in Boston, in Europe, in every part of the world—north, south, east and west,—and say, "Lo, I am with you always," and "I, Who am the perfect law; I, Who was able to be true to that divinity within Myself ; I am that resurrected life in you; I am He that is living and was dead." He speaks within us and tells us that He is resident in each one of us, if we will but be still and listen, and "He that is living and was dead" says, "Behold, I am alive forevermore within you." Death did not touch Him any more than water wets the sands of the desert, when it is only in a mirage of an oasis.

Claim identification with Jesus Christ. Let us learn to love His words, for they lead us into His mind, the mind that never was disturbed; the mind that never expressed a negative thought; the mind that never failed to be stayed on Omnipotence. Let us know that Jesus Christ does this for us! Let us answer His call —"Come unto me, all ye that labor and are heavy laden!" Let us, in the building up of our consciousness, feel the truth of these words, "I will give you rest by letting My consciousness be operative for you!" There is that One Undefeatable Self in you and in me. That Undefeatable Self is Jesus Christ, resident in every cell of our bodies. Let us feel the power in His name because it is the name of Divine principle—the name of Divine Love— the name of the Real You!

"Only believe," He says, "All things are possible to them that believe," and, "Lo, I am with you always"—your unfailing, unvarying, unbreakable faith; your resurrected life; your love that knows no unforgiveness; your peace that passeth all understanding; your consciousness of *"the Kingdom of God within you"* and Jesus Christ in His Kingdom—your Kingdom, my

Kingdom.

Let us be sure to make use of this gift! Let us *dare* to be still! Let us *dare* to become acquainted with His daring! Let us *accept* Him! Let us *feel* Him "If ye abide in Me and My words abide in you, ye shall ask what ye will and it shall be done unto you." *What an offer this is!* Let us believe that these words are true and that Jesus Christ is in His Kingdom; that He is in you and in me and in every part of our country—*in complete control*—in spite of appearance to the contrary. Let us trust in His power to control. Let us be still and know that His "Peace be still" is as powerful today as it was about two thousand years ago! Let us enjoy our Kingdom and the King, Jesus Christ!

*   *   *

A presentation of Jesus Christ's teachings and practice as interpreted by The Home of Truth is here offered to the world,— a presentation that is believed to be the primitive ministry of Christianity, which was given to the world for man's healing or salvation—body, soul and estate.

The chief teacher and founder is Jesus Christ. The great authority for our belief is the Holy Spirit within each one; and the church is the whole body of divine humanity everywhere. The text books are: First, the Four Gospels of Matthew, Mark, Luke and John, especially the words of Jesus Christ; second, the remaining books of the Bible; and the third, all other Scriptures and writings that have blessed humanity. Our family is the whole of humanity visible and invisible, and we are all brothers and sisters with one Father and one Mother, whose name is God.

Realizing that the church of Christ is that perfect body of humanity that does not need to be organized or held together by rules and strictures, the workers of this presentation have formed no new church or creed, but have seen that the homes of the nation are the spiritually natural places for worship and the healing and teaching ministry. The true home is the representation of Heaven. And that happy, innocent, wise and loving interior state which is the real Kingdom of Heaven, externalizes itself most naturally, as a home of comfort, harmony and bliss. Such homes are the beginnings of Heaven upon earth, promised by the Spirit and prophesied by the Christ.

Two or three souls, consecrated with all their love of heart, soul, mind and strength to God the Good, have been the starters of each one of the Homes of Truth. These teachers believe that God the Good is All in All, and that there is none to love or to be, to know or to work for but this One—in our neighbor, in ourself, or in the world; this being their interpretation of the greatest of all the commandments—Mark 12:29, 30, 31.

They believe that every good gift has been conferred upon us freely by our Heavenly Father, and that knowledge of Truth and its application, will reveal to us eternal health, unchanging prosperity, age-lasting life, and all the bliss of omniscient, omnipresent and omnipotent Love.

They believe that Heaven is within you, and that you are to manifest it on the earth, and need not wait to die in order to enter into its joys.

They believe that all men and women are innately good, and that all are alive, whether visible or invisible, and under the care and guidance of the loving Father, who knows no failure but will present Truth in all ways to His children until every one shall come to himself and to the joy for which his heart has been yearning.

The public ministration has three departments: Healing, teaching and worship.

The healing ministry is the same as that of Jesus Christ, who healed through knowledge and by speaking the word of truth, both silently and audibly. The Lord is the great physician with whom all things are possible, and to whom no disease is incurable. "I am the Lord that healeth thee."

No charge is made for any of the ministrations, for all the gifts of God are free, and we are all one family, whose members in the heavenly state are not under the law of barter, since buying and selling have no place in the realm of the Spirit. Love always expresses itself in gifts; and in loving our neighbor as ourselves, we give freely even as the Spirit has given to us freely. Therefore, nothing of the healing and teaching is priced or sold, but all are love gifts. The same privilege of free giving is accorded to those who come to the Home or love its ministry, and many give richly and generously to the work, in the form of money or other expressions of value.

The first of these Homes has been in existence for over fifty years, and thousands testify to the benefits in healing, both physical and spiritual, conferred upon them by the workers and healers. Through the meditations morning, noon and evening, there is a spiritual rhythm that maintains a spiritual atmosphere which stands as a background for many classes. Individual instruction and healing is carried on.

The Sunday School is an important feature. Also the schedule of lessons used to prepare teachers and healers for the ministry of Jesus Christ is an important feature of the Home of Truth idea. Residence in the Home during this preparation gives a wonderful opportunity for Christ unfoldment. There are always guest rooms in the Home, where anyone in sympathy with its ministry, can reside for a time, according to the good judgment of the household. The chapel is open to the public for meditations and readings. A fine Reading Room and Lending Library is another feature.

Each Home is independent of all the others, financially and in methods of ministry, and yet they are in perfect harmony as to the main ideas. The desire and aim of the workers is to maintain equality among themselves and to esteem all the work equally honorable. This is accomplished by working for God alone and being unmoved by the opinions, criticisms and ingratitude of people. The Lord within the people knows, and will finally be the only One to speak and act in response to the love and faith extended by the workers.

This Home aspires to be only one of all the homes of truth throughout the earth, and its most earnest desire is that every home shall be a healing center, where anyone who loves the truth may find spiritual refreshment; instruction and counsel without money and without price;—where they may be healed physically and morally, and become themselves instruments of blessing to hasten the day prophesied in Jeremiah 31:34, when "they shall all know me, from the least of them unto the greatest of them, saith the Lord," and (Isaiah 11:19) "the earth shall be full of the knowledge of the Lord as the waters cover the sea." "He which testifieth these things saith Surely I come quickly." Rev. 22:20.

IDENTIFICATION WITH THE POWER OF GOD
BY HENRY VICTOR MORGAN

Rev. Henry Victor Morgan, Pastor of the Church of the Healing Christ, Tacoma, Washington, and Poet Laureate of the 1.N.T.A., is known as "the man with a million friends." For many years a minister of the Universalist Church, he has subsequently devoted thirty or forty years to the healing ministry in the Church of the Healing Christ. Mr. Morgan publishes *The Master Christian* and is author of: *Cosmic Consciousness and World Healing, The Pathway of Prayer, Soul Powers and Privileges, The Healing Christ, The Master Powers of Man, Path-way of Blessedness*, and numerous booklets.

THE most surprising thing about this article, to many readers, will be its simplicity. And yet something is here given out of my long experience in the healing ministry that may open to all who enter into the spirit of it, a way into a kingdom that beggars the glory of Solomon's.

This lesson has not only appealed to beginners but has brought words of praise from many who have studied long and earnestly. I am now sending it forth on wings of love to all readers of this book, as my love offering to the world, praying earnestly that all who read may enter more fully into that Place of Power where miracles are born.

* * *

"He that believeth on me, the works that I do shall he do also; and greater works than these shall he do, because I go unto my Father."—john 14:12

The realization of two great truths is all that is essential to a successful Healing Ministry.

First and Foremost: It is essential to know, not merely to believe, that God is all there is or can be; that He is the animating Life of the universe; that as the earth rests in the soft arms of the atmosphere, so does man rest in the bosom of God.

The Second Great Truth: Man is God's image and likeness. Therefore, every power attributed to God must, by the very nature of things, be embodied in "His image and likeness."

It was the application of the Principle contained in these two statements that released me from a limitation caused by an accident, and which had held me in bondage from the time I was twenty-one until I was thirty-seven, a condition for which the doctors knew no cure. In the hour of my greatest darkness, when even hope was almost dead, a little pamphlet on spiritual healing was given me which contained, in substance, these words:

Man is in God's image and likeness. Therefore, the truth about God is the truth about spiritual man. This is the truth that Jesus said would make you free.

Something within me said: If this is so, I will never have another convulsion. I seemed to hear a Voice saying: "It is true and you never will." Nearly forty healthful and health-giving years have passed since then and I never have.

I had found an *available* God.

Man is in the image and likeness of God. Than this there can be no higher truth. If God is our Father, then all the qualities of the Father's mind must inhere in the son. Surely we have not known what we are. God's image has not been expressed. Man is still in the making. We have resources on which we have not drawn.

It is only as we catch sight of our God-like origin that we can overcome the flesh and rise to dominion. No stream can rise higher than its source. No thing can be evolved that is not involved. Man cannot become what he is not by nature. *But this vision of dominion is in the soul of man.* We must reverently realize that as is the Father so is the son, and claim our inheritance as sons of God and brothers of the Christ.

This is the basis of all right thinking. He who meditates on the truth of God's image in the soul will find that he has touched a stream of power before unknown. As is his thought, so will be his expression. To think of God is to realize strength. To become an imitator of God is the Christ way of attainment. When Jesus said: "I and my Father are One," he revealed the secret of mastery to all the sons of men.

After my healing, a new world of divine possibility opened before me. I could understand the feeling of Paul, when the scales fell from his eyes and he saw Life in the Light of the Spirit. The news of my healing soon brought many to me seeking help. I then discovered a wonderful thing: *that by simply holding people in mind and thinking earnestly on the Power that healed me, many marvelous cures were made.* Later I took classwork in nearly every phase of the metaphysical movement, but I have found in all my studies no higher method than this.

The secret of healing power is to know and practice the presence of God's image in every man. We must know that as God is limitless in power, so is man when dwelling in the secret place of the Most High. How strengthening to man is the knowledge of the indwelling God. It is the assurance of things hoped for. To this faith nothing is impossible. It is health to all our flesh just to realize that the Life of God is perfect in every cell of our body.

Live in this thought and the stream of God's omnipotence will flow through your every act and word. You will become vitalized by your own controlling idea. You will call out in men the power you KNOW to be there. You will become magnetized by divinity and your word and thought will be creative. You will be in direct touch with the Father of Light and in that Light there will be no darkness. You will heal the sick by your very presence.

You will awaken in others the Power of God, to which all things are possible. God is available Power here and now. The Father stands back of all men and women who recognize Him in all their ways. "It is not I but the Father . . ." forever sings the soul inspired with the Divine Idea.

I love to refer to this method of identification with God as a system *that has foundations whose builder and maker is God.* In my classwork, I have found three rules to be beneficial:

First: While giving a spiritual treatment, dismiss all thought of yourself. Know that it is not you who are giving the treatment, but *"the Father which dwelleth in you."*

Second: Blot out all memory of what your patient has told you concerning his limitations.

Third: Having called your patient's name and having identified him with the Power of God, fill your mind with the Perfection, Omniscience and Love of God. Realize what Emerson meant when he said: *"When the mind of the devotee is caught up until he sees the thing as it is in God, then is the miracle wrought."*

One of my first remarkable experiences in healing was that of a young man affected with typhoid fever. The case appeared hopeless at the time I was sent for. At that time, I had not taken any class lessons in healing, so I simply realized: "The power that healed me is healing you," and in half an hour the fever was gone, *consciousness restored, and healing followed.*

I give another instance to show how *all who have faith* can take part in the healing ministry. In a city in Nebraska, I gave one lesson-lecture on "Healing by the Power of God." A young woman who bad never before attended a healing meeting, brought a friend who was afflicted with goiter.

All the time I was talking, she kept repeating: *"The power he is talking about is now healing my friend."* So great was her faith that she expected the goiter to be gone before the lecture was over, but it was not. Six weeks later, however, it had disappeared entirely and there had been no further treatment of any kind. This leads me to say that while healing is instantaneous in consciousness, its *appearance* is often made manifest in time.

What marvels we would witness if all persons who attend meetings where God is recognized as able to do exceeding abundantly above all we ask or think, *would hold in mind those whom they want helped!*

At first, I thought it was necessary to see personally those who needed help. I kept office hours. Later I discovered that those who wrote or telegraphed, and whom I had never seen, often received greater help than those whom I saw daily. I now know that *since God is omnipresent, man (who is in His image and likeness) is also omnipresent.* The time is coming when the word *absent* treatment will be obsolete, *for while our mind is on God we are omnipresent in God.*

*   *   *

As a man thinketh in his heart, so is he. As long as we think poverty is the *will of God*, so long will we be poor. We may even pile up millions of dollars and still be poor in consciousness. My own release from the poverty consciousness came while applying the principle of meditation as given in this statement:

"Words born from a high soul consciousness will awaken in whosoever repeats them, in prayerful meditation, the consciousness from which they sprang."

While meditating on the words of Jesus: *"All that the Father hash is mine,"* it was given me to see that as all the air is mine, and the sun is all mine, so I could say: *"Every dollar in the world is mine this minute."* From that day to this, I have never known what it was to lack any good thing. All my needs have been *abundantly* supplied according to His riches.

If we can only be still and know that we are channels through which God works, the right word will be given us. We need take no anxious thought. We need only to obey. When the word is given *in the silence*, then and only then can we say: *"The word of God in me is instant and powerful and it always works."*

For attaining the consciousness of God as infinite supply, I have found these statements most helpful: *"All that the Father hath is mine."*—*"My God will supply all my needs according to His riches."*—*"I am permanently conscious of unescapable prosperity."*—*"I know the things I stand for are dear to the heart of God; therefore, God is my instant and everlasting supply."*

*   *   *

For those who practice the Presence of God and identify themselves with the Eternal, *the best is always yet to be*, for they travel the pathway of Infinite Enlargement. They become like that on which their minds function. Their polarization is changed from man-limited to God-limitless. They have found the Secret Place of the Most High. Their thought of God forms a healing and protecting aura. They receive celestial instruction. They are guided from within. For attaining this intuitional insight, I have found meditation on this statement useful:

"I have within me, by reason of my divinity, a faculty for direct inspiration and unerring knowing."

Whoever you are, *for intuitional realization and treatment,* realize that you are the beloved of God; that you are now in the beginning with God; that you will ever be in the beginning with God. That the healing power of God's love fills every cell of your body with Life, Health, Strength, Truth and Action.

Realize that God is the Health of your mind, the loving support of your body and the glorious fulfillment of every true desire; that the Great Soul needed an organ in you, and that all your needs have been provided for from before the foundation of the world; that the thing you have always desired to do is the Voice of your ability, calling you to do it.

Then will the world see you the strong, the radiant, the advancing child of God, glorious in strength, and bringing health and blessings wherever your footsteps lead. Then will you know you are identified with the Power of God.

THE TRANSFORMING POWER OF MIND
BY VILLA FAULKNER PAGE

Villa Faulkner Page, founder of the Fellowship of Life Abundant, now leader of the Metaphysical School of Health at 60 Gramercy Park, New York City, was born and reared in New York State. Was graduated from State Normal Training School, Cortland, N.Y. Teacher of psychology and pedagogy in a State Normal School, New Paltz, N.Y. Six years associated with Charles Oliver Sahler, M.D., of Kingston, N.Y., America's great pioneer in psychotherapy. Student of Judge Troward in England in 1914. Author of the booklets: *Prayer, With the Master Builder, Christmas with the New Year, Truth Which Makes Free, Poems of Truth and Beauty, Bran Rudyn: A Song of Life.* Member of The Woman's Press Club of New York; The Pen Women's Club; The Federation of Women's Clubs; Daughters of the American Revolution.

THE New Thought Teaching is based upon the knowledge and practice of the Thought Power vested in us as Humans.

The words of Paul of Tarsus—"Be ye transformed by the renewing of your mind, that ye may prove what is the good and acceptable and perfect will of God"—becomes effectual in life today; through the instrumentality of Thought, man expresses his spiritual activity; and as he learns to control and direct thought he can be freed from suffering, disease, lack and limitation.

The oft-repeated Bible words: "As a man thinketh in his heart so is he" prove the truth; knowing which a new experience, a new life, becomes the rule.

"Behold, I make all things new" is the teaching of our Bible; which means a New Thought, a New World for everyone who believes and practices the teaching.

Thus the New Psychology was evolved, teaching us to know the influence of mental states upon physical conditions as well as the influence of physical conditions upon mental states. For example: Fear causes pallor and tremor of voice; joy or humor causes laughter; grief causes tears. All are common experiences which to the thoughtful mind are evidences; and at last the fundamental, working hypothesis was found which holds that "mind and body, mental states and physical conditions are the dual aspects of something greater than either; viz: the opposite poles of one reality."

We never weary of reviewing the many examples and proofs of this Law, under which the whole universe is created. Thirty or more years ago a great Russian scientist related that under the microscope he had seen the white blood corpuscles (the phagocytes) in the individual illustrate the Law of Mind.

Their function is to wrap themselves about any germ which may have been taken in and carry it out of the system. "I have seen them, when the individual was under fear or dread, turn tail and run away. Later, when that individual had been infused with a good Dutch courage, they came back and resumed their work."

Law was given by Moses to the Chosen People coming out of slavery. In fullness of time came love, the manifestation of the Christ "begotten of God."

Solomon writes: "The true beginning of wisdom is discipline and the care of discipline is love, and love is the keeping of its law."

Understanding is born of love. One who knows how to use understanding and knowledge has wisdom.

Again we turn to the words of Solomon, man of wisdom: "She, (Wisdom) is the breath of the power of God, and a pure influence flowing from the glory of the Almighty, therefore can no defiled thing fall upon Her, for She is the brightness of the Everlasting Light, the unspotted mirror of the power of God and the image of His goodness; and remaining in herself— she maketh all things new, and in all ages entering into holy souls she maketh them friends of God and Prophets." (Apocrypha)

The New Thought was hailed as a Pathway to release from the tribulation to which man is subject. "In the world ye shall have tribulation," said the Master, "but be of good cheer, I have overcome the world."

Gladly, reverently, we entered on the Pathway—proving at each step in this simple beginning, that Perfect Law of Jehovah which converts the soul. What joy to be told that in each one may the Christ be born! ("My little children, of whom I am again in travail until the Christ be born in you" said Paul to the Galatians.) Then, may be the transmutation by which "we become what we are"! ("Ye are Gods, though ye die like men!" said the Prophet.)

"But," said the man of Human Wisdom, "you are what you are, and so do you remain! It is Character that determines what you are! And 'character' is derived from the Greek word Karakos which means a scratch on a metal. A man will always be what he is in character!"

"Then our endeavor to help men and women to be better is useless?" one asked breathlessly.

"What one is, that he remains!" said the man of Human Wisdom.

In agony of heart the listener went away into prayerless darkness! "Why pray?" the sufferer would ask. "I am what I am, and that I must remain!"

Then came a day of hope! ("He giveth His Angels charge over thee to keep thee in all thy ways.") The way was pointed and made open by one by whom was known "the Truth that makes free!"

"Because I live ye shall live also," said the Master. "Christ in you the hope of glory," said Paul. In other words, the Supreme Intelligence-Power, that all-knowing Power is in the "Human Man," and when awakened, man

says with the Master, "The Father and I are One I" "All Power is mine."
"I—if I be lifted up will draw all men unto me." (The Christ or God Con-
sciousness "lifted up," or expanded.) "We have the mind of Christ," said
Paul. "All things are yours and ye are Christ's and Christ's is God's."

One step further! From Ancient Wisdom we learn that G---O---D is the
hieroglyphic spelling of that which is the Great Motivating (directing) Intelligence of All the Universe—of All Universes! The Omniscience.

Then "All is Mind." Then "There is no High"—"There is no Low,"
"There is no Great," "There is no Small." "There is only God."

This one Intelligence—God or Being—(The "Ain Soph Aur" —or Limitless Light, of the Kabbalah) is dual in aspect. It is Force (that which can
change the place of things) which in Activity is Energy and when focalized
is Power. This is the Father-God.

The second Aspect is Creativeness or Love or Understanding or Consciousness. This is the Mother-God.

That which is born of these is the Son. (1. That which can move; 2. That
which can be moved; 3. That which is moved.) This the Trinity:—Father,
Mother, Son.

Every perfected manifestation therefore, on whatever Plane of Being is
in Balance, or, "Fifty-Fifty."

The Great Reality in all is—Being—that which is without Beginning or
End—the Alpha and Omega—the Invisible.

The great Actuality is the manifested being.

Intelligence or Mind directs and controls all manifestations on all planes,
according to Law.

That Law which holds the Atom in place, in perfect operation is the
same Law which governs and controls the Solar System.

Verily:—"The Law of Jehovah is perfect restoring (converting) the Soul;
the Testimony of Jehovah is sure, making wise the Simple; the Precepts of
Jehovah are right rejoicing the heart." (Ps: 19)

Man's goal, then, is to attain unto that Perfect Wisdom which insures Perfect Manifestation.

Thus, as we learn how to read our Bible, we find it a Storehouse! The Great Text Book of all Life or Being. It teaches that "Truth which makes free!"

In its Allegorical style as written—(the style peculiar to the Orient) are given the Truths of all Science: Physiology, Psychology, Metaphysics and the Mysteries. The New Thought is based on those Truths, again we repeat.

To illustrate: We are shown by our Masters of Research that the Book of Genesis is the Recital of the building of Man's body and the focalizing therein of God-Intelligence.

The story of Noah, his three Sons, the Ark, the Flood is but that which the New Psychology gives: Noah, the Great Life Principle; Shem, the Conscious or Objective Mind; Ham, the Sub-Conscious or Habit Mind; Japheth, the Super-Conscious Mind. The Flood—that flood of Understanding poured into Man as the Ages advanced.

Mind is Creative so there are born, (allegorically) sons, daughters, families, nations; or Ideas, thoughts, words, actions. As all these are Positive or Constructive all relations are happy and peaceful. As they are destructive Wars occur.

Therefore: "Be ye perfect as your Father in Heaven is perfect." "All things are yours—and ye are Christ's and Christ's is God's."

In the Bible's Allegory we learn that the Garden of Eden represents the Perfect Plan of Manifestation: Adam the Earth man—Eve, the Soul.

The Four Rivers of Eden: Pishon, Gihon, Hiddekel, Euphrates—typify the Four-Fold Nature of Man :—Physical, Astral, Soul, Spirit. Again is the Four-Fold Nature presented in the Vision of Ezekiel;—and lastly in Revelations—(21-16)—the New Jerusalem that "lieth four square, and on each side three gates and each gate a pearl."

Let John ("who dwelt in Patmos, for his Savior's sake") tell of the opening of the Seven Seals—and then we are shown that they but typify the Seven Centers of Mind Action;—Solomon's version of which being: "He gave unto Man the five Operations of the Lord to which was added in the sixth place the Power of Illumination for the Understanding thereof, and in the Seventh place the Power of Speech for the interpretation of the Cognitations thereof."

The Master, Jesus the Christ, in teaching shows the Path of Attainment, of Manifestation.

His the Science, the Knowledge, the Understanding, the Wisdom, the Love! The Son of Man—begotten only of God; the God Consciousness in Him, the Christ even as promised! "The Word made flesh!"

Let us note also that this Practice is but the following of the Noble Eight-Fold Path of Ancient Wisdom: "The Right Belief, the Right Thought, the Right Word, the Right Action, the Right Means of Livelihood, the Right Exertion, the Right Remembrance and Self-Discipline, the Right Concentration."

*   *   *

The Pathway to all Truth is Prayer. Hence must we learn how to pray—and how to "continue constant in prayer." ("Whatsoever ye ask and pray for believe that ye have it and it shall be done unto you.")
This Contact through Prayer or Meditation or the Silence then releases one from the influence of Sensation, Emotion, Objective or Mortal Thought, Desire, Will.

"But thou when thou prayest enter into thine inner Chamber, and having shut the door, pray to thy Father who is in secret, and thy Father who is in secret shall reward thee openly."

Through relaxation, concentration (the Silence) there is contact with the Real Self—or the God self—the Christ within. Then is Peace. Then are the Life Forces released—Nature's Harmony—(the God Harmony) is restored. "Dis-ease" is removed, Health is reestablished, transformation is attained. ("Be still and know that I am God"). Peace, Harmony, Love! Wisdom is born. Guidance in all ways is given. Perfect manifestation in Thought, Word, Action follows.

The secret of all success lies in the utilization of every power, every faculty, every law and process of nature for the attainment of an ideal. So long as that ideal embodies all the elements that make for the peace, comfort, happiness and development of the individual and through him the race of man generally.

*   *   *

How may one teach, train, treat another, so as to release in him the Life Forces—and secure for him health, happiness and power to win success?

First: No two people are alike. Therefore all work must be given in accord with the Soul's Law of the Individual.

We cannot compel; we can impel.

Certain principles obtain in all teaching. It is well to bear them in mind in whatever phase of the work.

First; begin with the Known and proceed to the Unknown.

Second; begin with the Simple and proceed to the difficult.

Third; from the visible proceed to the invisible.

The great factors to be employed: Relaxation of Mind and Body; and mental treatment, oral and silent to be given.

The thoughts to be considered are of a perfect condition. Examples:

1. In real self all is quiet.

2. The blood flows evenly from head to foot: Peace—Peace, Peace.

3. Life in you is perfect.

4. Life, Love, Peace now enfold you and permeate you. Peace —Peace— Peace.

5. You are God's dear child.

In my personal experience many hundreds have been restored to health. So-called "incurables" have been made perfectly well.

Mental as well as physical cases responded quickly—(after years of treatment Abroad as well as in America.)

A physician, suffering with asthma so intense that the heart was displaced, was relieved in precisely two minutes by the above process.

A boy of 14 years—a dwarf—was made to grow to normal height. He is a celebrated physician today.

The most virulent diseases, as cancer, tuberculosis—blood poison—etc. have been completely restored.

Psychic cases—as obsessions, have been restored.

Insomnia, Melancholia, Fixed Idea, I have seen completely restored.

Every aspect of physical or mental disorder can thus be reached. There is Hope for all.

> "There is an inmost centre in us all
> Where Truth abides in fullness; . . .
> And to know
> Rather consists in opening out a way
> Whence the imprisoned splendor may escape,
> Than in effecting entry for a light
> Supposed to be without."

THE LAW OF LOVE APPLIED TO BODY AND AFFAIRS
BY BLANCHE MARIE PETERS

Blanche Marie Peters, Ms.D., founder and leader of the Radiant Life Fellowship, was born in New York City. Mrs. Peters, who is nationally known as a writer for prominent metaphysical magazines, lives in Syracuse, New York, where she devotes her time to writing, lecturing and teaching.

NEW Thought is a practical, scientific mental system of regeneration. This system of redemption for the whole man is based upon divine laws. Since God-Mind must be contacted through mental faculties, man must learn to control his thought processes, his mental actions and reactions. By training his mind to "think God's thoughts after Him" man may overcome his mortal tendencies and be lifted up into his true spiritual state, as the offspring of his heavenly Father. He expresses his highest Self increasingly as he grows in love, wisdom and understanding.

This process of spiritual rebirth in the individual is brought about by his acknowledging that of himself (on his human level of consciousness) he does not have power, but only as he is lifted up (to the consciousness of his true identity as a son of the living God) can he attain his divine inheritance of health, joy and abundance. Seek ye first his kingdom, and his righteousness (the right use of his laws); and "all these things shall be added unto you," is the promise. Emerson informs us that "Great men are they who see that spirituality is stronger than any material force; thoughts rule the world."

SELF-HELP THROUGH SELF-KNOWLEDGE

The chief aim of the New Thought movement is to help people to help themselves. First, by teaching the student what God is and how to develop a better understanding of Him. Second, by aiding him to a realization of his oneness with his Real Self or God in him. Third, by explaining in a simple way the scientific principles which are the fundamental laws of life. Fourth, by presenting working formulas for the application of these rules, showing him "just how" they should be used. Fifth, by teaching him his true spiritual unity with other individuals through the Christ Spirit inherent in each. Sixth, by instructing him in the science of prayer, or silent communion with Divine Spirit within him for consolation, upliftment, greater wisdom, renewal of faith, more life, power, harmony and peace, the realization of which helps him in the demonstration of health of body, tranquillity of mind, and the successful adjustment of his outer affairs.

MAN A CO-CREATOR WITH GOD

By acquiring an understanding of the benign laws of God man may attune himself with his heavenly Father's purposes of good for all. Thus he becomes a cocreator with God and may bring into his experience inspiration, joy, life and peace of mind; harmony, power and perfection of body; satisfaction in his environment and success in his affairs.

We must learn to live in love, harmony, and cooperation with others. This means a surrender of the selfish ego and a blending of our will with the divine. The intellect must become a servant of God.

We must learn to place first things first—GOD FIRST. In order to help us to do this, it is a good thing to declare: *"I allow my body to be ruled by my mind; I surrender my mind to the control of my soul; and I yield my soul to the guidance of God."*

In reality each individual is a law unto himself. He may exercise his prerogative of choosing for himself what he will think. The majority of people know but little of spiritual Truth, consequently they believe only what the senses tell them and judge entirely by objective appearances. Therefore it is important that each of us immunize himself against race consciousness by the repetition of words and statements which represent spiritual Reality.

This act constitutes a lifting process which helps us to rise above mortal limitation into the pure Light of Spirit where all is good. By this ascending action we clear the way for divine Law to operate in our affairs, which automatically dissolves the error condition, whatever it may be, into its native nothingness, and our Father's perfect divine Plan becomes manifest.

Using statements in line with Truth may be likened to working the controls in an airplane causing the ship to rise in the air. Instead of coasting along on the bumpy ground at a limited speed, with many obstacles in the way we, by the means of spiritual Truth, may ascend into God-Mind where there are no obstructions or limitations. In this consciousness we absorb wisdom, life, love and power and bring it back with us when we "land" on the "earth" or meet the seeming material condition.

AN AFFIRMATION TO BANISH WORRY AND FEAR

"I let go of all anxiety and fear. I drop all disturbing thoughts from my mind. I relax and place all my affairs in the hands of my loving Father to work out satisfactorily for me. I send kind thoughts and blessings to everyone without exception.

"Tomorrow will be a new day. I shall be a new being. I wash the slate clean of all discouragements, disappointments and regrets. Thank God for a new opportunity each day to start my life afresh. I forgive myself and all others. I expect only good things to happen. I look only for health, happiness and prosperity for all. I praise God for His goodness!"

In my experience in the application of spiritual Truth for myself and others I have found many good methods of applying divine Law for the healing of the body, mind and affairs. The following are brief outlines of two methods which I have found most effective.

How To Use the Law of Love by Radiation
FOR HEALTH, HARMONY AND SUCCESS

1. Relax. Repeat some high inspirational statement, slowly and thoughtfully, such as The Lord's Prayer.

2. Address the Creative Spirit of Universal Life thus: "Loving Father, pour Thy healing, harmonizing and prospering love through me that it may glorify Thee."

3. Think of the Creator as the Great Sun of Love and feel yourself enveloped by warm, soothing rays of Light shining upon you.

4. Take a slow, deep breath, lifting your chest and at the same time imagine these rays penetrating into your whole body.

5. While holding your breath think of these rays or radiations going out from you, like rays from the sun. You may direct them to anyone you desire to help, heal, bless or protect, or for whom you desire to establish harmony. Lastly send these love rays to all people and things in the world.

6. Feel your whole body filled and surrounded by LIGHT. Then think, "Love . . . peace be unto you in the name of Jesus Christ."

7. After a few minutes of this practice, say, "I thank thee Father, that Thy love has accomplished Thy Divine purpose. It is done."

This practice will completely transform your life if used regularly with sincerity. Be sure you have no ill-will or fear in your mind while using this exercise. Have your mind as much like the benevolent mind of God as you can imagine. Watch its miraculous operation as you become proficient in its use. It makes you a direct channel and instrument of God and is the quickest way of becoming attuned with Him.

Often when doing this for another the user himself is healed, because the substance of Love flowing through his body cleanses, opens closed channels, dissolves growths, soothes pain, destroys disease germs, and harmonizes the whole body. Besides this, it radiates out into the affairs with its freeing power and conquers difficulties, adjusts differences, summons quick assistance, opens closed doors, redeems, blesses and enriches the life of the user. As ye give (out) so do ye receive, is the law. Be very sure you do not see the patient as he appears to be in his perhaps imperfect outer form. Lift up your vision and see him as the perfect spiritual being that he is in Reality.

Another method of healing which I use is called the Absolute Method. In using this method of Metaphysical or Christ Mind Treatments, as I call them, for the healing of physical disease or for the solution of any problem, we do not deal with person, thing, time, circumstance, condition or anything in the manifest world. We deal wholly and solely with Divine Spirit. The practitioner invokes the Christ Spirit and Spirit does the work. Words must be filled with Spiritual meaning before they have healing power. Jesus said, ". . . the words that I speak unto you, they are spirit and they are life."

As an illustration of this, when we desire a certain program on the radio, we must set our dial to accord with the wavelength of the station we wish to tune in to. The Christ-Mind "station" is continually "broadcasting" or sending out healing power, peace, love, comfort, etc., but in order for us to receive its beneficial ministrations we must attune our minds to the same QUALITIES as the Christ Mind. When we have adjusted our minds to the proper "wave-length" we receive the "program" and send it out. This is the work of the healer who sets his or her mental dial to transmit the healing power.

I find that there are a number of mental operations that go to make up a scientific healing Treatment. The healing program which I use is divided into ten principle steps for the benefit of the student. In reality there is a consciousness, not easy to describe, that includes all these steps in one.

TEN STEPS TO DEMONSTRATION

1. RELAXATION—a thorough loosening up of every mental and physical tension.
2. SERVICE—a desire to serve humanity as God's agent.
3. PRAYER—the acknowledgment of the One Mind—God —ALL IN ALL.
4. LOVE—the Christ Spirit of compassion and impersonal love.
5. FAITH—in God's instant response to true prayer.
6. PEACE—the Silence—fourth dimension of Spirit.
7. REALIZATION—vision of PERFECTION existing eternally.
8. ACCEPTANCE—of what has been asked for, here and now.
9. THANKSGIVING—joyful gratitude to the Father for His goodness.
10. ACTION—acting in accordance with the realization.

Much of the success of a healing treatment depends upon the patient's faith or spiritual receptivity. Jesus told those whom He healed, "Thy faith hath made thee whole." Therefore, it is of utmost importance that the patient prepare for his healing by purifying his mind of all malice, worry, unforgiveness, fear and discouragement. A spiritual law which must be conformed to is embodied in the following text, "If two of you shall agree on earth as touching anything that they shall ask, it shall be done for them of my Father who is in heaven." It should be obvious that the healer cannot agree with the patient that he is sick. Therefore, the patient must agree with the practitioner that in Truth he is a perfect spiritual being, this of course referring to the Self of him which God created and called "very good."

The healer does not try to heal the sick patient, he knows that there never has been any other man in Truth than the one created in the image and likeness of his Creator and who always has been sinless, whole, pure, and perfect. When the patient agrees, through faith, with the inspired consciousness of the practitioner, the healing is instantaneous. Another important point for the one desiring healing is, that his help comes from God within himself and not from his practitioner. By acknowledging that his healing comes from God he is correctly polarized to the Source of his good.

To be sure, the healer is the agent of the Father through whom he makes his contact with the one seeking the healing. This is sometimes made through another person near to the patient who acts as "center of faith" when the patient is unable to ask for the healing himself, and sometimes by means of a letter or other vehicle. These are the outward and visible signs by which two persons' minds are brought into attunement and cooperation with each other and with God, so that the laws which govern the healing processes may operate.

When giving a treatment for a patient (absently or in his presence) I do not try to analyze the cause of his difficulty, since in the Absolute there is no cause for error. Then, too, the intellectual or reasoning part of the mind must be absolutely silenced to give way to the spiritual or inspirational part. Neither do I take the diagnosis of the patient's ailments into consideration. I turn absolutely to the healing Christ and the Christ power does the work. I take no responsibility for the establishing of the Word, nor personal credit for the healing. I give all the glory to God.

My attitude toward my patient is not one of cold indifference to his physical and mental suffering, but one of compassionate understanding, for I realize that his troubles are very real to him. Nor do I have a weak sympathy for him, which is destructive in effect. I have perfect faith that the healing laws work when the conditions are fulfilled by both the healer and the patient. In using the Absolute method of healing I neither deny nor affirm the Truth because I KNOW, and this conviction of perfection being all there is in reality, now and always, is the switch that operates the law.

In giving a healing treatment I endeavor to rise in consciousness above the sense realm into the pure White Light of the Christ Mind, thereby *making a contact between the Christ Mind in me and in my patient.* This starts the healing forces flowing through his whole body, relieving him of his ailment, whatever it may be. It does more than this because it goes beyond the patient's body into his environment and adjusts his affairs to harmony and abundance. This whole process is a divinely natural one, and not supernatural, for in man's true state he should be expressing health, joy and plenty. If these conditions were not already established in the realm of Spirit, they could not be brought into manifest form through the operation of Divine Law.*

*The author wishes to acknowledge quotations in part or in modified form from some of her artides in Nautilus Magazine; also from a twenty-five lesson course of instruction by the author called, "Christ Heals Today," published by the College of Universal Truth, 20 East Jackson Blvd., Chicago,

THE HEALING POWER OF TRUE SPIRITUAL VALUES
BY HERBERT E. RODWELL

Herbert E. Rodwell, D.D., Founder and Leader of the Church of Divine Science, Daytona Beach, Florida, began his healing work in South Africa thirty-seven years ago. The increasing number of students and patients that have come to him during his ten years work at Daytona Beach attest to the validity of his teaching.

AFTER thirty years of personal experience, first as an investigator into spiritual truths, then as a teacher and practitioner in the metaphysical field, I know that God as a Living Presence can be felt and known. I know there is an intelligent Law and a Creative Power which can be demonstrated through spiritual consciousness. •

Generally we form our ideas of God and the spiritual universe from what has been taught us, but too frequently such speculative theories possess little or no practical value. We all feel that Jesus Christ must have been a past master not only in the art of understanding spiritual values, but in the more dynamic act of using such values in meeting human needs. Always the Christian world has accepted this, but it has not come to everyone that the science and art practiced by Jesus was, and is, available to all.

I started my inquiry into spiritual truth, as I presume most of us do, feeling that I already understood what Jesus had taught, but when I came to place my personal beliefs beside his accomplishments I knew that I had but little of real value. I finally discovered that all beliefs and theories must give place to actual, demonstrable knowledge, so that one may possess these values as a vital part of his spiritual Self. Each must discover for himself the meaning of the truths which Jesus taught and demonstrated.

It has been my privilege to do this in some slight measure, and the results which have been obtained could not be committed to the printed page because of their amazing and astounding nature, but there are many persons who can testify with one that many of the wonders wrought in the days of Jesus have been experienced in their own living.

According to any experience which I have had, I am certain that God cannot do anything for me other than as I permit Him to work through my own consciousness. I feel I should make this more explicit and state that God works through me only as I become consciously aware of such working. The result, I am certain, is an effect of a Creative Law in the universe which always works in accord with Its own nature, no matter how urgent our needs may be.

I see now that there are many stages of thought through which we must pass before we can develop that true spiritual consciousness by which the humanly impossible easily can become accomplished. I feel that one of the fundamental propositions which we must all accept, is that each one of us knows God only for what God is to us. No matter how much we may believe in the Absoluteness of God, such belief remains but a speculation until the truth of its meaning becomes established in our own spiritualized consciousness.

I believe that God actually incarnates Himself in the souls of men, and that the one who has spiritual understanding is forever, in a certain sense, becoming God. That is, he is forever incarnating God power. It seems to me that an increased embodiment of God power must go on indefinitely so that things now undreamed of will be possible tomorrow. "Eye hath not seen, nor ear heard, neither have entered into the heart of man, the things which God hath prepared for them that love him."

The urge to push forward never diminishes and my feeling is that that which is greater lies ahead. There is a constant thrill as I anticipate the wonder of the eternal tomorrow.

I have found that extreme laborious methods are not essential, but really hinder us, in our spiritual work. God cannot labor even in mind and neither can the Spirit-filled mind enter into labor. After much sincere study in this direction, I was amazed to discover that Jesus often did not even pray when he accomplished what have been called wonderful and miraculous things. Prayer is too often thought of as a labor of the soul, and often is mingled with great human limitations. That is, we are liable to pray for that which we feel we do not possess. Thus, in a certain sense, the prayer of petition becomes an impediment in the great healing ministry. The discovery of this most significant fact led me to the disuse of prayer as a petition and to the necessity of replacing this attitude by something more effective. This something more effective was a deeper realization of the Indwelling Spirit.

I became convinced that since everything centers in God, I must let the Divine Spirit express Itself through my consciousness in greater measure. In this matter I sought wisdom from the Infinite Mind and was encouraged to follow what I believed was the example of Jesus Christ. I am confident that results have justified my conviction since many definite healings of most extreme cases of disease have taken place; sometimes by a mere personal conversation, at other times through the means of a letter, and again I have seen diseases healed with no other sign than the patient taking a long breath and giving expression to a deep sigh of contented acquiescence.

My method has been based upon the teaching and the works of Jesus, because I have found them the most practical and the clearest, and because his methods are without stress or strain. Paul said, "I know whom I have believed, and am persuaded that he is able to keep that which I have committed unto him." It has ever been my desire to reach the mystical conclusions which I am certain Jesus must have arrived at. Not as a result of pleading with God, but that deeper passageway of seeking first the Divine Kingdom, I have come to understand that supply is a state of consciousness and I no longer take thought regarding my needs. My consciousness of God is my infallible supply.

The consciousness of God as the One Unfailing Source of all good allows of no compromise. As the years have gone by beliefs have fused into a living consciousness, a complete and dynamic acceptance that the Kingdom of Heaven is at hand. I do not feel, however, that I possess any spiritual values which are not available to all mankind. The fishermen of Galilee had equal rights with the learned scholars of the world. The fatted calf awaits every prodigal who returns to the Father's kingdom. The supreme necessity is to train one's mind to receive the good that is stored in the invisible universe, as a matter of sequence and not of effort.

A toleration for all religious beliefs and convictions should be carefully considered, because all roads lead to the Infinite. There can be nothing gained by attempting to destroy any good that already exists. As we who have attained a more mature spiritual attitude have discarded our childhood toys, so will every one finally discard the lesser and accept the greater. The truth is not a competitor, and the enlightened mind rises by its own momentum. Subtlety and subterfuge are of no avail. Nothing less than a fearless acceptance of truth, as exemplified by Jesus, will or can meet human needs. "Father I thank Thee," and "I know that Thou dost always hear me," when uttered with deep spiritual conviction will accomplish the seeming impossible.

It seems to me that the first requisite toward spiritual enfoldment is a sincere desire to know God as a living intelligent Power within the Self. In the quest for spiritual enlightenment, I know of no substitute for silent meditation, which may be assisted by the reading of a good book or by the consideration of some statement of spiritual truth that seems to fill the present need. Mere words are of little value and often hinder as much as they help. God is Spirit, and in conscious spiritual meditation many have felt and known wonderful things that have been revealed to them in this silence. "Be still and know," means exactly what it says, for in this stillness is the consciousness of the Almighty.

There is a tremendous value in spiritual feeling. All through my experience I have noted its wonder-working power. In tune with the lower aspect of mind, we easily feel happiness or sorrow, health or sickness, wealth or poverty, because the lower mind is a tomb to its dualistic belief and experience. In the upper reaches of our thought, however, we tune into the pure unitary Cause, to the God Who is One, perfect and within us.

I am fully persuaded that the transmission of good from God is through the mind of man, when this mind is consciously centered in Divine Spirit, and accepts itself as a vehicle through which wonders may be made manifest. To illustrate this, may I refer to a case of cancer of the stomach which had been diagnosed as fatal. A letter written direct to me brought a direct appeal to save a patient's life. This letter awaited an answer until I knew by an *inner feeling* that the case was met. I asked for an immediate diagnosis of the case. This was done and I received a telegram stating that no cancerous condition could be found. Experience has convinced me that high spiritual states of consciousness are conveyed to the sick with tremendous healing power.

There is a definite *Science of Mind* which is based on an Eternal Principle, but I have never found a *science of method* in this healing ministry. No two cases respond alike. Jesus used a variety of methods to meet the desired end. I have found this the most effective way of working.

Imagine a crippled child, whose feet were drawn out straight by spinal meningitis, receiving an instant and perfect healing! She is now a married woman. Who, as a person, or what, as a power, is sufficient to accomplish such a result? Surely not merely a system of methods, *but rather a spiritual awareness of God as Absolute Power, Intelligence and Law can bring such things to pass*. We must all feel that nothing is impossible with the Indwelling God.

So long as a worker senses any doubt, there can be no response from the Spirit. The victory is to the courageous. There can be no final power but God, and man living in the consciousness of the Spirit is a vehicle for the use of that Power.

THE OMNIPRESENCE OF CREATIVE ENERGY
BY ERVIN SEALE

Ervin Seale, now minister of the Church of the Truth, New York City, was born in Washington, and went to public schools in Canada and Spokane, after which he attended Gonzaga and Washington State. Graduate of the University of Metaphysics, and ordained in the Church of the Truth. Has been a member of I.N.T.A. Board, a Field Secretary, District President for Washington, and Chairman of the Committee on the Constitution.

THE term "New Thought" when used to denote a new and original system of thinking, is not entirely descriptive since our thought is not in this sense new. It is as old as the hills to which the psalmist lifted up his eyes for help, and has been known in all ages and all climes. But whenever or wherever it has been known it has brought newness and freshness to human life. It is a discovery of every soul and therefore new to it.

It is the awakening of the individual from a sleep wherein he dwelt in bondage, to a consciousness of his inherent and eternal freedom. He is free not because someone or something has made him free, but because he has come under the influence of a "new thought" which seems to initiate a movement in consciousness and induce the flow of creative power. This modern metaphysical movement teaches the individual to think new thoughts about his world, the universe, God and man, and thereby set new forces in motion to create new and better conditions. These forces are, as Emerson says, "inexorable and execute themselves."

The shortest and best statement of this creative process was made by Quimby, the unlettered New England clock maker, who rediscovered for our time the potency of a new thought. He said, "I discovered that if I *really believed* a thing, the effect would follow whether I was thinking of it or not." This is the creative process; in other words, whatever the mind accepts as being true, becomes a belief and this belief automatically sets in motion these inexorable laws which execute themselves. Thus, new thought is not a system of thought manipulation, but a manner of thinking and feeling which calls into action in the life of man, a healing and regenerative power. It sees, with Jesus Christ, that we cannot by taking thought add one cubit to our stature. But we can by taking thought convey ourselves to the place in consciousness where something else takes hold and begins to translate our thought into form or action. Thus, as Jesus said, "The Father Indwelling, he doeth the works." Or, to speak in terms of logic, the mental and spiritual process in man is purely syllogistic, meaning that what the conscious mind or surface self thinks and accepts as true, the subconscious or deep self also accepts without debate and without reasoning or even any sense of right and wrong and begins to act upon it. This has been adequately demonstrated by scientific experiment and observation and has been fully explained in the vast literature of the field. Therefore, it is sufficient in this article to indicate its direct application in the life of the individual.

It is obvious that there are only two forms of belief: one is a belief in that which appears to be so from an objective standpoint; and the other is a belief in that which is inherently and internally true. This latter is what we call in New Thought the Truth of Being. A belief is a conviction, or at least an intellectual assent generated by the vision. What the mind sees inspires its thoughts and these thoughts become its belief. If man looks at the negation in his world, namely, sickness, war, the limitation, these inspire his thinking and form his beliefs and by the creative process of mind which we are here describing, he perpetuates such conditions in his immediate world. If, on the other hand, he turns his attention from these and obeys the commandment of the prophet to "look to the rock whence ye are hewn and to the pit whence ye are digged," he beholds the Father who is Spirit. Since no one can see Spirit in the sense that he sees physical objects, he must "see" the Father with the understanding. This understanding is, that Spirit is beyond time and space and limitation of any sort. It is changeless, deathless. It is infinite. Because it is infinite it is One and because it is One it must be everywhere. If it is everywhere it is All. It is Life itself. Life means expansion, progression, perfection. When the understanding "sees" this, then by the same creative process of mind by which he created his limited, obstructed world man will bring forth an experience of freedom and joy in accordance with the Truth of Being which he has been visioning. The method by which we hold the mind to this higher visioning is the discipline of New Thought. It is called prayer or treatment.

Prayer and treatment are the tools by which we condition the consciousness with the Truth of Being, by directing the vision and attention continually upward. This is not a forceful act of the will but a gentle acceptance of the promise, "Draw nigh unto me and I will draw nigh unto you." To facilitate this process we usually make statements or affirmations about the Truth of Being. These may be made silently or audibly. Such a statement might be: "God is All and God is Spirit. Spirit is Life. Life is all there is. It is a throbbing, vital, active Presence in which I live, move and have all my being." Gradually the individual becomes aware that there are not two beings, that there is not God and man but that there is just one life, movement and intelligence and that, "That Thou art, I Am."

At the same time he understands that there is not good and evil but just one Power moving in two directions, now upward and now downward, and each movement induced by the upward or downward visioning of man. This is the place of realization where thoughts and perceptions become realities. It is at this point that man's part as an individual in the creative process ceases and the movement of the Universal begins. Something within us begins to move in response to and confirmation of our statements of Truth. Our treatment or prayer has induced the flow of the creative energy which was always omnipresent and instantly available and abundantly responsive.

Thus we see that the creative cause of anything is in Life itself, and that once the human mind accepts any proposition as true the creative forces move into action to manifest the effect of that belief or acceptance, whether it be for good or for evil. It is automatic, inexorable and eternal.

Let man look, then, to the perfection of his source, to the rock whence he was hewn. Let him look long enough for it to inspire his thinking and feeling and so establish in consciousness his complete identity with that which sent him forth. All the powers and forces of the universe are working for him and with him now to do him good. That which he is seeking is seeking him with as much diligence as he is seeking it, therefore let him be at rest from seeking after it. In quietness and confidence shall be his strength and with the poet he may smile to know "God's greatness flows around our incompleteness, round our restlessness His rest."

THE SCIENCE OF MAN
BY SHELDON SHEPARD

Sheldon Shepard, A.M., LL.B., Litt.D. Degrees from University of Missouri, University of Chattanooga, University of Southern California. Formerly practicing attorney, Professor in Pomona College, President of The University of the West (Long Beach). Author and Producer of *The Long Beach Miracle Plays, The Passion Play of Youth, etc. Author of Life-Building Faith, Dreams Against The Sky, The Abundant Life*, etc. Contributor to many periodicals. For the last 14 years, Minister of the First Universalist Church of Los Angeles. Founder of *The Science of Man*, and Director of *The Institute of Man*, 1363 South Alvarado Street, Los Angeles, California.

THE purpose of The Science of Man is to integrate the various aspects of personality and daily living into the understanding of life as an expression of the One Universal Spirit. Proceeding from the proposition, "In the beginning Spirit—" it recognizes the inner life as the determining influence for every one. Believing that a part of the high function of thought is the organization and direction of all natural forces, The Science of Man views the rightly organized life as an instrument of Spirit.

Metaphysics is that high practice of the mind when it searches for the inner nature and the ultimate reality of personality, of experience and of existence. No life can be complete, no mind alert, without attempting those heights. If sometimes the climber slips, and hangs perilously over unknown chasms, it is still better to dare the high, wild winds of the dangerous, but fascinating, mountain-tops. Metaphysics implies a sense of the deep reality and power which underlies phenomena.

The sublime truth which is sought by all its forms is eternal and unchanging. The most real element of any person's life is that Divine Something within him which holds capacities of which he has not yet dreamed. Within each of us is the Infinite Light and Love and Power in which we live and move and have our being. Our thought may be, not a few chemical and magnetic processes, not the shallow sounds of a limited personality, but the Father speaking within, the Limitless, the Untold, the Unfathomable.

Of each of us it may be true as of Jesus, "I and the Father are one." Every day of modern science leads progressive researchers and explorers nearer to ideas which fit into these elemental metaphysical interpretations of existence.

The Science of Man is not an attempt to cheat the universe, not a process of grabbing the inside spiritual track, an attempt to get within the gates without paying the price of a ticket. It is not a scheme to find success without achieving it; to secure health without building it; to arrive at blessedness without cleating blessing.

True metaphysical superiority over things consists partly in the capacity to find the fullness of life without them. Ghandi is near the truth when he declares that freedom consists in the ability to be independent of possessions and circumstances. A sound metaphysics will reveal the treasures of the kingdom within, to which outer benefits are incidental. Though all the things we need come from the true spiritual life, they are not the main current of blessing, but attractive and useful plants which bloom upon its banks.

When we try to play the spiritual game by the rules of selfishness, we fail. If one wishes to live for the sake of possessions and demonstrations, for domination, it is far better to play the game of life in accordance with the rules of the selfish, materialistic world. Time spent in prayers and meditation for selfish ends would yield more if used in planning, scheming, manipulating and working.

Metaphysics is the revealer of the deeper life to which everything else is incidental. The kingdom of God is not to be sought in order to gain other objectives, but pursued for its own sake. The test of spiritual attitudes is not in demonstration, but in their own worth, satisfaction and power.

Inner realization comes to one, not to enable him to avoid the necessity of studying the laws of living, mastering his appetite, straining his muscles at mighty tasks, pulling with his soul against the tides of his time. It awakes within him, rather, to enable him to come to these daily challenging tasks with deeper wisdom, greater strength and more joy. It is not to take us away from life, but to thrill us with successful forays into all its territories.

One has to be very careful that his religion avoid becoming selfish. Salvation for the purpose of securing for oneself the blessings of Heaven is a miserable aim for righteousness. Metaphysics for the purpose of securing health and success is a glorified selfishness.

We seek to discover the Universal Reality, not to use it as a secret of self-satisfaction, but in order to become universal. We look for available power so we may become superior to all things. We explore the Kingdom of God for the purpose of extending its reign. Not the individual is the aim, but the Universal. We seek not for ourselves, but for all. We pursue the best, not for the sake of our selfish uses, but with the object of creating the best everywhere.

Health, success, happiness and usefulness are the natural, unfailing results of such pursuit of the best. They are fruits, not themselves cultivated, but dropping bountifully from the tree of the good life.

The knowledge and practice of Metaphysics should include these elements of understanding and technique:

Realization of the Spiritual Nature of Everything.

Recognition of one's own thought and emotional life as the directors of all creative force.

Responsibility of every individual for all that he is and for every thing which happens to him.

Control of all one's thinking.

Mastery of emotions.

Understanding that the Universal Spirit, with capacity for Perfect Expression, is the student's truest self.

Use of this knowledge in daily living.

Organization of the entire life on a plan in harmony with, and as an agency for, the Universal Spirit.

The Science of Man Metaphysics presents all these elements in a practical unity. The organization of all one's life in harmony with its nature is a high spiritual procedure. Recognition of our oneness with the Unseen Source of all is only one of our techniques of demonstration. Discovery that all attainment is potential within us is the bugle call which arouses us to action. Divine expression of ourselves has its laws of operation which should be studied and put into action.

The human is an expression of the Divine, of the Universal, the Eternal. Life did not begin; it will not end. The creativeness of the universe belongs to you. Good or evil may be made by you.

There are two processes of spiritual development and use of spiritual forces. One is realization of the grandeur and beauty and power of one's real nature, the recognition of the God within. The other is the organization of life for the expression of its purposes.

This combination adds to the fervor and flavor of existence, as well as all its power. If one has a high ambition, a goal toward which he wishes to drive, does it mean more or less if he organizes all his activities round it? When one has a great love, does it mean more or less if he lives conscious of it, and in all his ways is inspired by it, and lives in accordance with its beauty and vitality?

So it is with the spiritual concept of life. It means more as one has it in mind in every bit of his activity, and places all his thought and action at its disposal. He who thinks of the body as the temple of the spirit has an added joy in keeping it fit, trim and worthy. The mind is an instrument of the spirit, and therefore adds to its own worth and creativeness the fineness of an instrument for the ultimate producer. The heart is more than just an element of personal power to be kept right; it is a channel for the expression of the Universal. The integrating soul presents not only its own capacity; it is the maker of a way for the Divine.

For proper radio reception there are three essentials. There must be a broadcasting station, sending forth the vibrations of the program we wish to hear. Then there must be a tuning in to the waves. This requires an apparatus for the purpose of adjusting our reception so that we receive that which we desire. Also knowledge of the broadcast and the methods of receiving the program, though occasionally by accident we pick up delightful entertainment or helpful information. And finally, it is necessary that the radio-receiving set be in good condition and satisfying operation.

At any one of these points, radio reception may break down, giving an unfavorable result. If there is a station broadcasting that which we wish to receive, we must tune in to the proper wavelength and we must provide a satisfactory radio. Perfect broadcasting may be missed entirely by failure to tune in. How often have we said, "I did not know that program was on the air!" Or, "I forgot to tune in." Occasionally the tuning is inaccurate and results correspondingly unsatisfactory. Sometimes we have had the misfortune to have static develop in the midst of important broadcasting, or have failed to get clear, pleasing reception.

For the human being, there is a Divine Broadcast of that which he most desires. The vibrations which are the essence of all our needs are always going forth. God's station never goes "off the air." Spirit operates on a twenty-four hour basis. By accident we pick up much of this program. All life and expression are by virtue of its presence.

But life's reception is greatly expanded by knowledge of the broadcast. When one learns that God's wisdom, love and power are always pouring upon him, he immediately begins to take to himself more of the available presence.

The first part of our spiritual program is recognition of the vital fact that the broadcast is on. This realization brings a great thrill. To know that God's program is always available is in itself a spiritual experience of high order. Just to be aware of it, to have it in consciousness, has its own value. All life seems better because we know God is at work.

But this by no means completes the spiritual experience. One may appreciate the fact that a program is regularly available, may enjoy the possibility of hearing it as a value in life, and yet seldom tune in to its information, beauty or inspiration. Too often religious people rest on the conviction that God is "in his heaven" without doing anything positive to cooperate, or to receive his program of well-being.

We have to know how to tune in, and we must proceed to tune in. Exercises of faith, hope, love, expectation, understanding are processes by which we open our lives to the Divine Blessing. Vibrations of health, energy, peace, joy and power press upon us all the time. We may tune in by the use of right thoughts, attitudes, emotions and action.

But with a perfect broadcast, with knowledge of the wave length and correct tuning, one may still have poor reception because of a poorly working instrument. Static may make beautiful voices sound harsh, conflicting sounds may interfere with understanding, or the tones may be ruined by the quality of the radio. So with understanding of God's availability, with tuning by prayer, faith and love. One also must furnish the practical instrument of the good life.

It is true that faith and love, rightly understood, involve the good life. But it is sometimes easy to think of them as only mental and emotional processes. They should have their complements of actions in harmony with

God. Love must express itself in forgiveness, in service, in observance of Divine Law, faith shown forth in courageous action and confidence, hope in expectation of the best.

With these elements, we may receive the Divine Presence sufficient for all needs. Knowing the availability of God's program, tuning in with thoughts, affirmation and prayer, and furnishing a well-ordered life as the instrument of the expression of the Eternal, the harmony and beauty of the Infinite are expressed through us. As in a real sense the radio program to which we listen is in our rooms, so God is in our lives.

A true spiritual understanding leads to two special victories: More Strength and Better Conditions. In the first place, it puts into the believer's life something which makes it possible for him to carry the load which is upon him. And in the second place, it helps in the solving of all the pressing problems of life; it is a force to put to work in the achievement of a life worth while. It makes things better.

In experience, there is not much difference between having a burden lightened and having strength increased. To careless observers, the lightening of the burden seems to be the greater blessing. And people everywhere exhaust themselves seeking ways to lighten their loads. But the understanding ones know that a greater boon is the strength to make burdens seem light.

The reason the second is a greater blessing than the first is that the lightening of the load leaves one still weak for whatever may come. But the strength to carry the burden remains as an asset in future situations.

The two rewards of spirituality mentioned—the solving of problems and the strength to carry on—come from the same sources. A right method of lightening loads comes from an inner strength. Then one goes forward with his problems solved, and with an accumulation of power to prevent their arising again.

In the practice of The Science of Man, three specific techniques are used to bring the student into the fullness of The Abundant Life.

I. The teacher or practitioner brings the student's attainment into the realm of his own "fervent, effective prayer." "Treating" by realization of the Oneness of Spirit as the creative canal of all things, we place everything within the Unseen Power.

II. The student is led to a corresponding use of his own consciousness, looking to the inner kingdom as the realm of cause. He is taught the use of that faith which is the determining influence in his life. The creative forces of his own inner being are set in the direction of his goals.

III. In the Science of Man interpretation of thought, action and all life as instruments of Spirit, the student is led to self-organization and self-direction which develop mastery of mind and body as instruments of spirit. We develop a unity which puts every minute of the student's action, in all spheres, into tune with his spiritual aspirations.

These results are, of course, obtained by the use of all available methods of instruction and help. We engage in lectures, classes, personal instruction, publishing, correspondence, coaching and healing.

As a part of the New Thought movement, Science of Man students look to the realm of thought and feeling as the cause of the world's distress and as the source of its healing. We are preparing for the New Day which soon will follow this dark night, and we believe that we are building its foundations.

WHO IS GOD?
BY ELIZABETH TOWNE

Elizabeth Towne, author, lecturer, teacher, editor and publisher. One of the pioneers in the field of New Thought, intimately identified with it in every section of the United States, having published (Elizabeth Towne Publishing Co.) most of the writings of the prominent New Thought teachers of the past twenty-five years. Actively engaged in club and political activities in her own state. Ordained minister and always a crusader for that which she believes is right. Editor and publisher of *Nautilus Magazine*, which she founded in 1898 and which is affiliated with the International New Thought Alliance. Past president I.N.T.A.

WHY, *you* are God. And you. And you. And I AM God. And everybody, the whole two billions of us on earth—everybody is God. Not one of us alone—not Jesus the Christ alone—he was the "first *born* of many brethren"; all children of one God. God, the I AM of everybody on earth, or whoever was on earth, or ever will be!

Can I put my finger on God in me? Sure. My CONSCIOUSNESS is God—not a little piece of God, but the FULNESS of God.

And the same is true of you, and you, all round the world. The fulness of the infinite God is YOU—your *consciousness*. Not a little piece of God, but the FULNESS of God, is you.

Go into the silence in consciousness and dwell upon this truth. You are conscious of whatever you think of in the world, and there is nothing in the universe so far away or so big aroundlthat you cannot think it in consciousness. Try it!

Go into the silence and see if your consciousness can be made to compass anything, even to the uttermost parts of the universe, conscious or unconsciousness—see if your consciousness can compass ANYTHING beyond the reach of itself, of consciousness. No. You can think the highest thoughts that God himself has expressed to the world through Jesus Christ and through all the prophets from the beginning of time to the present! Not one of His thoughts is too big or too wonderful *for you* to reflect upon. Your consciousness is the Whole Infinite God, and there is nothing high or low, from the bottom of Hell to the highest point in Heaven or the outermost rim of the universe and back again!— *which is not in your* consciousness, and all you have to do is to *get acquainted with your consciousness* and call from its vasty deeps the qualities and the particularities of expression, of God. Of your I AM, of your God-self.

And remember that you have no God-self, no self of any kind EXCEPT GOD IN HIS FULNESS.

Now, be still and KNOW your 1-AM-God.

Your nature is the nature of God, and there is no great healing that ever was done on earth that *you cannot do*, if you dwell in God and declare HIM as your SELF, and do His works in your thoughts. If you do this as Jesus did you can "decree" anything and it shall come to pass. Just as Jesus Christ did.

In that model prayer which Jesus gave to the world, you find these words: "Our Father who art in heaven (*heaven is within us, you know*), hallowed be thy Name": what do you think "hallowed" means? It means literally '*holied*, or *wholely*. "Name" means literally "nature." So, those words mean, "Holied be thy NATURE within me."

And then Jesus prayed: "Thy kingdom COME on earth as it is in HEAVEN, Thy will be DONE on earth (now!) as it is in HEAVEN"—in the 1-AM-God within you. And within All of Us the world round.

Don't you see that that is a "DECREE" uttered by Jesus in the self-consciousness of himself and the Father as ONE?—he *decreed* that the fulness of God in man—all men and women!- that the fulness of God reigning, *good-willing* through All of Us, shall be done on earth as it is in heaven within us—where the Son (sun!) and the Father are one, indivisible, omniscient, omnipotent, omnipresent, and able to decree and bring to pass ANYTHING according to the Good-Will of the father in the Son— in all mankind.

Now, you simply can-NOT know the fulness of the I-AM-God while you carry in your consciousness a resentment against anybody or anything, any condition, any organization, nation, country or creed, in your mind. Why?

It is because the I AM within you is INFINITE and must be infinitely expressing itself, Himself, in your consciousness if you are to reach that state of clear consciousness of God which is able to DECREE and manifest what you desire. "Be ye perfect GOD-WILL, AS the Father in heaven (in you and in all creatures) is perfect, for he maketh his LOVE, his light, his appreciation, his good-will and loving kindness to shine upon the unjust as well as the just." That is what Jesus said, and what he meant.

If you would successfully decree the works of God as Jesus did, then you must have the CONSCIOUSNESS of God as Jesus had it. Don't think for a minute that God made you any purer or better or higher (or lower, for that matter) or more holy than anybody else that God made.

Remember that in order to do the works that Jesus did, "and greater works than these," you have to BE God, the Infinite God —*in your consciousness*. And from that vantage point you can stand upright and decree any good thing and it will come to pass. When you go into the silence, *you go into God in your consciousness*. The longer you stay in God in your consciousness, the more nearly infinite does your consciousness of God become! And therefore your decree becomes more glorious, more full of FAITH IN GOD, more potent to change the consciousness of any other human being who is full of the false consciousness of himself as the NOT-God. See?

All you need to do in this world is to cultivate the consciousness of yourself as GOD in his heaven within you, until none of these not-God ideas will clutter up your CONSCIOUSNESS: i.e., your God-faith, your God-will, your love, wisdom, divine power to create after God's infinite pattern.

Instead of creating after the little one-sided, partisan, anti-this and anti-that stuff which has been cluttering up our consciousness in times past—ever since the time when we were literally as little children "beholding the face of the Father" at all times. And now that we are tempted by the world's wars to think these partisan things within the spaces of our GOD-CONSCIOUSNESS —now is the time we should be more on our guard to live in the consciousness of God and what he sent Jesus Christ to this earth to proclaim: "GLORY TO GOD in the highest (everywhere and at all times and places!) and PEACE on earth and *Good-Will* to man!"

Our job is to do what Jesus did: (1) LIVE in the kingdom of God within, live in the consciousness of God in his heaven within us, and (2) make our decrees according to God's infinite and perfect Good-Will to man.

The more we live in this consciousness, the more firmly it becomes a habit, the fewer *words* we are obliged to say in the direction of any one person whom we are trying to heal. From the fulness of this inner God-consciousness, our word is the Infinite Word which creates *instantly* that whereunto we send it. Your word goes instantly from your divine consciousness to the divine consciousness in the one you are treating. And, my friend, I have learned by experience that you can get better results by speaking the word to whole families, whole groups, whole nations, and the Whole World!

Your consciousness is God. "THINE is the power and the glory forever."

I know of no treatment that is more effective than The Lord's Prayer for bringing about that clear *state of consciousness* in which your WORD of health, happiness, and prosperity is DECREED for anybody, and for all bodies in the world.

"Glory to God in the highest consciousness and on earth Peace, Good-Will—GOD-Will—to man."

When Moses went to lead the children of Israel out of slavery to the Egyptians he announced to them "I AM *hath sent me.*"

God is the one eternal, infinite Spirit which sent Moses and Joshua, and Abraham before him, and Job and Jesus and you and me, each with his own divine urge to do that particular service-to-mankind for which the I AM within hath sent him.

Jesus said, "As I AM in this world *so are ye*"—and "I AM sent me to do HIS works"—"I-AND-THE-FATHER are ONE I-AM"—"I AM come that ye might have LIFE," as I do; *for the LIFE of YOU is the I AM of you, and of All of Us*, pasty present and to come.

"I AM that I AM" was the first name and revelation of God to man—"I-AM that I-AM," which is *"the Light that lighteth every man* (and woman) *that cometh into the world."*

God in Jesus, and in you, and in me is the I AM THE LIGHT of every one of us, and that same God is the one and indivisible I AM THE LIGHT of each and all.

And when, and as we turn our back to the I AM LIGHT of us, how deep is the darkness within us.

The first decree, or Word, of God was "Let there BE Light— and there *was* light." In other words, Let all creatures *be aware* (or conscious) of this LIGHT WHICH I AM—in each and every soul. And it is recorded in John 1:1 to 5, that "In Him (God, the I AM) was LIFE and *this Life was the LIGHT of men."*

When Daniel found himself in the den of lions (Dan. 6) he looked *above* the lions to the Light of the I AM GOD of him, and no harm touched him.

When you are dropped into a den of destroyers do you continue in *awareness of the den and the lions?* Or do you *turn away* and lift up your eyes to the I AM THAT I AM which is *God-and-You together*, One Spirit, One Indestructible Life and Light of You, and there believe that you receive that which you desire— that which YOU AM!

You remember that Jesus tells you to "go into your closet and *shut the door*" leaving all the worries outside, so that in the silence of your "closet" you will become aware of *just* GOD, your infinite I AM LIFE, LIGHT—I AM NOW All Good.

God is your *I Am Awareness, your consciousness; to be conscious of your Godness* is to *DISSOLVE your troubles and LET God give you the desires* of your heart.

What you hold in your consciousness, your awareness, *is what sticks to you like a leech; for YOUR awareness of your troubles is the LIFE you breathe into them!*—Turn your awareness to God, your I AM and the Good You Desire, and your I AM LIFE brings them into being.

It is just like a tree growing—the tree turns its sap away from the outer crop, to the I AM center, and then pushes it upward again into a new leafing and fruiting.

Things exist by your awareness of them. If you don't like them turn your awareness away from them to the I AM INFINITE-NEW-GOOD of you, and start a new crop. The old crop will wither and drop away for lack of I AM LIFE, exactly as leaves and berries drop off trees in autumn.

And now consider Jesus' Story of The Judge Who Neither Feared God Nor Regarded Man: This parable of Jesus fits everybody in the world, as well as the judges on the Supreme Court Bench, and all the other thousands of court benches. And it especially fits all the lawmakers and the law administrators of our country. And that includes you and me, for *every voter is a judge of candidates and measures* for the public good. In every question supported, in every candidate voted, we play the part of judge—are we the unjust judge, advocating and voting for our own personal comfort? Every man (and woman) is his own judge and his decrees must include justice for All of Us.

Here is Jesus' story itself, as translated by Dr. Charles Cutler Torrey of Yale, in his "The Four Gospels," *St. Luke 18: 1 to 8*; the story of the Unjust Judge:

"Jesus gave them a parable to the effect that they must always pray and never despair. In a certain city, he said, there was a judge, who neither feared God nor regarded man. There was a widow in that city, who kept coming to him and saying, Give me justice of my adversary. For a time he would not; but at length he said to himself, Even though I neither fear God nor regard man, yet *because this widow troubles ME* I will give her justice, lest she wear ME out by her perpetual coming. And the master said: Hear what the unjust judge says! and will not God give justice to his elect who cry to him day and night, even if he is slow to anger in their behalf? I tell you, He will give them speedy satisfaction."

Did you get anything new from that reading? I did. It suddenly dawned on me that in commending the woman for her faith Jesus included the fact that her faith in her cause *impelled her to keep on demanding justice of that unjust judge!*

Jesus did not compare GOD to an unjust judge. What Jesus said amounted to this: Keep on praying to God, *believing in the justice, the rightness, the will-of-God-ness, of the thing which* you are praying for, and go on *acting out your faith* by demanding action of the "unjust judge" who has control over it.

In other words, have faith in God and in the justice of the thing which you desire, and *then keep on ACTING as if you had this faith*. The poor widow *ACTED*, by going again and again to the door of that "unjust judge," making her plea so strong and so often that finally the judge's *inertia*—for that is exactly what it was: not meanness, but inertia—his habit-inertia melted and *he too became active* in securing that which was just.

The widow's faith-action eventually fired the judge to action— like one torch firing another; like one Spirit firing another Spirit to action. That is a perfect picture of what you and I must do in order to move the "unjust judges" to show mercy and do justice to the near-dispossessed people of our country. The poor widow showed the steps exactly, and that is what Jesus told the story for.

Here are the steps: (1) the poor widow had faith in God and the justice of her claim; (2) she kept right on making it hot for that judge, who was *not in the habit* of granting such requests as the widow was making of him—except for the special privileged ones. He thought the widow was too small and unimportant for a great judge to bother with.

If we do nothing but have faith in GOD, *without waking up* those inactive ones we will go right on having conditions which favor a few thousand important folks while we disregard the giving of justice to the millions of unimportant folks.

We all must learn to value and to deal justly with common folks; "God must have loved the common people, he made so many of them." (Abe Lincoln)

And God must have loved the "unjust judges," for they include All of Us by turns.

THE SECRET OF SUCCESSFUL LIVING
BY RALPH WALDO TRINE

Ralph Waldo Trine, internationally known for his: *In Tune with the Infinite*, published in almost every language as well as in Braille for the blind and an. edition in Esperanto. Born in Northern Illinois. Graduated from Knox College with degree of A.B. receiving that of A.M. two years later. A year at the University of Wisconsin and graduate work in the Department of History, Political and Social Sciences at the Johns Hopkins University prepared him for his life long work as author, teacher, and healer. In addition to his first book: *In Tune with the In finite*, three or four of his other books have sold more than one-half million copies. One of the greatest living writers of metaphysical literature. He now resides in Hollywood and is writing vigorously at least six hours a day.

WE HEAR much today, both in various writings and in public utterances, of "the spiritual life." I am sure to the great majority of people the term *spiritual life* means something, but something by no means tangible or clear-cut. I shall be glad indeed if I am able to suggest a more comprehensible concept of it.

First let us note that in the mind and teachings of Jesus, there is no such thing as the *secular life* and the *religious life*. His ministry pertained to every phase of life. The truth he taught was a truth that was to permeate every thought and every act of life. It is we who make arbitrary divisions of it.

In seeking to define the spiritual life, it were better to regard the world as the expression, the manifestation, of the Divine Mind. The Spirit is the life; the world and all things in it, the physical, to be moulded, raised, and transmuted from the lower to the higher. This is indeed the law of evolution—the God Power that is at work, and *every form of useful activity that helps this process of lifting and bettering is a form of Divine activity.* If, therefore, we recognize the One Divine Life, working in and through all—the animating force and therefore the Life of all— and if we are consciously helping in this process, we are *spiritual* men.

One of the great secrets of successful living is unquestionably the striking of the right balance in life.

The material plane has its place, and an important one it is, too. Fools indeed were we to ignore, or attempt to ignore, this fact. We cannot, however, except to our detriment, put the cart before the horse. *Things* may contribute to happiness, but things alone cannot bring happiness—and sad indeed, and crippled and dwarfed and stunted becomes the life of anyone who is not capable of realizing this fact. Truly, life indeed is more than meat and the body more than raiment.

All life is from an inner center outward. As within, so without. As we think we become. It is, therefore, for us to choose whether we shall be interested primarily in the great spiritual forces and powers of life, or whether we shall be interested solely in the material things of life.

But there is a wonderful Law we must not lose sight of. *It is to the effect that when we become sufficiently alive to the inner powers and forces, to the inner springs of life, the material things of life will not only follow in a natural and healthy sequence, but they will also assume their right proportions. They will take their right places.*

It was the recognition of this great fundamental fact of life that Jesus had in mind when he said: "But rather seek ye the kingdom of God; and all these things shall be added unto you," meaning the kingdom of mind and spirit made open and translucent to the leading of the Divine Wisdom inherent in the human soul when that leading is sought, and when through the right ordering of the mind, we make the conditions whereby it may become operative in the individual life.

It is our eternal refusal to follow Jesus by listening to the words of life that he brought, and our proneness to substitute something else in their place, that brings the barrenness that is so often evident in the everyday life of the Christian. We have been taught to *believe in Jesus*; we have not been taught to *believe Jesus*. This has resulted all too often in a separation of Christianity from life.

A man may be a *believer in Jesus* for a million years and still be an outcast from the Kingdom of God and His righteousness. But a man *can't believe Jesus*, which means following his teachings, without coming at once into the Kingdom and enjoying its matchless blessings both here and hereafter.

The great value of God as taught by Jesus is that God dwells in us. It is truly Emmanuel—God with us. The Law must be observed—the conditions must be met. "The Lord is with you while ye be with him; and if ye will seek him, he will be found of you." . . . "If any of you lack wisdom, let him ask of God, that giveth to all men liberally, and upbraideth not; and it shall be given him. But let him ask in faith, nothing wavering." That there is a Divine Law underlying prayer ("ask in faith") that helps to release the inner springs of wisdom, which in turn leads to power, was well known to Jesus as his life so abundantly proved.

His great aptitude for discerning the things of the mind and spirit enabled him intuitively to realize this, to understand it and to use it. There was no mystery, no secret, no subterfuge on the part of Jesus as to the Source of his power. It was the truth of this inner kingdom that would make men free that he came to reveal. "The words that I speak unto you I speak not of myself: but the Father that dwelleth in me, he doeth the works." . . . "... for as the Father hath life in himself; so hath he given to the Son to have life in himself."

How many times we are told that Jesus withdrew to the mountain for his quiet period, for communion with the Father that the realization of his oneness with God might be preserved intact. And the distinct statement he made, in speaking of his own powers, was ".. . and greater things than these shall he do," showing clearly the possibilities of human unfoldment and attainment, and proving clearly that this Divine source of wisdom and power is the inheritance of every human soul.

Not that problems and trials will not come. They will come. There never has been and never will be a life free from them. Life isn't conceivable on any other term. But the wonderful source of consolation and the source that gives freedom from worry and freedom from fear, is the realization of the fact *that the guiding force and the moulding power is within us*. It becomes active and controlling in the degree that we are able to open ourselves so that the Divine Intelligence and Power can speak to and can work through and for us.

By the same token that judicious physical exercise induces greater bodily strength, an active and alert mental life induces greater intellectual power. So the same general law is true in regard to the development and the use of spiritual power and the losses resulting from this neglect are almost beyond calculation. How strange it is that this most important of all activity—that which has to do with life itself—we neglect most of all!

A modern writer of great insight has said: "The understanding that God is, and *all there is*, will establish you upon a foundation from which you can never be moved." *To know that the power that is God is the power that works in us is knowledge of transcendent import.* To know that the spirit of Infinite wisdom and power which is the creating, the moving and the sustaining force in all life—thinks and acts in and through us as our very own life, in the degree that we consciously and deliberately desire it to become the guiding and the animating force in our lives; and to open ourselves fully to its leadings, is to attain the state of conscions oneness with the Divine that Jesus realized, lived and revealed, and that he taught as the method of the natural and normal life for all men.

If we would have the leading of the spirit—if we would be illumined by divine Wisdom and energized by divine Power— bringing the affairs of the daily life thereby into Divine sequence, we must observe the conditions whereby these leadings can come to us, and in time become habitual.

There is perhaps no more valuable way of realizing this end than to adopt the practice of taking a period each day for being alone in the quiet, a half hour, even a quarter hour; stilling the bodily senses and making oneself receptive to the higher leadings of the spirit—receptive to the impulses of the soul. This is following the master's practice and example of communion with the Father.

Now that value of prayer is not that God will change any laws or forces to suit the numerous and necessarily the diverse petitions of any. All things are accomplished through law, and the law is fixed and inexorable. In the realm of spirit the law is as definite as in the realm of mechanics. The value of prayer, true prayer, is that through it one can so harmonize his life with the Divine order, that intuitive perceptions of truth and a greater perception and knowledge of law becomes his possession.

It is with great pleasure that I recall a visit I once had with Dr. Edward Emerson of Concord, Emerson's eldest son. Happily I asked him in regard to his father's methods of work—if he had any regular methods. He replied in substance: "It was my father's custom to go daily to the woods—*to listen*. He would remain there an hour or more, in order to get whatever there might be for him that day. He would then come home and write into a little book—his 'day book'—what he had gotten. Later on when it came time to write a book, he would transcribe from this, in their proper sequence and with their proper connections, these entrances of the preceding weeks or months. The completed book became virtually a ledger formed from his day-books."

When man becomes centered in the Infinite, he is redeemed from the bondage of the senses. He lives thereafter under the guidance of the Spirit, and this is salvation. It is a new life he has entered into. He lives in a new world, because his outlook is entirely new. He has brought his own personal mind and life into harmony with the Divine mind and life. He becomes a coworker with God. He is now living in the Kingdom of Heaven.

To establish this connection, to actualize the God-consciousness, that it may not be for one transcendent moment, but that it may become constant and habitual, so that every thought arises, and every act goes forth, from this center—this is the greatest good that can come into the possession of any man. There is nothing greater, for it is none other than the realization of Jesus' injunction: "Seek ye first the Kingdom of God and his righteousness and all these things shall be added unto you."

What I am trying to say, in as many ways as I know how, is that there is a divine sequence running throughout the universe. To come into the conscious, vital realization of our oneness with the Infinite Life and Power—the source of all life and power—is to come into the current of this divine sequence.

There is a mystic force that transcends any power of the intellect or of the body, that becomes manifest or operative in the life of man when his divine Self-realization, his God-consciousness, becomes awakened and permeates his entire being. To repeat—we can bring our minds into rapport, into such harmony and connection with the infinite divine Life and Power, *that it speaks in us, directs us, and therefore acts through us as our own very selves.*

It is ours, then, to act under the guidance of this higher wisdom, and in all forms of expression, in every act of life, to live and to work, augmented by this higher power. The finite thereby becomes the channel through which the Infinite can and does work. Coming thus into harmony with the Infinite, brings us in turn into harmony with all about us, into harmony with all the universe. And above all, it brings us into harmony with ourselves, so that body and soul and mind become perfectly harmonized, and when this is so, life becomes full and complete. We are awake to our possibilities and powers as true sons of God, and the Christ becomes enthroned in our lives.

To find one's center, to become centered in the Infinite, is the first great essential of every satisfactory life; and then to go out, thinking, speaking, working, loving—living from this center.

UNITY
BY ERNEST C. WILSON

Dr. Ernest C. Wilson, minister of Christ Church, Unity in Los Angeles, has been for over twenty years a contributor to Unity publications as well as many secular periodicals. He is the author of eight published books besides numerous booklets and magazine articles. Most of this time he has been affiliated with Unity's International Headquarters in Kansas City, during which time he has served as minister, teacher, lecturer, and editor-in-chief of all Unity publications. He is still a member of the Editorial Staff of Unity School of Christianity, and a member of the faculty of the Unity Training School at Headquarters. Dr. Wilson has lectured in Europe, the Orient, Hawaii, and the United States. He founded the British Unity in London, England, and the Unity Center in Honolulu, Hawaii.

THE central principle of Unity is oneness, the unity of all things; unity of the soul with God; unity of all religions; unity of man with man.

Unity is not primarily a church, but it can scarcely avoid becoming one to a certain degree. Charles Fillmore's idea of Unity is that it shall be primarily a school of religious thought.

By Unity ideas we simply mean interpretations of the Christ message that Unity has had a major part in promulgating through prayer, Unity publications and its teachers. The Great Teacher, we feel, brought Unity into the world, and we believe it will stand as long as we recognize its spiritual purpose and work steadfastly for that purpose.

An Oriental teacher has said that "light is good in whatsoever lamp it shines," and we who seek to be followers of the Way, as Christianity was called in early times, try to be alert to discern that light of Truth wherever it may shine, and are grateful for it. We do not limit our approval to those who adopt the same religious customs and terminology used in Unity, but instead we strive to reach past outward differences and praise the good wherever we find it in institutions and persons.

We feel that ritual, creed, and terminology must be secondary in the sight of God, and that those who seek to put God first should put God first all the way along.

One of the distinctive things in the Unity teaching is that it is the divine birthright of every child of God to have complete harmony, which, of course, includes perfect health and abundance. This is based on the assurance of Jesus Christ that the Truth of God is not only to help us with spiritual problems, but to help us with every need that we might have. One of the great things that Jesus Christ came into the world to do was to free mankind from the obsession of suffering and lack, and the conviction that it should be bowed down under the harsh limitations of a material world; in fact, quite as much as to free mankind from the darkness of ignorance and distressing thoughts.

In applying Unity teachings we make bold the claim to Jesus Christ's promise that we shall have whatsoever things we desire, and that the price of these things is righteousness, or the right use of them, a basis essential to prosperity and its circulation and exchange.

Unity emphasizes the healing power of prayer as did Jesus Christ, but it does not emphasize healing as much as it does teaching, nor did the Master. We believe in the healing power of the Spirit through prayer on the testimony of the Psalmist who said (Psalms 107:20), "He sendeth his word, and healeth them."

However, Unity does not oppose the use of medicine, but affirms the use of intelligence and quickened understanding in meeting all human problems. It blesses all who seek sincerely to minister to the wellbeing of mankind, and prays with nurses and physicians and surgeons with their patients.

Although Unity believes that God works mightily through human agencies to accomplish His good for man, we know that His power is not limited to material agencies or remedies. We know that no human agency could ever bring health to sick bodies if it were not for the indwelling presence and power of the Spirit.

Unity does not encourage students to depend upon some one else instead of physicians. It teaches them to depend on God. The ministry of Unity School is one of instruction and prayer; instruction in the simple teachings of Jesus Christ, and prayer with and for its correspondents and readers that they may find and understand and follow the guidance of God.

The Society of Silent Unity is a department of the Unity School, and is a consecrated group who pray daily with those who request help in prayer, sending them letters and other literature of an instructive nature. Day and night there are always workers on duty, in faithful remembrance, and to answer letters, telephone calls, telegrams, and cablegrams as they are received. These communications to Silent Unity are held in strictest confidence, and the names of the correspondents are never mentioned. Silent Unity never advises students to take any outward course of action nor to refrain from doing so; it prays that they may be divinely guided and asks them to pray to the same end, casting aside all personal prejudice and selfish desires. By "watching and praying" we strive to "attain unto the unity of the faith, and of the knowledge of the son of God . . . unto the measure of the stature of the fullness of Christ."